The Children's Television Community

LEA's COMMUNICATION SERIES
Jennings Bryant and Dolf Zillmann, General Editors

For a complete list of titles in LEA's Communication Series, please contact Lawrence Erlbaum Associates, Publishers at www.erlbaum.com

The Children's Television Community

Edited by

J. Alison Bryant
Nickelodeon/MTV Networks

LEA
LAWRENCE ERLBAUM ASSOCIATES, PUBLISHERS
2007   Mahwah, New Jersey   London

Copyright © 2007 by Lawrence Erlbaum Associates, Inc.

Lawrence Erlbaum Associates, Inc., Publishers
10 Industrial Avenue
Mahwah, New Jersey 07430
www.erlbaum.com

Cover design by Tomai Maridou

Library of Congress Cataloging-in-Publication Data

The children's television community / edited by J. Alison Bryant

      p. cm.

Includes bibliographical references and index.

ISBN 978-0-8058-4996-7 — 0-8058-4996-3 (cloth)
ISBN 978-0-8058-4997-4 — 0-8058-4997-1 (pbk.)
ISBN 978-1-4106-1445-2 (e book)
1. Television programs for children.   I. Bryant, J. Alison.
PN1992.8.C46C45   2007
791.45'6523—dc22   2006042315
                                                                          CIP

Books published by Lawrence Erlbaum Associates are printed on acid-free paper, and their bindings are chosen for strength and durability.

Printed in the United States of America
10   9   8   7   6   5   4   3   2   1

For my father—

my best friend and favorite coauthor

Contents

Preface

Unlike most books on children's television, which look at how children receive television programming and how it affects them, this book looks at the process of creating children's television, focusing on the "behind the scenes" that ends up on the screen. Children are a "special" audience and creating and supporting (politically and financially) programming for them raises a number of issues that are unique. Unlike "regular" television programming, which can be assumed to be a primarily economic venture targeted to a general audience, children's programming has to take into account the special cognitive, emotional, and developmental needs of its audience. This alters, or should alter, the way in which programming is created, marketed, distributed, and critiqued. This also changes the nature of the "players" in the process.

The concept for this book began as I was conducting research on the coevolution of these players, or organizations, that make up the children's television community in the United States. I quickly found that because of the special nature of children's television programming: (1) there are a greater number of key organizational players to consider as part of the process, (2) the relationships among these organizations are complex, and have changed (often dramatically) over the past 50 years, and (3) the perspectives that people in each of these groups brings to issues in children's television can be both surprisingly different and similar. This book, therefore, attempts to address these issues by emphasizing the varied set of actors whose creative, financial, political, and critical input go into children's television, and giving each of them a voice in this volume.

The authors in this book, most of whom have had vast experience in the day-to-day inner workings of the children's television community, offer incredible insight into how children's television is created, distributed, marketed, advocated, and regulated. They are the content creators, programmers, marketers, concerned citizens, and academics who have affected the evolution of children's television over the past 30 years. Through their chapters, they give their insider perspectives on the history, state of the art, and future of children's television. The blending of these diverse perspectives offers a comprehensive picture of children's television.

Part I of this volume provides an overview of the children's television community. Mitroff and Herr Stephenson (chap. 1) give an overview of the evolution of children's television in light of major societal events and changes in the larger entertainment industry. Bryant (chap. 2) looks at the evolution of the children's television community and provides macrolevel organizational explanations for why children's television has changed in the way that it has. Alexander and Owers (chap. 3) consider children's television as a business, giving the economic background necessary for understanding the complex production and distribution processes that are described in Parts 2 and 3 of this book.

Part II focuses on the production of children's television. London (chap. 4) outlines the process of creating and producing children's television programs, highlighting issues, concerns, and challenges that arise during the process. Fisch (chap. 5) focuses on the production of educational programs, looking at a range of production models and the integration of educational content and empirical research into the production process. Stipp (chap. 6) ends this section by reflecting on the experiences of NBC in integrating academic advisors into the production process.

Part III concentrates on how children's television is distributed and marketed. Simensky (chap. 7) provides insight as to how the Public Broadcasting System approaches children's television and the unique challenges that PBS faces. Kalagian (chap. 8) offers the cable networks' side of programming, discussing how various networks have approached children's programming and the key factors that affect cable. Tashjian and Naidoo (chap. 9) explore the complex interactions and interplay between children's programming and successful children's product retail sales. Finally, Rockwell (chap. 10) rounds out these perspectives by exploring the implications of the rapid technological changes that are occurring for what children will see on their screen(s).

Part IV is written from the perspectives of the policymaker, the advocate, and the concerned citizen. Kunkel (chap. 11) provides a cutting-edge perspective on the current state of regulation in children's television. Montgomery (chap. 12) reviews the actions and impacts of the major policy advocacy groups that have been part of the children's television community over the past five decades. Kleeman (chap. 13) builds on the discussion of advocacy by looking at the importance of industry-engaged advocates. Finally, Herr Stephenson and Banet-Weiser (chap. 14) end our tour of the children's television community by looking at how children's television constructs its audience, focusing in particular on the issue of obesity.

I am greatly indebted to the wonderful authors in this book for taking time out of their hectic schedules to collaborate on this project. Early conversations with many of them helped shape the original prospectus for the book. As the book has evolved, their willingness to provide detailed background, in-depth descriptions, and personal narratives in their chapters has enhanced this volume beyond any hopes I originally had for it. This has truly been a group effort.

Many thanks also go to the wonderful folks at Lawrence Erlbaum, Associates, especially my editor Linda Bathgate and assistant editor Karin Wittig Bates, who continue to be a pleasure to work with. My colleagues in the Department of Telecommunications at Indiana University, where I did most of the work on this project, also deserve a round of praise for their support and encouragement. In addition, I would like to thank my family members (Jennings, Sara, Todd, and Adrienne), who are an amazing support net and cheering section, even when my ideas seem a bit crazy—I couldn't do it without you. Finally, a special "thank you" goes to Jennings, to whom this book is dedicated, who has supported this project from day one on so many levels—colleague, confidant, editor, mentor, sounding board, and just plain-ole' dad.

—*Alison Bryant*

I

UNDERSTANDING THE CHILDREN'S TELEVISION COMMUNITY

1

The Television Tug-of-War: A Brief History of Children's Television Programming in the United States

Donna Mitroff
Rebecca Herr Stephenson
University of Southern California

The history of children's television programming in our culture spans only about 50 years. Dr. Mitroff's career as a practitioner in the industry has spanned nearly half of this time period. She began watching TV as a child when television was a new, exciting addition to family entertainment. Ms. Herr Stephenson's career in the industry is just beginning; however, she grew up during the years when the presence of television and the choices in children's television programming were ubiquitous. We have had remarkably different experiences with children's television programming and yet we share the belief that there is a constant interplay between what is happening in society at large and in the broadcast and cable industry and that this interplay frequently has a trickle down effect on the content and themes of children's television programs.

This chapter attempts to outline the major societal events that have occured during the lifetime of the mass media in the United States and draw connections between these events, the structure and products of the entertainment industry (with a focus on the television industry), and children's television policy and programming. It is important for readers to note that we are not historians. The historical overview sections of this chapter are not intended to serve as complete analyses of American history. Rather, they are intended as snapshots of American history during different decades. These historical snapshots are provided for the purpose of orienting readers to the major events and societal trends of the historical periods. Furthermore, this is neither an exhaustive investigation of all themes and examples present in children's programming nor a definitive examination of the relationships between the cultural forces and the products of the entertainment industry. Rather it is the first product of a line of research we plan to expand in future work.

The first part of this chapter explores the overarching premise that all media is a reflection of the context in which it is produced. As a cultural artifact, media, like art or literature, reflects cultural concerns, societal trends, philosophical, moral, and religious beliefs, and reactions to world events. Media produced for children is certainly not exempt from the impact of context. Perhaps because of its perceived educational duty, children's media has, in several instances, reflected societal changes and concerns before those same elements appeared in general audience programming. The story of children's television in the United States is one of a delicate balance between governmental regulation, advocacy by concerned citizens, and reactions by those in the industry. By and large, the children's television industry has stepped up to the challenge of assisting children in understanding and adapting to a changing society, and continues this work in the face of the challenging issues encountered by children (and adults) today. There is, however, constant negotiation between the desire to shape children's programming around children's educational, informational, and socioemotional needs and the perpetuation of television as a business.

In the second part of this chapter, we present a more detailed analysis of the way in which the children's television industry has addressed the issue of violence. We look at three examples of industry reactions to violent events in society and present a variety of strategies employed by producers in the children's television industry to help children understand, cope with, and learn from violent events.

To provide an overview of how society and the children's programming arena have interacted over the years, we have developed a timeline (see Fig. 1.1). The timeline illustrates important events within American history, media history, and policy, and television programming for children. Discussion of the timeline will focus on the interplay between events and societal trends, public policies (in particular those related to the regulation of television), and the content of children's television programs. This interplay is illustrated with a variety of examples drawn from children's programs within each historical period.

PART I: EXAMINATION OF THE TIMELINE

The 1920s and 1930s

American Society and the World Scene. The 1920s were years of transition in the United States. The end of World War I left many Americans disillusioned and unsure of the value of their sacrifice. The resurgence of business power and the expansion of industry brought a wave of materialism that made some question whether the idealism and social consciousness of the previous progressive era was lost. Nevertheless, the 1920s were a time of prosperity. Skylines expanded upwards, roads were built to accommodate additional automobiles, and new homes were erected to house the growing population. The national census of 1920 showed greater population density in urban centers than in rural areas; the impact of this demographic change was felt throughout the 20th century. The prosperity felt by some Americans was not a luxury of all citizens, however. Discriminatory legislation against new immigrants attempted to slow population growth in urban areas. Prejudice against ethnic minorities, particularly African Americans, was prevalent in several regions of the country, allowing the spread of the Klu Klux Klan beyond the south. Conservative morality tangled with science in the inflammatory Scopes Trial, and was felt again in 1918 when the passage of the 18th Amendment made prohibition the law of the land. The stock market crash of 1929 marked the end of the prosperity of the early years of the decade and signaled the beginning of the Great Depression. Unlike previous depressions, the impact of the Great Depression was felt most sharply by the middle class—the same people who had benefited most from the postwar economic boom. The New Deal programs enacted by Franklin Delano Roosevelt offered hope to the struggling middle class, promising work programs and protection of investments. Although unemployment remained relatively high through the end of the 1930s, the basic economic system survived. By the end of the decade, the focus of the nation was drawn to the growing threat of international aggression from the three totalitarian countries: Germany, Italy, and Japan (McDonough, Gregg, & Wong, 2001; Schlesinger, 1993).

The Entertainment Industry. The history of children's television programming begins with the story of the first two forms of electronic entertainment to permeate society: movies and radio. As movie theaters and radio stations developed during the 1920s and 1930s, children were a major target of both forms of media. The Saturday matinee was

1920   1930   1940   1950

American Society and the World Scene

- (1929) Stock Market Crash
- (1929-1939) The Great Depression
- (1933-1939) New Deal Legislation
- (1941-1945) World War II
- Baby Boom
- Growth of suburbs
- (1955) Montgomery bus boycott
- (1957) Sputnik launch
- McCarthyism/Communist paranoia
- Cold War begins

The Entertainment Industry

- Movie theaters grow in popularity
- Introduction of radio (mid-20s)
- (1930) 50% radio penetration in U.S. homes
- (1927) Radio Act
- (1929) NAB Code of Ethics
- (1934) Telecommunications Act
- (1939) Television introduced at Chicago World's Fair
- (1941-1956) television licenses halted due to WWII
- "The Golden Age of Television"
- (1950) ABC launches Saturday morning kids' block
- (1951) NAB Television Code
- Color TV arrives (mid/late '50s)
- Juvenile delinquency hearings (late '50s)

Children's Programming

- Snow White and the Seven Dwarfs (1937): first family film
- Little Orphan Annie ('31-'40)
- Captain Midnight (radio) ('38-'49)
- The Small Fry Club ('47-'51)
- Howdy Doody ('47-'60)
- Mr. I. Magination ('49-'52)
- Kukla, Fran, & Ollie ('48-'71)
- Rootie Kazootie ('50-'54)
- Ask Mr. Wizard ('51-'65)
- Ding Dong School ('52-'59)
- Captain Midnight (tv) ('54-'56)
- Mickey Mouse Club ('55-'59)
- Gumby ('56-'67)
- Lassie ('57-'74)

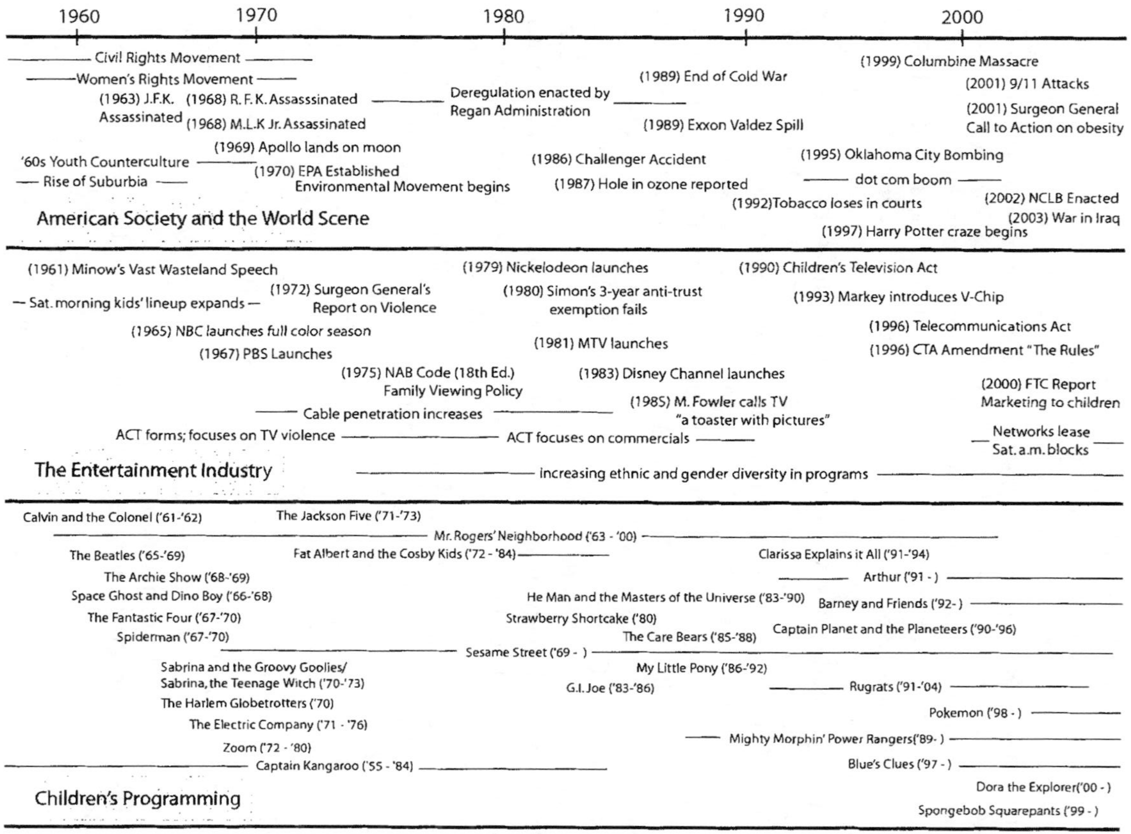

FIGURE 1.1   History of Children's Programming

Timeline markers: 1960 — 1970 — 1980 — 1990 — 2000

American Society and the World Scene
- Civil Rights Movement
- Women's Rights Movement
- (1963) J.F.K. (1968) R.F.K. Assassinated
- Assassinated (1968) M.L.K. Jr. Assassinated
- (1969) Apollo lands on moon
- '60s Youth Counterculture
- (1970) EPA Established
- Rise of Suburbia
- Environmental Movement begins
- Deregulation enacted by Regan Administration
- (1989) End of Cold War
- (1989) Exxon Valdez Spill
- (1986) Challenger Accident
- (1987) Hole in ozone reported
- (1995) Oklahoma City Bombing
- (1999) Columbine Massacre
- (2001) 9/11 Attacks
- (2001) Surgeon General Call to Action on obesity
- dot com boom
- (1992) Tobacco loses in courts
- (2002) NCLB Enacted
- (1997) Harry Potter craze begins
- (2003) War in Iraq

The Entertainment Industry
- (1961) Minow's Wasteland Speech
- (1972) Surgeon General's Report on Violence
- Sat. morning kids' lineup expands
- (1965) NBC launches full color season
- (1967) PBS Launches
- (1975) NAB Code (18th Ed.) Family Viewing Policy
- Cable penetration increases
- ACT forms; focuses on TV violence
- (1979) Nickelodeon launches
- (1980) Simon's 3-year anti-trust exemption fails
- (1981) MTV launches
- (1983) Disney Channel launches
- (1985) M. Fowler calls TV "a toaster with pictures"
- ACT focuses on commercials
- (1990) Children's Television Act
- (1993) Markey introduces V-Chip
- (1996) Telecommunications Act
- (1996) CTA Amendment "The Rules"
- (2000) FTC Report Marketing to children
- Networks lease Sat. a.m. blocks
- Increasing ethnic and gender diversity in programs

Children's Programming
- Calvin and the Colonel ('61-'62)
- The Jackson Five ('71-'73)
- The Beatles ('65-'69)
- The Archie Show ('68-'69)
- Space Ghost and Dino Boy ('66-'68)
- The Fantastic Four ('67-'70)
- Spiderman ('67-'70)
- Fat Albert and the Cosby Kids ('72-'84)
- Mr. Rogers' Neighborhood ('63-'00)
- Sabrina and the Groovy Goolies/ Sabrina, the Teenage Witch ('70-'73)
- The Harlem Globetrotters ('70)
- The Electric Company ('71-'76)
- Zoom ('72-'80)
- Captain Kangaroo ('55-'84)
- Sesame Street ('69-)
- Strawberry Shortcake ('80)
- He Man and the Masters of the Universe ('83-'90)
- The Care Bears ('85-'88)
- G.I. Joe ('83-'86)
- My Little Pony ('86-'92)
- Clarissa Explains it All ('91-'94)
- Arthur ('91-)
- Barney and Friends ('92-)
- Captain Planet and the Planeteers ('90-'96)
- Rugrats ('91-'04)
- Pokemon ('98-)
- Mighty Morphin' Power Rangers('89-)
- Blue's Clues ('97-)
- Dora the Explorer('00-)
- Spongebob Squarepants ('99-)

established to provide entertainment for a young audience. Early on, these matinees showed short films and newsreels. However, as the popularity of films in the youth market was demonstrated, studios began to produce family films. The family film genre was initiated with Disney's release of *Snow White and the Seven Dwarfs* in 1937 (Paik, 2001).

By the middle of the 1920s, movies had become an important form of entertainment for American families (Paik, 2001). However, the privileged status of film was challenged by the introduction of radio. By the end of the 1930s, half of the homes in the United States had radios and listening had become a family affair. As the penetration of radio increased, its major source of revenue shifted from the sale of radios to the sale of commercial airtime. The establishment of networks proved to be an efficient system for a group of stations to share costs and provide larger audiences to advertisers. Thus, the network model was firmly ensconced by the end of the 1930s (Alexander & Owens, 1998).

Regulation of this new national medium was enacted in 1927 with the Radio Act, which established the concept of the airwaves as public property, and mandated the creation of the Federal Radio Commission (FRC). In an effort to avoid further governmental regulation, the National Association of Broadcasters (NAB) developed a Code of Ethics and Standards for Commercial Practice, a self-regulatory act that was put into place in 1929. The Code prohibited "offensive material," "fraudulent, deceptive, or obscene matter" and "false, deceptive, or grossly exaggerated" advertising claims (McCarthy, 1995). The Code was employed alongside the FRC mandate. The FRC was disbanded when Congress passed the Communications Act of 1934 and shifted responsibility for the regulation of radio to the Federal Communications Commission (FCC). The Communications Act of 1934 mandated serving the "public interest, convenience, and necessity" as the basis for granting broadcast licenses. Defining the public interest, particularly as it relates to groups with special needs (such as children) has been a challenging and contentious process (Minow & LaMay, 1995). Debates over the public interest obligations of broadcasters resurface regularly. In recent years, the argument has become increasingly complicated by new technology and media conglomeration.

Despite concerns over regulation and serving the public interest, radio continued to grow throughout the 1920s and 1930s. It was soon demonstrated that children would follow serial dramas, identify with fantastic characters, laugh at comedy, and most importantly, influence family purchasing patterns. Radio producers and sponsors began to view children as a valuable audience and programs specifically for children increased. Although mainly intended for entertainment and to advertise the sponsor's product, many of these programs contained references to societal concerns. For example, the program *Little Orphan Annie* addressed the collapse of the economy, unemployment, and labor unrest. *Captain Midnight* told the story of Captain Jim Albright, a brave aviator in World War I, and thus encouraged nationalism and gratitude for the efforts of military personnel. Captain Midnight, as well as the Green Hornet, Tarzan, the Lone Ranger, and Buck Rogers became immortalized figures in American culture through radio programs, and many have reappeared in other media forms, including comic books, television shows, and animated films.

At the end of the 1930s, a technology was introduced that would challenge the status of both film and radio. Television was exhibited for the first time at the 1939 World's Fair in Chicago, with the promise of the electronic delivery of news and entertainment in both audio and visual form directly to American homes. However, the growth of the television industry was stalled at the beginning of World War II when the FCC stopped issuing broadcast licenses because of the need to direct efforts into the development of technologies for the war effort (Barnouw, 1990).

The 1940s and 1950s

American Society and the World Scene.   America's participation in World War II began in 1941 when the Japanese attacked Pearl Harbor and continued through September 1945. The war was almost unanimously supported by the American public despite domestic injustices perpetrated by the government, such as the internment of Japanese Americans in work camps. The surrender of Germany and Japan to allied forces secured the United States' position as a world power, and the postwar years were marked by a growing economy and widespread prosperity. Large numbers of returning servicemen took advantage of the G.I. Bill of Rights, which enabled them to attend college and buy homes, setting the stage for the huge baby boom in the United States. The Interstate Highway Act of 1956 connected the sprawling suburbs that surrounded every city. The 1950s were good years for the growth of the White middle class in America. African Americans, in spite of their service in the armed forces during World War II, were not equal participants in the growing middle class. Their frustration fueled the boycott that launched the civil rights movement and introduced the country to the Reverend Martin Luther King Jr.

The era also brought the commencement of the Cold War defined by the arms race between the United States and the Soviet Union, and the policy of containment of the spread of Communism that included America's entry into the Korean conflict in 1950. Paranoia over Communism set off a wave of suspicion, which led to searches for Communists living in America. Spearheaded by Senator Joseph McCarthy and the House Un-American Activities Committee (HUAC). The anti-Communist crusade came to be known as "McCarthyism," and invaded the government, the entertainment industry, higher education, and the literary community. America's confidence in its political, technological, and educational superiority over the Communist system was shaken when the Soviet Union launched Sputnik into the earth's orbit in 1957 and set off the "Space Race." The new mood in America set the stage for a change from the old order to the new youthful energy of the Kennedy era (Alexrod, 2003; Schlesinger, 1993).

The Entertainment Industry.   The FCC resumed granting television station licenses in 1946. The following decades saw a decline in movie attendance and radio use, and an extremely rapid penetration of television set ownership, leading to the designation of the 1950s as "the Golden Age of Television" (Barnouw, 1990). Programmers, advertisers, and networks quickly learned that children often influenced parents' decision to purchase a television; therefore, providing programming for children became a priority in the early years of television. By 1950, 10% of American households owned a television set. By 1955, set ownership was up to 67% of U.S. households (Baker & Dessart, 1998).

The first NAB Television Code, adopted in 1951, was almost immediately attacked by the ACLU as illegal censorship. It contained explicit content restrictions on displays of violence and sexual content (Minow & LaMay, 1995). By the end of the 1950s, television was no longer the darling of the public. Widespread concern about juvenile delinquency led to hearings on the link between children's behavior and the images shown in popular television programs. Chaired by Senator Estes Kefauver, who also authored a Reader's Digest article entitled "Let's Get Rid of Tele-Violence," these televised hearings raised the level of public awareness and concern about violence and television (Hoerrner, 1999).

In 1947, *Small Fry Club*, the first daily 30-minute program designed specifically for children, went on the air. The show's host, Bob Emery, later played Buffalo Bob on the *Howdy Doody* show which debuted in December, 1947. (Davis, 1995). Howdy Doody, the marionette star of the program, was so popular that in 1948 he received more write-in votes for President of the United States than the independent candidate (Stark, 1997). In these early days of television, programming for children was not restricted to Saturday morning nor limited to hours before and after school. Many shows, such as *Mr. I. Magination, Kukla, Fran and Ollie*, and *Super Circus* were aired in the evening and viewed by both adults and children. Fischer (1983) reports that Mary Hartline, who appeared as the baton twirler on *Super Circus,* was so popular that she became "a topic of conversation throughout the nation" (p. 23). Rootie Kazootie, a Little Leaguer who appeared on national television from 1950–1954 as Little League Baseball was skyrocketing in popularity, illustrates the appearance of popular themes in programs.[1] Not all programming aired during this time was originated by the networks; frequently, a show created by a local station would move to the national networks. One example is *Space Patrol*, which was first shown locally in Los Angeles and later was aired nationally on ABC (Fischer, 1983).

As the Baby Boom generation grew up, fueled by a steady diet of children's television programming, shows were introduced that contained allusions to Cold War concerns, including surveillance, secret agents, and post-war paranoia. These shows reflected the rampant anti-Communism sentiment of the McCarthy era. The popular radio drama *Captain Midnight* reappeared on television and was on the air from 1954 until 1956. *Captain Midnight* was a unique opportunity both to expound Cold War themes and create consumer loyalty to the sponsor, Ovaltine. The Ovaltine Company made it possible for children to see themselves as special by providing for them the opportunity to send in box tops from Ovaltine and receive a secret decoder ring (Davis, 1995).

The 1960s and 1970s

American Society and the World Scene.   In his January 1960 state of the Union address, President Dwight D. Eisenhower predicted that 1960 would be "the most prosperous year in our history" (Schlesinger, 1993, p. 556). Indeed, both the 1960s and 1970s brought the continuation of unprecedented growth in the American economy. The rise in per capita disposable income fueled the spread of "suburbia," and the growth of labor unions raised the living standards for blue-collar workers. University populations exploded as the Baby Boom generation grew up and went off to college. President John F. Kennedy captured the imagination of the younger generation with the Peace Corps, the Space Program, the Youth Conversation Corps, and a domestic Peace Corps. However, the shadows cast by the Vietnam conflict, civil rights violations, race riots, political assassinations, and the continuing and deepening Cold War highlighted by the Cuban Missile Crisis made these decades some of the most tumultuous in the nation's history. These decades introduced society to women's liberation, the environmental movement, sit-ins and antidraft protests, student unrest, and the youth

---

[1] see http://www.pspb.org/smallballpressroom/pdf/Little_League_history.pdf

counterculture, embodied by Woodstock in August 1969. By the mid-1970s the nation was riveted by the Watergate scandals and public confidence in government was irreparably shaken. The optimism that characterized the start of this period disappeared. The election of Ronald Reagan in 1980 was viewed hopefully, as the sign of a new era (Alexrod, 2003; Schlesinger, 1993).

The Entertainment Industry.   The rapidly growing entertainment industry was a significant part of the economic growth of the 1960s and 1970s. By 1960, ninety percent of U.S. households had television sets. The three major networks, ABC, CBS, and NBC, were solidly established. The Corporation for Public Broadcasting (CPB) was created by Congress in 1966. The Public Broadcasting Service (PBS), launched in 1967, featured 3 hours of daily programming. Color television arrived in the early 1960s and NBC launched its first season of color programs in 1965. Despite an incredible amount of success and forward momentum, the entertainment industry also was subject to increasing criticism. In 1961, Newton Minow, the newly appointed Chairman of the FCC, declared television's offerings a "vast wasteland." His speech stunned the broadcasting industry, and is still frequently quoted by critics of television (Minow & LaMay, 1995).

Sparked by public concern over societal violence, President Johnson created the National Commission on the Causes and Prevention of Violence in 1968. The commission's eight branches investigated various areas of concern, one of which was the mass media. The commission presented a quantitative and qualitative examination of the violence in entertainment television, demonstrating that violence was not only pervasive, but glamorized and portrayed as an acceptable means of resolving conflict. Although the work of the commission was criticized for including speculations on effects not supported by the data, it did prompt further research, which resulted in the 1971 Report of the Surgeon General of the United States, a collection of studies on the effects of television violence. Despite this governmental concern about media violence, news footage from the battlefields of Vietnam and protest sites around the country depicted actual violence more gruesome than previous fictional accounts (see Cole et al., 1996).

Despite the horrific images depicted on the nightly news and the numerous protests and rallies staged by outraged young people, much primetime network programming seemed to deny that this turmoil existed. Musical variety shows such as *Shindig* and *Hullabaloo* provided a "very scrubbed down, nonthreatening version of youth culture" (Hilmes, 2003, p. 81). Similarly, several programs from the early 1970s depicted young people in traditional institutions such as *Storefront*

Lawyers, The Young Lawyers, and *The Interns.* These sanitized depictions of youth were quite different from those portrayed on the news.

During the 1960s the techniques for advertising to the child audience were reexamined. Whereas early television programmers and advertisers viewed children as an important audience because of their potential influence over family purchasers, by the 1960s, advertisers shifted their focus to adult viewers. Because of this, prime time air increased in value and children's shows, primarily cartoons, were relegated to Saturday morning because of their inability to attract advertisers willing to pay increased rates. Within the confines of Saturday morning, cartoons were shown that had been produced for theatrical release and recycled for television broadcast—a great departure from the prime-time programming of earlier years (Mittel, 2003). Despite this temporary drop in program quality, the establishment of Saturday morning programs was a significant step in segmenting the television viewing audience. This segmentation has enabled advertisers to target adult viewers in primetime and ultimately has encouraged programmers to create age-target, educational, and entertaining programming for child viewers.

Once Saturday morning proved to be a profitable timeslot for reaching the child audience, production of original cartoons began. Cartoons such as *The Beatles* and *The Archie Show* attempted to emulate the musical variety shows popular in primetime. More prominent, however, was the trend toward superhero cartoons, from *Space Ghost and Dino Boy* to *The Fantastic Four. Spiderman* was introduced in 1967, followed by *The Batman/Superman Hour* in 1968 (Fischer, 1983). Superhero cartoons can be read as a reaction to societal concerns over crime and violence. However, most shows contained a substantial amount of violence. Superhero shows were among the first genre to portray empowered females. Both Gravity Girl from *Birdman and the Galaxy* and the Invisible Girl from *The Fantastic Four* possessed superpowers. However, it was not until 1970 that a female character with magic powers, Sabrina from *Sabrina and the Groovy Goolies* (later renamed *Sabrina, the Teenage Witch*) starred in a show of her own (Fischer, 1983).

Heather Hendershot (1998) writes in *Saturday Morning Censors,* "U.S. broadcasters regulate themselves largely out of fear of federal (FCC and Congressional) intervention" (p. 32). Increased governmental concern about media violence, as demonstrated by the large number of commissioned studies, urged broadcasters to self-regulate content. Standards and Practices (S&P) departments were enlarged, and increased regulation of violence was seen in both general and children's programming (Hendershot, 1998). By 1970, many of the superhero series of the late 1960s had been cancelled, and shows such as *The*

Heckle and Jeckle Show, Hot Wheels, and *H.R. Pufnstuf* (pp. 273–279) had taken their places (Fischer, 1983). This gradual lessening of violent cartoons represents a positive reaction to concerns over television violence on the part of the entertainment industry.

The effect of the civil rights movement eventually filtered down to the children's programming arena. Proof that a change was needed can be found in the short-lived (1961–1962) series *Calvin and the Colonel.* This program was an adaptation of the popular radio series *Amos 'n' Andy,* in which two White men in blackface played stereotypical African American characters. Such racial stereotyping was forbidden in radio and television programs by the early 1960s, so *Calvin and the Colonel* attempted to sidestep the issue by recasting the characters of Amos and Andy as a fox and a bear. However, the characters maintained the same stereotypical voices and the storylines mimicked those of the *Amos 'n' Andy* programs (Fischer, 1983). A more positive reaction to the civil rights movement can be seen in the creation of the show *Fat Albert and the Cosby Kids,* which was added to the CBS Saturday morning line-up in response to the 1971 Best Report that charged children's programs such as *The Jackson Five* and *The Harlem Globetrotters* with inadequately portraying the Black experience. *Fat Albert* relied on input from social scientists and educational consultants to capture the real issues facing African American children living in urban settings (Davis, 1995). According to Lou Scheimer, President of Filmation Studios, the early plots were "not too edgy" but after the show caught on, there was the "opportunity to do something really interesting and worthwhile" through the introduction of prosocial content to Saturday morning (McLees, 2004: pp. 7–12). One example of the important but "not too edgy" topics addressed in the series is found in the episode "Smoke Gets in Your Hair." In this episode, one of the neighborhood kids takes up smoking cigarettes, and the other kids must deal with pressure to try smoking as well.

Yet another example of the impact of the civil rights movement on raising the consciousness of the industry can be found in the relaunch of *The New Mickey Mouse Club* in 1976. The series originally aired from 1955 to 1959 with an entirely White cast. When the "new" version was launched, its cast of Mouseketeers included minority characters (Davis, 1995).

The suburban experience arrived on television in the extremely popular animated take-off of *The Honeymooners*—*The Flintstones.* This "beautiful parody of suburban life" (Fisher, 1983, p. 112) occupied a primetime slot from 1960 to 1966. Similarly, the Hanna Barbera character Secret Squirrel, alias Agent 000, parodied the popular character James Bond, Agent 007, who was himself a Cold War parody (Fischer, 1983).

The activism of the era found expression in the children's television arena with the establishment of Action for Children's Television (ACT) in 1968. ACT was established primarily to advocate for better quality, less commercial children's television. ACT managed to get attention from the FCC, the press, and the public by being "confrontational but less threatening" than other female-dominated interest groups of the era (Hendershot, 1998, p. 67). The work of ACT led the FCC to establish a permanent children's unit and issue a Children's Policy Statement in 1974. Action for Children's Television continued its work for the next two decades and Peggy Charren, its cofounder, continues to be a voice for quality children's television to this day. (See Montgomery, chap 12, this volume, for more on ACT and advocacy in children's television.)

The launch of Public Broadcasting in the late 1960s brought with it several innovative efforts in children's programming. The best known is *Sesame Street*. Premiered in 1969, *Sesame Street* was designed to attract and educate young children, particularly those in minority groups and those in poverty (Minow & LaMay, 1995). Another highly innovative program from this era is *Zoom*, which first aired on PBS in 1972, Targeted at elementary school-aged children, *Zoom* featured a multicultural, live-action cast of children who engaged in songs, skits, and games. *Zoom* extended the PBS mission of educational programming to older children and offered a format different from the cartoons that dominated the programming for this age group (Davis, 1995).

The 1971 Surgeon General's report led to the adoption of the NAB Code in 1975. In its 18th edition, the code contained a family viewing policy—a requirement that programs containing violent content be scheduled after 9:00 p.m.. That policy was challenged in 1975 by the Writer's Guild of America (WGA) in a suit that charged that the policy was not voluntary industry self-regulation, but rather policy coerced by the threat of government regulation. Further, the WGA asserted that the policy violated First Amendment rights. Although the decision in favor of the WGA was eventually vacated, the decision undermined the NAB Policy and after the next challenge (1982), the entire Code was discontinued.

In 1972, cable, or CATV, created originally to bring clear reception to remote areas, began offering new programming services with the launch of HBO. By the end of the 1970s, several unique programming services were launched and the rapid penetration of cable was underway (Dirr, 2001).

The 1980s and 1990s

American Society and the World Scene. When Ronald Reagan took office in 1981, the morale of the country was low, the economy was in trouble, major industries were faltering, and Americans were being held hostage in Iran. The public was eager for Reagan's optimistic message of patriotism and hoped for an economic revolution. "Reagonomics" were characterized by deregulation, budget cuts, and tax breaks. New economic programs employed "trickle-down" economic principles that reduced taxes for the wealthy in hopes that their increased investment would create employment opportunities for others. The economy steadily improved until 1987, when the stock market plunged, sending the country into yet another economic crisis.

International affairs included the bombing of the U.S. Embassy in Beirut, the invasion of Grenada, and finally, the beginning of the end of the Cold War. In 1987, while the country celebrated the 200th anniversary of the Constitution, President Reagan was condemned for the Iran Contra Affair. Major events held the public's attention: Tylenol poisonings, the Challenger accident, and the rapidly advancing AIDS epidemic. When George H. W. Bush was elected President in 1988, the economy was struggling and the unemployment rate was high. Bush's single term as President included the end of the Cold War in 1989 and a successful campaign in the Middle East, the Persian Gulf War in 1991. In 1992, William Clinton was elected President.

In the midst of an economic boom fueled by the dot-com craze of the mid-1990s, the country reacted to terrorist attacks perpetrated by both foreign terror groups (1993 World Trade Center bombing in New York City) and U.S. citizens (Oklahoma City bombing and the Unabomber). The O. J. Simpson murder trial and the Monica Lewinsky scandal captured attention at home and abroad for months on end. Children surprised adults with an appetite for reading when the Harry Potter phenomenon took off in 1997. The Exxon Valdez oil spill, the effects of El Niño, research into depletion of the ozone layer, and a major earthquake in Los Angeles brought environmental concerns to the public's attention. The campaign against the effects of tobacco took hold, precipitating big tobacco's losses in a number of court cases. An epidemic of school shootings throughout the 1990s culminated with the massacre of 12 people at Columbine High School in 1999. The decade and the century ended with the country split ideologically and politically, a reality that was illustrated by the stalemate in the election of 2000 (Axelrod, 2003; McDonough et al., 2001; Schlesinger, 1993).

The Entertainment Industry.   The governmental focus on deregulation throughout the 1980s led to the elimination of the NAB Code of Ethics. However, public concern about media impact (particularly that of violent media) remained strong. In 1980, Senator Paul Simon proposed a 3-year antitrust exemption to permit network cooperation on the development of a voluntary set of content standards or a code of ethics. The networks challenged this antitrust exemption, and ultimately Senator Simon was forced to rescind his request for exemption, thus leaving television content under the control of market forces.

Broadcast networks faced competition from the growing cable industry, which reached more than 50% penetration of the audience by the mid-1980s (Pecora, 2004). Dedicated channels such as MTV, The Weather Channel, and C-SPAN provided cable subscribers access to targeted programming around the clock, reducing viewer dependence on network schedules. The widespread adoption of the VCR beginning in the early 1980s also contributed to a changing dynamic for television viewing. VCR penetration increased greatly in the mid-1980s, with an estimated 50% penetration rate by 1987 (Sterling & Kitross, 2002).

The stiff competition set forward by cable and VCRs, combined with increasing costs of production and a focus on creating programming for syndication led to a great number of daytime game shows and talk shows. In primetime, made-for-television movies and miniseries proved to be popular, and new dramatic techniques were tested in programs such as *Hill Street Blues*, *L.A. Law*, and *St. Elsewhere*. Allusions to Cold-War concerns resurfaced in a handful of series such as *Mission: Impossible*, *The A-Team*, and *Hawaii Five-O* (Barnouw, 1990).

In 1984, NBC premiered *The Cosby Show*, a weekly situation comedy about the Huxtable family. The show was a huge success, earning top ratings for the 5 years between 1985 and 1990, and pushing NBC to into the leading network spot for the first time (Sterling & Kittross, 2002). *The Cosby Show* painted a very different picture of the life of an African-American family than most shows of the period, and in this depiction, the show reflected the progress made in interracial affairs in the United States in the 20 years since the beginning of the civil rights movement. The Huxtables, a large, upper middle-class family stood in sharp contrast to characters in earlier shows such as *Amos 'n' Andy*, which portrayed highly derogatory caricature of African Americans, and *The Jeffersons*, which depicted the challenges of African Americans who were "movin' on up" to traditionally White neighborhoods (Barnouw, 1990).

Also in 1984, the FCC voted to allow unrestricted commercial airtime, a decision that left the number of commercials shown in any given program to the discretion of the broadcaster. As children's shows did not bring in the same amount of advertising revenue as popular shows for family or adult audiences, networks began to discontinue many shows created specifically for young viewers. Engelhardt (1986) cites a drop in the average time allotted to children's programs from 11.3 to a mere 4.4 hours per week. This drop in network children's programming opened up a place for inexpensive animated shows based on licensed characters such as *He-Man and the Masters of the Universe* and *Strawberry Short-cake*; thus, the program-length commercial was born.

By 1985, at least 40 licensed character-based programs were on the air, a testament to their economy and popularity. These programs, which included *The Care Bears*, *My Little Pony*, *Thundercats*, and *G.I. Joe*, were of debatable educational and aesthetic quality, but were inexpensive to produce and effective means for advertising character-based products (Engelhardt, 1986; Seiter, 1995). Further, they are an obvious product and reflection of the laissez-faire economic policy of the time.

Alongside the rapid growth of cable channels for adults throughout the 1980s came a handful of cable channels targeted at children. The first of these was Nickelodeon. Launched in 1979, Nickelodeon grew quickly, employing an unorthodox strategy: network branding. Pecora (2004) writes, "[U]nlike the networks and syndicated programmers, whose program characters promoted a licensing character concept, Nickelodeon created a concept around the cable channel" (p. 25). The focus on branding has driven Nickelodeon's selection and creation of programs since its early days and has been a huge factor in its success at becoming *the* network for kids (Simensky, 2004).

Nickelodeon's original programming from the 1980s and 1990s demonstrates a conscious effort to sensitively portray the realities of teenage life. Programs such as *Fifteen*, *Who's Afraid of the Dark*, and *Clarissa Explains It All* dealt with issues such as multiculturalism, relationships with family and friends, and drug, alcohol, and tobacco use. Not only are these issues of great importance to the programs' teen audience, they reflected societal concern with interracial relations, family values, and the "War on Drugs" campaign launched by the Federal Government. As Sandler (2004) describes, "[t]he mature handling of teenage issues in all these shows [intended for teens] further solidified the components that made up Nickelodeon's brand essence. Nickelodeon could be goofy and messy, and at the same time sensitive and relevant" (p. 49). The "goofy and messy" side of the network was exemplified in its venture into original animated series in 1991 with the introduction of "Nicktoons". The first Nicktoons (*Rugrats*, *Doug*, and *Ren & Stimpy*) followed the lead of Fat Albert in that they focused on real life, rather than fantasy and superheroes—a welcome departure from traditional cartoons filled with violence in the wake of school shootings and controversy over violent video games (Sandler, 2004).

The environmental movement appeared in children's programming in 1990 in the form of *Captain Planet and the Planeteers*. The environmental movement began in the mid-1970s, and grew throughout the 1980s and early 1990s, fueled by scientific research, outcry over environmental disasters such as the Exxon Valdez oil spill, and celebrity advocacy (R. London, personal communication, February 10, 2005). The five Planeteers, chosen by the Spirit of the Earth to protect it and its inhabitants, were each given a ring capable of controlling one of the elements. When combined, the rings summoned Captain Planet, the show's progressive superhero. The show's tagline, "the power is yours!" emphasizes individual responsibility in stewardship of the environment.[2]

In an attempt to rein in children's television after the deregulatory period of the 1980s, The Children's Television Act was passed in 1990. The Act posited a solution to the ever-increasing concern about the content and availability of children's television, stipulating that any station wishing to renew its broadcast license had to provide proof that children's educational and informational programming was part of its program schedule. This attempt at self-regulation on the part of the industry was unsuccessful. Because it lacked clear parameters for the content, amount, and scheduling of such programs, it was vulnerable to abuse. Therefore, in 1996, the Children's Television Act was amended with stricter guidelines defining educational/informational (E/I) programming. "The Rules" required broadcasters to air 3 hours of regularly scheduled, clearly identified E/I programming per week. However, by the time the Act was strengthened and amended, cable channels such as Nickelodeon had established a loyal viewing audience uninterested in the meager offerings of the networks. Broadcasters lost huge numbers of child viewers, and most began to look for ways to get out of the children's programming business.

2000 to 2005 and Beyond

American Society and the World Scene. The new millennium began with a great deal of waiting. The world held its breath in anticipation of widespread chaos incited by fears of the Y2K technical glitch—and exhaled gently when no chaos resulted. The nation also endured a month-long protracted dispute over the 2000 presidential election, which ultimately required a Supreme Court settlement to confirm George W. Bush as the 43rd President of the United States. The first 5 years of the decade have witnessed a struggling economy, high gas prices, and decreased employment throughout the country. The national climate underwent another radical shift following the September 11, 2001 terrorist attacks in New York City and Washington D.C. The effects of the tragedy were profound. President Bush launched the "War on Terror" in October, 2001 and deployed troops to Afghanistan in search of Al Qaeda and its leader,

---

[2]see http://www.tvtome.com/CaptainPlanetandthePlaneteers

Osama Bin Laden. In the meantime, the United States became a nation obsessed with fear. The Department of Homeland Security was established to manage domestic policy related to security and the Patriot Act was enacted with little debate or revision. In March 2003, the United States invaded Iraq; this military action did not have the level of international support that followed the invasion of Afghanistan attacks, which strained the relationship between the United States and other world powers. Hussein was quickly removed from power; however, up to this point in 2005, winning the peace in Iraq has proven elusive. In addition to coverage of the war, several major scandals, including Enron, WorldCom, the winter Olympics in Salt Lake City, and the Catholic Church, have dominated the news.

The lives of children have also undergone great changes in recent years. The *No Child Left Behind* (NCLB) act, a major educational initiative mandated to public schools, gave many Americans hope for improved public education, but has been widely criticized by educators and administrators. Technology use has soared for children of all ages. Cell phones, wireless Internet, innovative gaming systems, and portable music players such as iPods have integrated technology into kids' everyday existence.

The Entertainment Industry. The new millennium was marked by sweeping changes in the entertainment industry. The impact of the nation's struggling economy was felt by studios and networks, as profits fell and production costs soared. Triggered by the success of *Survivor* in 2000, the industry increased production of reality shows. Reality programming is less expensive to produce than most dramas or sit-coms and the format lends itself to corporate sponsorship and prominent product placement, advertising strategies that have become important due to personal video recorder (PVR) technologies such as TiVo, which allow viewers to fast forward through advertisements (Fass & Kafka, 2003). In 2002, FOX revived the musical variety-show format with its hit show *American Idol*. Elaine Showalter (2003) commended the show for illustrating "how the postmillennial United States is changing with regard to race, class, national identity and politics" (p. 2) through its universal appeal. She writes, "[a]ppealing simultaneously to Marines, Mormons, gays, blacks and Latinos, and to every region of the country, *American Idol* has a legitimate claim to its label of reality TV" (p. 2). Because of this universal appeal, *American Idol* has been successful in creating a family viewing experience, a challenge rarely met by primetime shows.

In 2003, the FCC mandated new media ownership rules allowing greater consolidation of television station, radio station, and newspaper ownership. This policy negated previous antitrust legislation, and reinstated *vertical integration*, a structure that allows a parent company to control production, exhibition, and distribution of a property. Research conducted in reaction to the mandate by Children Now, an independent, nonpartisan advocacy group, asserted that media consolidation "diminishes the availability and diversity of children's television programming" (Children Now, 2003, p. 10). The Children Now report was only one piece of a large amount of criticism raised against the new FCC policy. This criticism and the resultant public backlash contributed to the Senate's decision to overturn the ruling.

In January 2004, 140 million people watching the Super Bowl halftime show were surprised by a brief exposure of Janet Jackson's breast during a dance routine with Justin Timberlake. The incident resulted in over a million complaints to the FCC, stiffer fines against broadcasters for violations of the agency's indecency rules, and a complete overhaul of the system for processing complaints (Ahrens, 2005).

The decline in the Saturday morning audience for network programs, the implementation of the Children's Television Act and Amendments, and the growth of cable, particularly cable channels dedicated to children, led the broadcast networks to decrease resources allocated to children's programming in the early part of this decade. Rather than producing original children's programming to satisfy the obligations of the Children's Television Act, networks employ one of two strategies. First, some networks lease the children's time-block to outside production companies. For example, 4 Kids Entertainment was selected to provide all children's programming for the FOX network while Discovery Kids supplies NBC with its children's programming block. A second strategy is repurposing programs from program providers within the parent corporation. For example, E/I-qualifying shows from Nick Jr. aired on CBS through summer, 2006, while shows from the Disney Channel provide the qualifying content for ABC. Both of these strategies are cost-effective ways for the network to meet CTA requirements.

Children's programs created in the last 5 years have increasingly reflected a national interest in interactivity. Although producers of children's television have always been cognizant of attentional processes and formal features that encourage active viewing, computers have shifted the standard from activity to interactivity. Anderson (2004) describes the model used by the Nick Jr. show, *Blues Clues,* to encourage interactivity in its viewers. First, the host directly asks children to participate. Then, children are given instructions on how to complete the task at hand. Third, viewers are given plenty of time to respond. Although this makes for a slow-paced show, the model has demonstrated its value in promoting attention and interactivity in the preschool audience. Other preschool shows, such as *Dora the Explorer* and the *Sesame Street* segment "Elmo's World," utilize interactive elements as well as direct references to computer use.

In September of 2000, the Federal Trade Commission (2000) issued a report entitled *Marketing Violent Entertainment to Children*. The report examined practices in the motion picture, music recording, and electronic game industries that have resulted in promoting inappropriate products, such as movies rated "R" due to violence, video games with an "M" for Mature rating, or albums with explicit lyrics, to children and youth. The report illustrated instances in which each industry violated its own system of self-regulation by promoting such products to children. These findings prompted plans in several branches of the industry to change marketing practices to conform with existing self-regulatory ratings systems (Caught Red-Handed, 2001).

Another area of focus in recent children's media is obesity. In 2001, *The Surgeon General's Call to Action to Prevent and Decrease Overweight and Obesity* was released. This report detailed the increased prevalence of overweight and obese people in the United States population, including children and adolescents, and cited a three-fold increase in overweight or obese adolescents since 1980. Inactivity was highlighted as a key contributing factor to the increase in obesity, and a direct link between media products (specifically, television and computer/video games) and inactivity was articulated (Department of Health and Human Services, 2001). The industry responded by rolling out a number of initiatives to encourage children to be more active. Nickelodeon's initiative "Let's Just Play" encourages physical activity, participation in sports and games, and a generally active lifestyle.[3] Through public service announcements (PSAs), the network encourages kids to turn off the television. Special events such as the Worldwide Day of Play, during which the network went off the air for 3 hours, substituting its regular Saturday-afternoon programming with graphics, and encourage kids to get active. In addition, the program provides grants to schools and community organizations for improved physical activity programs.[4] Similarly, Sesame Workshop has created an initiative called "Healthy Habits for Life," which provides information and activities for children and parents regarding physical activity, nutrition, and healthy habits.[5] Producers of goods and services attractive to children have also amended advertising campaigns to encourage

---

[3]see http//:www.nick.com/all_nick/everything_nick/public_letsjustplay2.jhtml)
[4]see http//:www.nick.com/all_nick/everything_nick/public_wwdop.jhtml).
[5]see http//:www.sesameworkshop.com/healthyhabits

activity and better nutrition. For example, Kraft Foods has committed to increase advertising of more nutritious products and revise product labels to increase clarity ("Kraft Foods announces marketing changes to emphasize more nutrious products" 2005). Nike has created NikeGO, a multilayered initiative to provide after-school and summer programs that feature physical activity, reinstate physical education classes in public schools that have had to reduce or eliminate the class, award grants for the creation of community programs to encourage activity, and support research into the "funding, advocacy, and program efforts aimed at reversing the current childhood health crisis of sedentary lifestyles and poor eating habits."[6]

The previous pages sketch a general outline of the interplay between societal events, government and industry policies, and the content of children's television. The examples presented are just a few of the many instances in which the industry has recognized a responsibility for assisting children in understanding and adapting to a variety of societal change. We now focus our attention on a specific issue: violence. In the next section of the chapter, we examine three different reactions to incidents of societal and media violence.

CASE STUDY: FOCUS ON VIOLENCE

The distinction of programming specifically for children, as well as the idea that children should be educated by television are related, prompted by the idea of childhood as a special stage of life. Prior to the societal changes enacted by industrialization, improvements in health care that lessened infant mortality, and the rise of the middle class, children were seen primarily as cheap labor. Little emphasis was placed on parent–child bonds, child-rearing techniques, or sentimentality toward children (Jenkins, 1998). As Lynn Spigel (2001) discusses in *Welcome to the Dreamhouse*, the Industrial Revolution in the United States sparked changes in adults' thinking about the status of children; in particular, it was recognized that children were not just little adults, that they needed care, education, and protection, and that adults had a responsibility for providing for children's needs. The development of a genre of literature and entertainment products specifically for children is one result of this shift in thinking. It is also one of the driving forces behind the perennial concerns over violence in media products consumed by children.

---

[6]see http://www.nikego.com

In each of the three cases that follow, different strategies are employed to address and manage violence; however, the issue is consistently addressed in a way that is sensitive to children's cognitive and emotional needs. One strategy is to facilitate conversations between children and adults about violence. This is a technique that aligns with child development research and traditional pedagogy, and is the method employed by Fred Rogers on *Mr. Rogers' Neighborhood.* Another strategy focuses on management of the content available to children. This is evident in self-regulatory efforts such as those enacted by Fox Family Worldwide[7] to reduce violence in its action-adventure programs and the collaborative effort within the children's television community to revise content guidelines in 2000. A third strategy works to build resiliency in child viewers by teaching life skills and coping techniques. It is not the intention of this chapter to rank or compare the effectiveness of these differing approaches. Rather, the goal is to highlight the variety of reactions to violence enacted by the children's television community.

Mr. Rogers' Neighborhood, a PBS show produced by Family Communications, Inc. in Pittsburgh, PA is renowned for its use of child development research in producing a show sensitive to the cognitive, social, and emotional needs of preschool-aged children. The longest running show on PBS, more than 900 episodes of *Mister Rogers' Neighborhood* were produced between 1968 and 2000. Each episode is designed to teach necessary skills for school, encourage healthy self-esteem and respect for others, and emphasize the values of family, love, and discipline.[8]

Early in the life of the show, Fred Rogers' deep concern for children led him to create a special episode of the in reaction to the 1968 assassination of Robert F. Kennedy (Rogers, 1968). The episode, which Rogers wrote overnight, was broadcast a few days following the incident and was shown in the evening to ensure parents' ability to watch with their children. The episode alternates between Rogers talking directly to parents (in the same way that he talks directly to child viewers) in the living room of his television house and a dramatization in the Land of Make-Believe. The vignettes in the Land of Make-Believe work to illustrate the power of play for children in understanding and expressing feelings about upsetting situations. The value of fantasy play for a child's cognitive

---

[7]During the period discussed in this chapter, Fox Family Worldwide consisted of a broadcast channel, Fox Kids, and a cable channel, Fox Family Channel. Fox Family Worldwide ceased to exist when the channel was acquired by ABC Disney in 2002 and converted to ABC Family.

[8]see http//:www.fci.org/mister_rogers_neighborhood

and emotional development is described by Piaget and Inhelder (1969) as "indispensable to his [the child's] affective and intellectual equilibrium" (p. 58) because it allows the child to assimilate new information into his or her existing understanding of the world. In this way, imaginative play is a valuable tool for development, and may be ultimately more valuable than other tools that help children cope by simply adapting behaviors to the new situation.

Sensitive subjects are regularly discussed on the show within the context of the Land of Make-Believe. This particular episode incorporates a second layer of fantasy, as the characters in the Land of Make-Believe pretend to reenact the assassination shown on television. Anxieties manifest in a variety of ways, ranging from Daniel Striped Tiger's generalized fears for his own safety to the anxieties that surface for X the Owl and Lady Elaine Fairchild due to their misunderstanding of the differences between pretending or wishing that something will happen, and acting in a way to carry out the action.

Exchanges between the human (adult) and puppet (child) characters in the Land of Make-Believe model coping and communication skills for children and parents alike. Additionally, this special episode contains segments intended specifically for parents. In these segments, Rogers attempted to help parents understand their roles in helping children deal with violent events, as well as the emotions leading to and surrounding violent actions. In this way, Rogers both taught coping skills and developed strategies for resiliency. In addition to having discussed and modeled these strategies, Rogers expressed his concern with graphic displays of violence on television, and issued a plea for parents to protect their children from such images.

The 1968 special was not the only time *Mister Rogers' Neighborhood* addressed the issue of violence. In 1981, prompted by several violent events, including John Lennon's assassination and the assassination attempts on Pope John Paul II and President Regan, Rogers created an episode entitled "Violence in the News: Helping Kids Understand." This episode featured interviews with children, who openly discussed the images in the news media that concerned or frightened them. The children who were interviewed were school-aged children, a few years older than the average viewers of the show. Intercut with the interviews was a story from the Land of Make-Believe, in which a sensational kidnapping is covered by the neighborhood news station. Allusions to practices by the real news media peppered the story, particularly references to replaying a dramatic clip numerous times for impact on the audience.

Both of these episodes approached the issue of violence in a developmentally appropriate and sensitive manner, and with a strong commitment to appropriate pedagogy. This is the same method used by Rogers in every episode of the program, regardless of the subject addressed. In the lifetime of the show, Rogers addressed many sensitive subjects for young viewers—from divorce to death to anxieties about being sucked down the drain of the bathtub, all with sensitivity, and concern for the well-being of kids.

In contrast to shows such as *Mister Rogers' Neighborhood*, whose status as a PBS show dictates educational content and exempts it from the need to generate profit, network children's programming occupies a place of constant tension, caught between the industry's perceived responsibility to provide safe and educational programming, and the network's status as a for-profit entity. Just as capitalist interests over-took public interests in the 1980s, resulting in program-length commercials, the capacity of violent programs to bring in high ratings and large revenues has again challenged the networks' commitment to serving the interests of children.

Within a network, the Broadcast Standards and Practices Department oversees the content of original and acquired programming. This department has the responsibility of creating, enacting, monitoring, and enforcing content guidelines that are aligned with FCC regulations, social and cultural norms, and the goals and brand identity of the network. This self-regulation is performed with the goal of avoiding external (e.g., Federal) censorship. In children's programming, the role of Standards and Practices Departments is particularly important and nuanced, as issues such as age-appropriateness, educational objectives, and family and community values must be given paramount consideration in the creation of programs (Mitroff, Ash, & Evans, 2001).

The Mighty Morphin' Power Rangers, a live-action show imported from Japan, began airing on Fox Family Channel during the 1993–1994 season, and continues airing (in various incarnations) to this day on ABC Family.[8] Despite concerns over its egregious displays of violence, the program consistently has made annual profits in the millions (Pecora, 1998). *The Mighty Morphin' Power Rangers* was in its seventh season when the school shootings took place at Columbine High School in Littleton, Colorado in April of 1999. Columbine was the most widely publicized of a series of school shootings in the late 1990s, particularly because of the connections made between the assailants and violent video games.

At Fox Family World Wide, Columbine served as a "last straw" in a long debate over the violence in some of the network's programs,

---

[8]see http//:www.ABCfamily.com

Power Rangers in particular. The Broadcast Standards and Practices Department was quickly charged with the task of revising existing guidelines for fantasy violence and action programs. Within weeks of the shootings, new guidelines were developed and approved internally. The new guidelines focused on avoiding imitable violent behavior in fantasy violence shows, the nonrealistic depiction of weapons (e.g. guns that shoot lasers rather than bullets), and the portrayal of consequences to violence. With the approval of the new guidelines, considerable changes were made to the network's action/adventure programs, including *Power Rangers.*

A similar revision of existing self-regulations was initiated by Mediascope in 2000. In a collaboration with DIC Entertainment, a media company specializing in children's entertainment products, a group of experts and industry representation were convened to review and revise a set of content guidelines for children's media that had been created at a similar conference in the mid-1990s. Both the original guidelines and the revisions were created primarily for the writers of DIC programs, particularly syndicated and straight-to-video programs, for which no other standards existed. The guidelines were made available to producers of any type of children's media in the form of a pamphlet titled *Special Considerations for Creators of Children's Media* (2000).

The "phamphlet" included guidelines for character and values, diversity and stereotyping, and conflict and violence. Each of the guidelines was carefully considered, as it was important for each guideline to be neither too vague (to satisfy the requirements of the advocacy groups), nor too specific (to allow for the creativity in production). The final outcome of the revision contained new emphasis on the need to avoid "[g]ratituous, graphic, or excessive violence—whether physical or psychological," a guideline that captured the current programming trend or increasingly graphic violence, and attempted to reshape the practices of children's media producers from within the industry (2000).

The internal self-regulations occurring at Fox Family and the establishment of the *Special Considerations for Creators of Children's Media* happened concurrently with a larger movement for self-regulation by the industry as a whole. In response to a mandate from the FCC, the industry released a scheme for content ratings in 1997. Despite criticism for inconsistent use and lack of parental education and awareness, the content ratings continue to appear on all children's programs.

As internal guidelines and content ratings attempted to regulate violent content primarily in fictional programs, the violence in everyday life increased with the terrorist attacks on the World Trade Center and the Pentagon on September 11, 2001. The news media, as it often does with striking graphic images, replayed the footage of the plane crashing into the Twin Towers and the collapse of the towers hundreds of times in the days that followed the attacks. As America struggled to comprehend and deal with these events, the huge number of casualties involved, and the uncertainty about safety, the entertainment industry reassessed its responsibility to its viewers in a time of such crisis. The action movie *Collateral Damage* was withheld from release for 5 months following the incident because of its plot about terrorism, networks reedited various shows to eliminate references to terrorism and jokes about airport security, and images of the Twin Towers were removed from scenes in several movies, including *Spiderman* and *Zoolander*. The events of September 11th have fueled episodes of several hour-long dramas, including *Law and Order* and *Third Watch* (Freeman-Greene, 2003) and have also been addressed in children's programming, in particular by four episodes of *Sesame Street* created to alleviate children's fears, help parents and children discuss the events, and teach resiliency and coping skills necessary for young children to deal with trauma (Mazzarino & Diego, 2003).

The four special episodes produced after September 11th focused on fire safety, loss, bullying, and diversity and inclusion. According to Rosemarie Truglio, the Workshop's decision to address general life skills rather than the specifics of the September 11th attacks was "informed by a group of mental health specialists and also by PBS's decision to keep PBS as a safe haven for children" (R. Truglio, personal communication, December 16, 2004). Each episode, in the sensitive and age-appropriate way for which *Sesame Street* is known, addressed the feelings a preschooler might feel in a trying situation.[9]

The issues of diversity and inclusion were identified as important topics to address because of concerns about prejudice and exclusion directed at children of some ethnic or religious backgrounds following the attacks. Loss was also identified as an important topic as some children experienced the loss of parents, siblings, or other loved ones as a result of the events of September 11th. The fourth episode in this series attempted to address the feelings of exclusion and fear some children felt after the attacks, and modeled several strategies for dealing with bullies that children could employ independently or with adult assistance (Truglio, Kolter, Cohen & Housley-Juster, 2005).

Sesame Street's focus on general, long-term strategies for resilience differs greatly from the approaches taken by *Mr. Rogers' Neighborhood,*

---

[9]These episodes were shown on PBS and also distributed in an outreach kit to parents and educators. The outreach kit contained information for parents on a campaign called "You can ask!" which encouraged parents to ask their young children what they are thinking and feeling in response to difficult situations.

Fox Family Worldwide, and the producers of the *Special Considerations* in addressing violence. Like the special episodes of *Mr. Rogers' Neighborhood*, the post-September 11th episodes were intended for parents and children to view together and use as a starting point for further conversations. As programs intended for preschoolers, both *Mister Rogers' Neighborhood* and *Sesame Street* have the luxury of assuming this high level of parental involvement. For older children, there is, as Amy Jordan (2001) reports, "an apparent discrepancy between what [violent programs] parents say they 'protect' their children from and what children actually watch" (p. 654). In this situation, self-regulation intercedes by limiting the content available to young viewers. Although this practice does raise questions about children's First Amendment rights, it is generally perceived by parents and industry professionals as a positive way of shielding children from exposure to violence.

CONCLUSION

Throughout this chapter, we have examined the context of children's television production. We have demonstrated that children's television programming reflects world events, politics, industry trends, cultural concerns, and societal trends. In this way, children's television programming is a reflection of the context in which it is produced. It is also a reflection of the manner in which we as a society value young people. As Baker and Dessart (1998) state, "the introduction of every popular medium in this country has been attended by grave concern over its potential dangers and by intense conflict over who will control it so that those dangers will bring no harm to the most vulnerable among us" (p. 155). Just as concerns arose over the introduction of radio programs and films for children, concerns about the potential dangers of television constantly have been weighed against the medium's potential for entertaining and educating children. These same concerns are now being raised about new forms of interactive media.

As was mentioned in the introduction, this chapter is intended to be the first phase of a larger line of research. Therefore, we propose some preliminary conclusions and questions, all of which warrant further examination.

First, we recognize the many disparate stakeholders who seek, both directly and indirectly, to influence the production and content of children's television. There is a constant tug-of-war between those who emphasize the educational and public interest responsibilities of children's television, and those who emphasize the need for children's television to sustain itself as a for-profit industry. This tug-of-war was highly evident in the deregulation of the 1980s, which resulted in the successful syndication of toy-based programs, but also raised heated objections from the advocacy community about the value and implications of program-length commercials.

Is this tug-of-war necessary for the growth of the industry? Does it act as a system of checks and balances, allowing producers creative freedom to experiment with innovative programming and content while providing reassurance to consumers that egregious practices will be protested, examined, and (usually) halted?

Second, we understand the implications of the production process. Programs targeted at children are made *for* children *by* adults. As Jenkins (1998) points out: "[c]hildren's culture is shaped by adult agendas and expectations, at least on the site of production and often at the moment of reception, and these materials leave lasting imprints on children's social and cultural development" (p. 26). The resulting products, therefore, are biased by the experiences and knowledge of creators who are many years removed from the experiences of childhood and often come from a different cultural or socioeconomic background than the audience. These creators infuse their own ideas, desires, and anxieties about childhood into the products they produce. Further, the creators of children's programming rarely are trained in child development or child psychology. With the exception of programs created for public broadcasting and some commercial preschool shows, program ideas rarely develop from the assessed needs of children in a particular age group. The primary implication of this process is that much children's programming is irrelevant to the developmental needs of the child audience.

It is also through the production process that certain agendas are privileged. In most cases, this has both positive and negative outcomes. For example, the protectionist agenda highlights the special needs of children, and advocates for media that meets those needs. However, it can also lead to restrictions on content that could be useful or beneficial for children. Another example is the representation of ethnic diversity. Some producers of children's programs have recognized the need for a diverse cast of characters, not only for teaching children about diversity, but also for attracting and maintaining an audience. As a result, ethnic diversity is better represented in children's programming than in primetime programming, although it is far from a fair representation, and is often wrought with stereotypes (Children Now, 2002). Are agendas such as these instrumental or detrimental to the production of children's programs? How far on either side of the tug-of-war is society willing to go? Would the content of children's programs change if program creators were trained in child development, psychology, or sociology? How can the experiences of *all* children be better represented on television?

Third, children are often used as political leverage. Jenkins (1998) asserts that "almost every major political battle of the twentieth century has been fought on the backs of our children. ... The innocent child carries the rhetorical force of such [political] arguments; we are constantly urged to take action to protect our children" (p. 2). Our research demonstrates that this is often true. For example, the televised congressional hearings on juvenile delinquency chaired by Senator Estes Kefauver in the mid-1950s raised the public's awareness and concern about the potential relationship between television violence and juvenile delinquency. However, it has been noted that Kefauver "knew a good bandwagon to lead when he saw one" and that he used the hearings to raise his own profile because of his aspirations to run for the presidency (Hoerrner, 1999, p. 10). Were similar motivations for raising one's personal popularity and profile behind the efforts of Senator Paul Simon in the late 1980's or Senator Joseph Lieberman's efforts in the 1990's to raise public awareness about sex and violence in the media? Do the benefits gleaned from the political leveraging of children for personal gain outweigh the questionable ethics and potential repercussions of the practice?

Finally, while we are encouraged by the picture of the children's television industry that has emerged from our investigation thus far, we saw a need to train more professionals versed in *both* academic research *and* industry practices. The work of such "translators" could ensure that the latest research in areas sailent to the production of media products. The end result of such a collabration would be more complex understanding of the "tug-of-war" we have discussed in this chapter, as well as more diverse and appropriate media offerings for the child audience. The interplay societal events, various stakeholder groups, and the producers of children's programming is essential to the growth of the industry and the continued development and perpetuation of a mediated society. Without such relationships, the evolution of the industry would stagnate, leaving children with a bleak set of offerings rather than the increasingly vibrant array of media choices they deserve.

REFERENCES

Ahrens, F. (2005, February 9). FCC aims to speed evaluations of indecency complaints [Electronic version]. *The Washington Post*, p. E01.

Alexander, A., & Owens, J. C. (1998). *Media economic theory and practice.* Mahwah, NJ: Lawrence Erlbaum Associates.

Anderson, D. A. (2004). Watching children watch television and the creation of *Blue's Clues*. In H. Hendershot (Ed.), *Nickelodeon nation* (pp. 241–268). New York: New York University Press.

Axelrod, A. (2003). *The complete idiot's guide to American history* (3rd ed.). Indianapolis: Alpha Books.

Baker, W., & Dessart, G. (1998). *Down the tube*. New York: Basic Books.

Barnouw, E. (1990). *Tube of plenty: The evolution of American television* (2nd ed.). New York: Oxford University Press.

Caught red-handed: Entertainment companies market violent material to children. (2001, July 29). *Stanford Business School News Release*. Retrieved December 11, 2004 from http://www.gsb.stanford.edu/news/grier_violent_entertainment.html

Children Now. (2003). *Big media, little kids: Media consolidation and children's television programming, a report by Children Now*. Oakland, CA: Author.

Children Now. (2002). *Why it matters: Diversity on television*. Oakland, CA Author.

Cole, J., Gregory, M., Suman, M., Schramm, P., Reynolds, J., et al. (1996). *Television violence monitoring report, 1995–1996*. Los Angeles, CA: UCLA, Center for Communication Policy.

Davis, J. (1995). *Children's television, 1947–1990*. Jefferson, NC: McFarland & Company.

Department of Health and Human Services. (2001). *The Surgeon General's call to action: prevent and decrease overweight and obesity* (DHHS Publication No. 017-001-00551-7). Washington, DC: U.S. Government Printing Office.

Dirr, P. J. (2001). Cable television: Gateway to educational resources for development at all ages. In D. G. Singer & J. L. Singer (Eds.), *Handbook of children and the media* (pp. 533–546). Thousand Oaks, CA: Sage.

Engelhardt, T. (1986). The shortcake strategy. In T. Gitlin (Ed.), *Watching television* (pp. 68–110). New York: Pantheon.

Fass, A., & Kafka, P. (2003, September 29). Ad infinitum? [Electronic version]. *Forbes, 6*.

Federal Trade Commission. (2000). *Marketing violent entertainment to children: A review of self-regulation and industry practices in the motion pictures, music recording, and electronic game industries*. Washington DC: Author.

Fischer, S. (1983). *Kids' TV: The first 25 years*. New York: Facts on File Publications.

Freeman-Greene, S. (2003, May 3). Twin tower drama [Electronic version]. *The Age*.

Hendershot, H. (1998). *Saturday morning censors*. Durham, NC: Duke University Press.

Hilmes, M. (Ed.). (2003). *The television history book*. London: British Film Institute.

Hoerrner, K. L. (1999). The forgotten battles: Congressional hearings on television violence in the 1950s. *Web Journal of Mass Communication Research, 2(3)*. Retrieved February 12, 2005, from http://www.scripps.ohiou.edu/ wjmer/vol102/2-3a-B.htm

Jenkins, H. (1998). Introduction: Childhood innocence and other modern myths. In H. Jenkins (Ed.), *The children's culture reader* (pp. 1–37). New York: New York University Press.

Jordan, A. (2001). Public policy and private practice: Government regulations and parental control of children's television use in the home. In D. G. Singer & J. L. Singer (Eds.), *Handbook of children and the media* (pp. 651–662). Thousand Oaks, CA: Sage.

Kraft foods announces marketing changes to emphasize more nutritious products. (2005, January 12). *Kraft Foods Newsroom.* Retrieved *February 5, 2005* from http://www.Kraft.com/new sroom/01122005.html

Mazzarino, J. (Writer), & Diego, K. (Director). (2003). You can ask! [Television series episodes]. In C. Delfico & C. Klein (Producers), *Sesame Street.* New York: Sesame Workshop.

McDonough, G., Gregg, R., & Wong, C. (Eds.) (2001). *Encyclopedia of contemporary American culture.* New York: Routledge.

McCarthy, M. M. (1995). Broadcast self-regulation: The NAB codes, family viewing policy, and television violence. *Cardozo Arts and Entertainment Law Journal, 667,* 680–683.

McLees, D. (2004). *A conversation with Lou Scheimer.* In *The Adventures of Fat Albert* [Promotional pamphlet included with DVD]. Thousand Oaks, CA: Ventura Distribution.

Minow, N. N., & Lamay, C. L. (1995). *Abandoned in the wasteland.* New York: Hill & Wang.

Mittel, J. (2003). The great Saturday morning exile: Scheduling cartoons on television's periphery in the 1960s. In C.A. Stabile & M. Harrison (Eds.), *Prime time animation: Television animation and American culture* (pp. 33–54). New York: Routledge.

Mitroff, D., Ash, L., & Evans, K. D. (2001). *Program policies, practices & standards at Fox Family Worldwide.* Unpublished handbook.

Paik, H. (2001). The history of children's use of electronic media. In D. G. Singer & J. L. Singer (Eds.), *Handbook of children and the media* (pp. 7–28). Thousand Oaks, CA: Sage.

Pecora, N. (1998). *The business of children's entertainment.* New York: Guilford.

Pecora, N. (2004). Nickelodeon grows up: The economic evolution of a network. In H. Hendershot (Ed.), *Nickelodeon nation* (pp. 15–44). New York: New York University Press.

Piaget, J., & Inhelder, B. (1969). *The psychology of the child.* New York: Basic Books.

Rogers, F. M. (Writer & Producer). (1968). R.F. Kennedy assassination special for parents [television series episode]. In *Mister Rogers' Neighborhood.* Pittsburgh, PA: Family Communications, Inc.

Rogers, F. M. (Writer), & Martin, H. (Director). (1981). Violence in the news: Helping children understand [television series episode]. In S. Newbury (Producer), *Mister Rogers' Neighborhood.* Pittsburgh, PA: Family Communications, Inc.

Sandler, K. S. (2004). "A kid's gotta do what a kid's gotta do": Branding the Nickelodeon experience. In H. Hendershot (Ed.), *Nickelodeon nation* (pp. 45–68). New York: New York University Press.

Simensky, L. (2004). The early days of Nickelodeon. In H. Hendershot (Ed.), *Nickelodeon nation* (pp. 87–107). New York: New York University Press.

Schlesinger, A. M. (Ed.). (1993). *The almanac of American history.* Greenwich, CT: Brompton Books Corporation.

Seiter, E. (1995). *Sold separately: Parents & children in consumer culture.* New Jersey: Rutgers University Press.

Showalter, E. (2003, July/August). Window on reality: *American Idol* and the search for identity [Electronic version]. *The American Prospect,* p. 65.

Special considerations for creators of children's media. Los Angeles: (2000) Mediascope.

Spigel, L. (2001). *Welcome to the dreamhouse: Popular media and postwar suburbs.* Durham, NC: Duke University Press.

Stark, S. D. (1997). *Glued to the set.* New York: The Free Press.

Sterling, C. H., & Kittross, J. M. (2002). *Stay tuned: A history of American broadcasting* (3rd ed.). Mahwah, NJ: Lawrence Erlbaum Associates.

Truglio, R. T., Kotler, J. A., Cohen, D. I., & Housley-Juster, A. (2005). Modeling life skills on *Sesame Street*: A response to September 11th. *Televizion, 18,* 15–19.

2

Understanding the Children's Television Community From an Organizational Network Perspective

J. Alison Bryant
Nickelodeon

There is no doubt that children's television in the United States and its political, social, and economic environments have changed dramatically since the advent of broadcasting. The previous chapter (Mitroff & Herr-Stephenson) gave a complete overview of how social change, changes in the entertainment industry, and changes in children's television programming and policies have coevolved since the 1920s. The chapter at hand builds off of that detailed examination, using network theories and analysis to elucidate changes in the structure of the children's television community over the past five decades in order to understand the impact of those changes. Unlike other analyses in this book, particular those written from industry insiders, this chapter takes a step back and tries to figure out, as a "outsider," what has happened to the children's television industry and why.

There are various ways that we could use network theories and analysis to understand the children's television community. We could look at the evolution of the interpersonal, or social, networks within the community over time, focusing on the relationships between key players or directors of organizations within the community. This type of research has a long-standing history in management research. A second network approach would be to look at the relationships over time between a particular set (or sets) of organizations within the community, such as the relationship among content producers or the relationship between content producers and toy companies. Academic and popular literature on the organizational or industry-related history of children's television has focused primarily at this level, looking at how particular players, such as Nickelodeon, or industries, such as advertising, have evolved within the children's television community.

A third approach, and the one taken in this chapter, is to look at children's television as the end-product of an organizational process that takes place within a coordinated set of organizational populations that create, distribute, defend, and support children's television. The process unfolds through the interactions of these populations, which is the evolution of the network, so that what decades of American children have seen on their television screen is the result of this macrolevel organizational coevolution. In this chapter, the children's television community is defined as the following set of populations: educational content creators, entertainment content creators, content programmers, toy tie-in companies, advertisers, governmental bodies, advocacy groups, and philanthropic organizations (See Fig. 2.1). These populations and their interrelations over time will be discussed in detail later in the chapter.

This analysis of the children's television community takes a macrolevel organizational perspective on how the relationships in the community have changed over time, and looks at the community from an ecological and evolutionary perspective. By looking at the community as a system or network that evolves over time based on internal dynamics as well as external pressures, we can get a enhanced assessment of how and why the community has changed the way it has; why the programming has changed over time; and what the current state of affairs may hold for the future. This chapter in many ways complements chapter 1 of this volume by examining the combined histories of the society, industry, and programming put forth in that chapter through a theoretical and analytical lens that helps understand those histories.

This macrolevel organizational network perspective takes into account all sides of the children's television equation, looking at how all of the different players interact over time as an organizational network and how these interactions alter the make-up of the community. In addition, this vantage point incorporates environmental variables, such as political, economic, and social changes, in order to understand how they affect change in the community. Using this perspective, we can better understand the changes in children's television. We can see how changes in the environment affect relationships within the community,

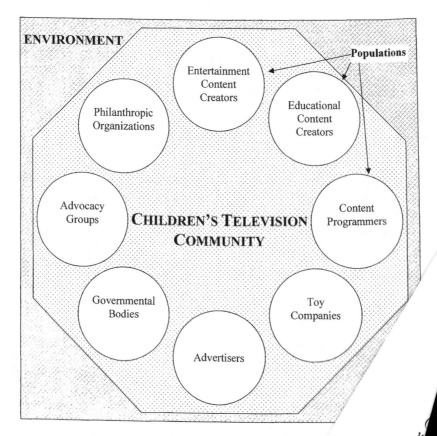

FIGURE. 2.1.   The children's television comm␍

and how these changes in relationships affect t␍
television programming at any given time.

The following sections outline a theoretica␍
to looking at this macroevolutionary persp␍
standpoint, a network perspective on com␍
from an analytical standpoint, the results␍
lined and network analysis of the data␍
the most pressing problems facing th␍
as identified by this research, are d␍

THE NETWORK, EVOLUTIC␍

Theoretically, this analysis ␍
going back to Hawley's sociolog.

relatively recently in the organizational science literature, which built on work in population ecology. Population ecology focuses on organizations as they form populations. A population is comprised of "all the organizations with the same form that are competing for resources" (Barron, 1999, p. 443). Populations are also often identified as being synonymous with industries (Aldrich, 1999). Within the children's television community, a population would be a particular set of organizations that fulfill a similar function, such as advertisers or advocacy groups. Each population, therefore, has its place within the larger organizational community.

But what exactly is a *community*? *Community* has been defined in almost as many ways as there are analyses of organizational communities (Aldrich, 1999; DiMaggio, 1994). Hawley's (1950) original sociological work on community ecology focused on relationships within geographically and temporally bound communities. As community ecology has been refitted from Hawley's original work for organizational scholarship, the definitions of community have moved from a geographically based scheme to a more functional approach (Ruef, 2000). That is not to say, however, that organizational scholars agree on how community should be defined, operationalized, or analyzed. In the past 20 years, *community* has been defined by looking at technology-based interrelationships between populations (Astley, 1985); competitive and mutual relationships between organizations (Barnett, 1994; Barnett & Carroll, 1987; Barnett, Mischke, & Ocasio, 2000); "populations whose interactions have a systemic character, often caused by functional differentiation" (Hannan & Carroll, 1995, p. 30); or populations organized around a "core," whether it be technological, normative, functional, or legal-regulatory (Aldrich, 1999; Ruef, 2000). This final definition is the one adopted in this analysis.

By understanding the children's television community through Ruef's (1999) definition— "a set of coevolving organizational populations joined by ties of commensalism and symbiosis through their orientation to a common technology, normative order, or legal-regulatory regime" (p. 301)—we view each of the populations as having a specific function and the relationships within the community network as being connected and changing overtime. Relationships between pairs of populations are not static, nor are they necessarily equivalent. The pair may have a mutually beneficial relationship (+,+), a predatory relationship, a fully competitive relationship (−,−), and many variations in between. In addition, populations may enter the community or leave, so the set of actors is not always the same. Therefore, over the course of the evolution of the community, the picture of the complete network changes dramatically.

Each population brings its own set of resources to the community, which can be economic, political, or social. In addition, the environment provides (or lacks) necessary resources for the community to survive, such as social or political legitimacy for public broadcasting or a strong economy. Populations within the community compete amongst each other for scarce resources and can coordinate to create new resources for the community.

Moreover, communities form based on interrelated functions and common goals. This is certainly the case for the children's television community. Because of its tie to a particular technology (television broadcast), the nature of content and programming for children, and the fact that the government has defined this as a "special-needs" group, children's television organizations are fundamentally different in function from other content, programming, or policy organizations. The resources necessary to sustain children's television, therefore, are different than for other forms of media or other economic industries. The community, in turn, may have a different historical evolution than other similar communities, such as the larger television community.

The children's television community functions are the creation, programming, defense, and support of children's programming. These functions help to protect the community from its environment. This is another tenet of community ecology—the community buffers populations from the environment (Barnett, 1994; Hawley, 1950, 1986). The creation of the community, therefore, ironically creates a certain amount of self-sufficiency. Hawley (1950) described the community, in its essence, as a "collective response to the habitat" or environment (p. 67). Organizations and populations within the community are sheltered from major environmental changes. Inclusion in such a community, therefore, is especially important for populations on whom the environment places strict or numerous constraints, or for whom environmental changes are unpredictable. In such situations, the community can act as a buffer from these constraints and changes, and can increase the number and amount of resources to which the population has access. The children's television community is an example of a community on which there are numerous constraints, especially as compared to the general broadcasting community. Current political and social climates can affect the ability of populations to support for programming for its "special" audience, and economic downturns severely affect funding for any targeted programming, especially well-produced (sometimes more expensive) children's programming. By forming relationships within the community, for example between content producers and philanthropic organizations (that are not a part of the larger television community), the community provides a buffer from these changes in environmental resources.

Although there are many ways to look at the evolution of a community, this chapter focuses on changes that can be elucidated through network analysis. At its essence, network analysis is about understanding relationships between a set of entities (Monge & Contractor, 2003; Wasserman & Faust, 1994/1998), and therefore fits the framework of community ecology well. We can view the creation, maintenance, and dissolution of the networks as the key mechanisms by which the community emerges, evolves, and (possibly) collapses. Within this evolutionary framework, a network perspective focuses on specific characteristics of the network to highlight changes in the community, specifically the changes in the *density* of the community relationships (the number of actual ties compared to the total number of possible ties), the changes in the *types* of relationships, and the overall changes in the *structure* of the network over time.

For the children's television community, therefore, we are interested in how membership within the community, the number and types of relationships among the populations, and the structure of the community as a whole have changed since programming explicitly created for children came on the scene. We look at how cohesive the community has been during different political and social environments (the density of the network); how the relationships between populations have changed in response to environmental or community changes; and how those changes, in turn, have affected what American children have seen on their television screen.

THE CHILDREN'S TELEVISION COMMUNITY

The populations in the children's television community are educational content creators, entertainment content creators, content programmers, toy tie-in companies, advertisers, governmental bodies, advocacy groups, and philanthropic organizations. Educational content creators create programs that are explicitly educational, such as *Sesame Street, Mr. Rogers' Neighborhood, and Blue's Clues* (e.g., Sesame Workshop, Family Communications Inc., Nick Jr.). Entertainment content creators create programs that are not explicitly educational, but are instead primarily entertaining, such as *Mighty Morphin Power Rangers or Pokémon* (e.g., Saban Industries, Pokémon USA Inc.). Before going on, it is important to note that although there is certainly overlap between these first two populations (and, of course, educational content must be entertaining and entertaining content is always teaching *something*), they have been separated in this manner because each has a different set of resources and function differently within the community. Moreover, their relationships with other populations over time are often significantly different.

Content programmers are the broadcast and cable networks that program children's television shows (e.g., ABC, Fox, WB, Discovery Channel, Nickelodeon). Toy tie-in companies create and manufacture toys that directly relate to children's television programs, either through direct sponsorship of the programs, such as Barbie™ in the 1950s, or by tie-in products sold through retail, such as Strawberry Shortcake in the 1980s (e.g., Mattel, American Greetings). Advertisers are companies that advertise their child-targeted products, such as sugared cereal and fast food, during children's programming (e.g., General Mills, McDonalds). Governmental bodies are federal and state regulatory, administrative, and legislative bodies that enact, carry out, and enforce legislation and regulations pertaining to children's television (e.g., Corporation for Public Broadcasting, FCC, Congress). Advocacy groups are organizations that monitor and advocate for improvements in children's television (e.g., Action for Children's Television, Center for Media Education). Philanthropic organizations are charitable organizations that financially and otherwise sponsor or support children's television programming (e.g., Markle Foundation, Carnegie Foundation, Ford Foundation). These eight populations create and share the resources vital to children's television. They also compete for these resources, especially in times where funding or political interest is scarce.

In the early years of the children's television community, as the role of television within the family and society was just beginning to be determined, the community was relatively small. Content programmers, entertainment content creators, toy tie-in companies, and advertisers, which were all hold-overs from the age of radio, were the only populations involved in children's television programming. Over-time, as the community evolved, other populations entered the community and altered the nature and resources of the community. For example, the entrance of educational content creators, such as Fred Rogers (later Family Communications Inc.) and Children's Television Workshop, and philanthropic organizations, such as Markle and Carnegie, on the national scene in the 1960s added to the public and social legitimacy of the community by showing a beneficial purpose of the community that differentiated it starkly from the rest of broadcasting.

The political and social climate of the 1960s, as well as the increased penetration of televisions sets into the home, created an atmosphere in which the effects of television, both beneficial and detrimental, became important issues on the public agenda. This change in the environment in which the children's television community was situated prompted governmental bodies and philanthropic organizations to join the community. These two populations proceeded to create the political, social, and economic resources necessary for the emergence of the educational content creators and advocacy groups into the community.

By the time 1970 rolled around, the network of populations within the community was set. The relationships within that network, however, changed continuously over the next three decades. The next sections delve into how to look at those changes from a network, evolutionary perspective and what that perspective tells us about the history, current state, and maybe even the future of children's television.

STUDYING THE CHILDREN'S TELEVISION COMMUNITY

In order to study the children's television community from a network evolutionary perspective, we need longitudinal, macrolevel network data. Unfortunately, unlike other types of organizational network data, this type of information cannot be easily gathered through financial records, industry histories, and the like. Instead, a triangulation of methods, including in-depth interviews, network data survey collection, and examination of historical records, are necessary to garner a complete set of evolutionary network data. Although a more complete discussion of the research project undertaken to gather this data is discussed elsewhere (Bryant & Shumate, 2006), a brief synopsis of the project is discussed here before reviewing what this type of research tells us about the evolution of the children's television community.

Data Collection

In-Depth Interviews.   Interviews were conducted with prominent citizens in the children's television community. The list includes both people who were integral to the foundings of the populations,[1] as well as those who have been prominent figures throughout the past 50 years. In total, 20 key players from all eight of the populations were interviewed. Each of the interviews was conducted in person at either the office or home of the participant and ran an average of an hour and a half long. The interviews focused on two major topics: details regarding the major events affecting the children's television community in the past 50 years and the changes in the relationships between the populations in the community during that time.

---

[1]Unfortunately, since the time period for this research extends back to the 1950s, there are several key players from the early days of the community who could not participate in the research.

Network Data Questionnaires.   Either during the course of the interview or after the interview, each participant was asked to fill out a questionnaire designed to collect network data on the community over time. The questionnaire was comprised of a set of ten matrices with the eight populations in the children's television community listed as the rows and columns. Each of the matrices corresponded to a particular 5-year time period within the 50-year history of the children's television community. In each of the matrices, the participant was asked to identify the type of relationships that occurred between the populations of children's television organizations during that particular time period. The participant then filled out the matrices, identifying which of four types of directional relationships each of the populations had with every other population during that time period. The four types of relationships were: no relationship, negative relationship, neutral relationship, or positive relationship.

Historical Records.   In addition to in-depth interviews and the network data questionnaire, several important historical texts regarding the history of the children's television community, and particular populations within the community, were examined for information regarding relationships between the populations. The texts used in the data collection either focused on the history of children's television in general (Calabro, 1992; Melody, 1973; Pecora, 1998; Schneider, 1987; Turow, 1981), or focused on a particular population of organizations within children's television (e.g., Action for Children's Television, 1988; Cross, 1997; Jarvik, 1998; McNeal, 1992; Polsky, 1974). As described in the following section, the information garnered from these texts was particularly important for the earliest time periods of the community, because personal accounts from those periods are harder to come by. Due to mortality issues, none of the participants had been active in the children's television community before the mid-1960s. Therefore, histories of the children's television community or particular populations within the community, particularly those published soon after the time periods they cover, were seminal in coding the network data.

Data Coding

The three data-collection methods focused on the 50-year period between 1953 and 2002. This time period was chosen for several reasons. First, and most importantly, the beginning of children's television is generally considered to coincide with the first airing of *Disneyland* in 1954 (Melody, 1973) or the first airing of the *Mickey Mouse Club* in 1955 (Schneider, 1987). In order to understand the emergence of the community, it is important to begin data collection before these first seminal events, in order to capture any important environmental events that may have spurred the emergence of populations and/or relationships between already existing populations. In addition, this allows the emergence of the community and of populations within the community to be examined. Moreover, the beginning date of 1953 was chosen in order to simplify data collection, so that the time periods to be used in the network data tool could be 10 five-year periods. For each of the 10 time periods, a complete network of relationships between the populations was created from triangulating the data. This yielded a total of 560 network relationships (ten 8×8 matrices, excluding the autonomous relationships). In addition, a set of key environmental events affecting the children's television community garnered from the interviews was created.

The emergence of the populations into the community was derived by looking at: the participants' opinions about when each population entered into the community, gathered during the interviews; and historical accounts of the community and of the individual populations. From these data, each population was assigned an "emergence" time period, in which they entered the community network. For example, the data indicated that educational content creators did not become a part of the children's television community until the creation of CTW in 1968. Therefore, the period of emergence for educational content creators was set as 1968–1972.

The second step in coding the data gathered in this research was to create a set of over-time matrices by triangulating the data collected. For each time period, those populations that had been identified in the first step as not yet entering the community and their corresponding relationships were coded as "No Relationship." Once these ties were coded, the rest of the ties were coded through triangulating three types of data: a consensus network derived from the network data collected from each participant, descriptions of the population relationships narrated in the interviews, and descriptions of the population relationships found in the historical records. This yielded the final set of 560 network ties, with excellent intercoder reliability. (For complete details on how the network data was compiled, coded, and recoded using network analysis software and interreliability was tested, please see Bryant, 2003.)

In addition to the network data, a list of community-level environmental events important in the history of the children's television community was also created in order to conduct the analyses necessary to test the hypotheses. In each of the interviews, the researcher asked the participants to identify the major community-level environmental events that affected children's television community. They were told that an environmental event was a political, economic, social, or technological event (Aldrich, 1999; Baum, 1996). In creating the list of key environmental events, the researcher reviewed each of the interviews and created a list of events mentioned by the participants. From this list, the researcher took the events that were mentioned most often by the participants (the other events were mentioned two or fewer times throughout the 20 interviews). The key environmental events and the time period in which they occurred are:

- Public Broadcasting Act of 1967 (1963–1967)
- Penetration of Cable (1983–1987)
- Children's Television Act of 1990 (1988–1992)
- Three-Hour Rule (Addendum to CTA in 1996) (1993–1997)

WHAT THE NETWORK DATA TELLS US

The network data created for the 10 time periods in the history of the children's television community was then analyzed using network analysis focusing on the changes in the community relationships overtime and the density of those relationships (see Bryant & Monge, 2006, for a complete discussion of the network density analyses). Figure 2.2 shows an overview of the network densities within the community overtime. Figure 2.3 shows the community network during each time period. There were three major findings based on this analysis, each of which will be detailed in the following section.

Emergence

The first finding is that, although the children's television community formed due to a technological event (Aldrich, 1999), the advent of television, the original relationships within the community were not novel. The children's television community emerged based on the relationships between entertainment content creators, content programmers, toy tie-in companies, and advertisers. Those four populations had already established strong mutual ties in the broadcasting arena during the earlier days of radio (Cross, 1997; Melody, 1973; Pecora, 1998; Schneider, 1987). As these populations created the children's television community, they retained the same fundamental relationships they had during the earlier era. By 1955, the children's television community had subsumed the resources of the children's radio community, and there were no children's radio programs (Pecora, 1998). Therefore, although the change in nomenclature to the children's *television* community was due to the technological event, the children's broadcasting community had already been established.

During the emergence of the community (1953–1967), the relationships between the populations were primarily mutual or positive. In the

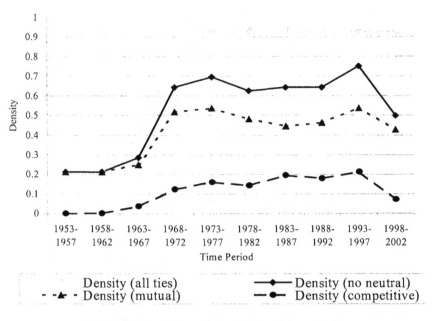

FIGURE 2.2   Network densities by time period.
Note. The "no-neutral" density was computed without the neutral ties, in
order to garner a more thorough perspective on the changes in the children's
television community. (See Aldrich, 1999, for more on this tecnique).

late 1960s and early 1970s, as more populations entered the community,
the number of competitive relationships increased. According to community ecology theory, this rise in competitive relationships is to be
expected, as there were now more populations within the community
competing over resources. This balance of mutual to competitive relationships stayed relatively stable through the 1970s and 1980s. In the
mid-1990s, however, there was a slight increase in the proportion of
mutual to competitive relationships again. This increase was only temporary, however, and by the final time period (1998–2002) the relationships within the community had dramatically altered, with fewer ties
within the community overall (lower density).

Changing Nature of the Community Ties in
Relation to Environmental Events

What do these changes in the community network mean? If we compare
the network changes with the key environmental events generated during

Mutual Ties   Competitive Ties

1953-1957

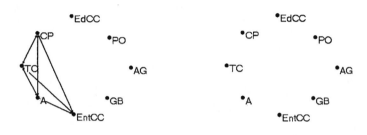

1958-1962

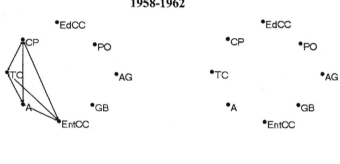

1963-1967

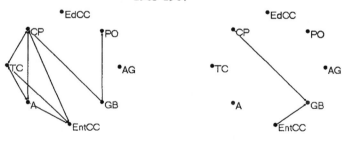

1968-1972

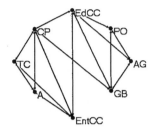
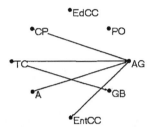

1973-1977

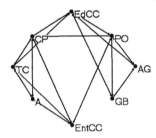
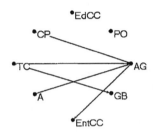

1978-1982

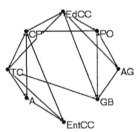
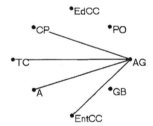

1983-1987

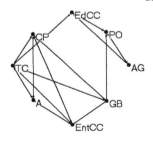
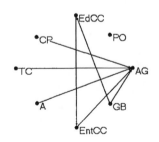

1988-1992

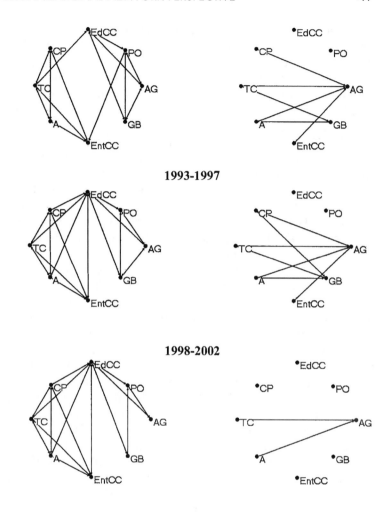

1993-1997

1998-2002

Legend:
    EdCC = Educational Content Creators
    PO = Philanthropic Organizations
    AG = Advocacy Groups
    GB = Governmental Bodies
    EntCC = Entertainment Content Creators
    A = Advertisers
    TC = Toy Companies
    CP = Content Programmers

FIGURE 2.3   Community network mutual and competitive ties during
each time period.

the data collection and the various interview and historical accounts of changes in children's television, we develop an interesting story of the evolution of the community.

The rapid growth in television's popularity in the 1950s fostered an economic environment that was flush with resources and short on competition. Although the four original populations created the basis for the children's television community, it was not until the political and social environment of the 1960s, and the corresponding "transformation of norms and values," that the children's television community had the resources to support the emergence or entrance of the other four populations (Aldrich, 1999). In this case, the community changed from a strictly commercial community focused on children as consumers to a community that recognized children as a special audience, not only with regard to niche advertising, but also with regard to developmental needs and susceptibilities.

Moreover, when we look at legitimacy as a resource available to the community, we see that the first 15 years of the children's television community were characterized by legitimacy based on the economic legitimacy of the larger broadcasting community. Children's television was considered a legitimate enterprise because it could garner advertising revenues during time slots that had been considered "ghettos," when adults would not be watching (Melody, 1973). In the mid- to late 1960s, as the political and social environment altered and the children's television community changed its focus, the goal of economic legitimacy became less central. In its place, sociopolitical and cognitive legitimacy moved to the forefront of the community. The vision of television as educator for children, especially disadvantaged children, became widespread (L. Morrisett, personal communication, April 1, 2003; Polsky, 1974). The actions of the educational content creators, advocacy groups, governmental bodies, and philanthropic organizations reframed the perception of children's television, so that the need for television specifically created for children became, as Aldrich (1999) puts it, "accepted as a part of the sociocultural and organizational landscape" (p. 30), and therefore gained legitimacy. This reframing of the perception of children's television and its alignment with the political and social climate of the time also fostered moral and regulatory acceptance of the community on the part of "key stakeholders, the general public, key opinion leaders, and governmental officials" (Aldrich, 1999, p. 30). This acceptance is the key to sociopolitical legitimacy (Aldrich, 1999). A large proportion of mutual ties fostered this attainment of legitimacy by an emerging community.

By the 1970s, the children's television community had reached a relatively stable state. The total number of ties within the community (network density) settled into a constant, high level. Although there were slight fluctuations with regard to the nature of the relationships between the pairs, from 1973 to 1993, the overall structure of the community remained relatively static.

During these two decades, two major environmental events were identified through the interviews. Based on community ecological theory, one would expect that these events would cause significant changes in the community networks. Neither event had a significant effect on the overall number of ties in the community, however. After further exploration, it seems as though both of these events, touted as being key turning points in children's television, were not significant catalysts for change within the community. The first event, the penetration of cable, was more of an ongoing process than a singular event. Although the critical mass of cable penetration—more than half of U.S. households—occurred in the mid-1980s, it has been a relatively steady increase from the mid-1970s until today. Closer examination of the analyses suggests that, although the number of ties did not change, the type of relationships between the populations altered greatly during this time period. The time period from 1983 to 1987 was the only period in which there was not a significantly greater number of mutual to competitive ties. This change in the nature of the ties is supported by the narrative and historical accounts of this time period, which highlight the deregulatory nature of the Reagan administration, the increasing competition in the marketplace due to Nickelodeon and the Disney Channel, and general doldrums of children's television programming in the 1980s.

The third environmental event was the passage of the Children's Television Act in 1990. There was not a significant change in the density of the community communication network between the period in which the Act was passed (1988–1992) and the subsequent period (1993–1997). This finding was not particularly surprising because, although many interview participants mentioned the CTA as an important event in the history of children's television, very few actually believe that it had any impact on either the children's television content that was created or the relationships between the organizations and populations of organizations. The most striking example of this comes from the head of the advocacy group oft-touted as being primarily responsible for passage of the Act, Action for Children's Television. According to Peggy Charren, "the law exists, but it's relatively meaningless" (personal communication, April 8, 2003).

The fourth environmental event, the Three-Hour Rule addendum to the Children's Television Act, corresponds with a significant change in the community network. By all narrative accounts by interview participants, as well as academic research (such as the studies conducted by Annenberg Public Policy Center in the late 1990s that looked at whether programming adhered to the new rules), the Three-Hour Rule had more impact than the CTA. By including specific requirements tied to license renewal, as well as incorporating several public accountability mechanisms, the ruling effectively created the "teeth" necessary for effecting change in the community. However, as we'll see in the next section, this change came at a time in which the community was just about to undergo a dramatic transformation.

Transformation

We see through the network analyses that there was a significant change in children's television community ties between the mid-1990s and early 2000s. In the mid-1990s, the community reached its highest point of cohesion, with a significantly greater number of mutual ties than competitive ties. It seemed as though the community was becoming self-sufficient. However, something happened to fundamentally alter the shape of the community over the next several years. The community began to transform.

The narrative data suggests that the children's television community is entering a recreation period similar to that of the early 1950s. Just as the increase in television penetration created the opportunity for the children's television community, and repositioned the first populations from the radio community to the children's television community, the recent increase in adoption of digital media and the Internet is creating a "new" children's *media* community (Corporation for Public Broadcasting, 2003). Resources, both economic and political, that were formerly earmarked for children's television have been reappropriated for new media endeavors (B. Sullivan, personal communication, April 8 2003; V. Rideout, personal communication, March 21, 2003; A. Cahn, personal communication, April 3, 2003; P. Miller, personal communication, March 24, 2003; K. Montgomery, personal communication, April 7, 2003). In the past 2 years, two of the most important advocacy groups, Center for Media Education and MediaScope, have closed their doors citing funding as one of their main obstacles (D. Mitroff, personal communication, December 12, 2003; see Montgomery, Chap. 12 this volume). Other advocacy groups, such as ChildrenNow, are trying to fill in the advocacy gap, but they are working with fewer resources due to the dramatic reduction of funding both by governmental bodies and philanthropic organizations (P. Miller, personal communication, March 24, 2003). Advocates for children's television today find themselves adrift in an ever-changing media environment. This environment has fewer resources (political, social, or economic) for television. In addition, trying to target succinct advocacy goals that can be made into successful public relations campaigns in such a large, ever-evolving environment becomes increasingly difficult.

In sum, we see that the fundamental changes in the technological core on which the children's television community has rested for the last 50 years will cause a re-creation of the community network similar to that of the 1950s. The penetration of digital cable, the convergence of televisions and PCs, and the rampant mergers and acquisitions within the children's media industry have made the definition of the community essentially obsolete. Over the next several years, we see the new media community emerge in much the same way as the children's television community did—with some carryover of populations and key organizations (albeit having undergone changes), and some new players added to the mix.

CONCLUSION

By viewing the children's television community through a network lens we garner a bird's-eye view of the community, and its outcome (children's television), has evolved. Viewing the community as a system or network that evolves over time, based on internal dynamics as well as external pressures, can change our elucidations of how and why the community has changed the way it has; why the programming has changed over time; and what the current state of affairs may hold for the future. Instead of explaining change (or lack of change) through the individual eyes of narrators that are situated within the community, we can understand how all of those perspectives interact.

What five decades of American children have seen on their television screen is the result of coevolution of a coordinated set of organizational populations that create, distribute, defend, and support children's television. Interactions within and between these populations aggregate into emergent phenomena that we see only at the community level. Understanding the organizational history of the children's television community, therefore, is the key to understanding why children's television has evolved in the way it has.

REFERENCES

Action for Children's Television. (1988). *ACT: The first 20 years.* Cambridge, MA: Action for Children's Television.

Aldrich, H. E. (1999). *Organizations evolving.* Thousand Oaks, CA: Sage.

Astley, W. G. (1985). The two ecologies: Population and community perspectives on organizational evolution. *Administrative Science Quarterly, 30,* 224–241.

Barnett, W. P. (1994). The liability of collective action: Growth and change among early American telephone companies. In J. A. C. Baum & J. V. Singh (Eds.), *Evolutionary dynamics of organizations* (pp. 337–354). New York: Oxford University Press.

Barnett, W. P., & Carroll, G. R. (1987). Competition and mutualism among early telephone companies. *Administrative Science Quarterly, 32,* 400–421.

Barnett, W. P., Mischke, G. A., & Ocasio, W. (2000). The evolution of collective strategies among organizations. *Organization Studies,* 21(2), 325–354.

Barron, D. N. (1999). The Structuring of Organizational Populations. *American Sociological Review, 64,* 421–445.

Baum, J. A. C. (1996). Organizational ecology. In S. R. Clegg, C. Hardy, & W. Nord (Eds.), *Handbook of organization studies* (pp. 77–114). London: Sage.

Bryant, J. A. (2003). From Networks to Nickelodeon to Noggin: A communication networks perspective on the evolution of the children's television community. Unpublished dissertation. University of Southern California: Los Angeles.

Bryant, J. A., & Monge, P. (2006). *The evolution of the U.S. children's television community, 1950–2000.* Manuscript submitted for review.

Bryant, J. A., & Shumate, M. D. (2006). *Network dynamics of a community: The case of Children's television.* Manuscript submitted for review.

Calabro, M. (1992). *Zap!: A brief history of television.* New York: Four Winds Press.

Cross, G. (1997). *Kids' stuff: Toys and the changing world of American childhood.* Cambridge, MA: Harvard University Press.

Corporation for Public Broadcasting. (2003). *Connected to the future: A report on children's Internet use.* Washington, DC.

DiMaggio, P. J. (1994). The challenge of community evolution. In J. A. C. Baum & J. V. Singh (Eds.), *Evolutionary dynamics of organizations* (pp. 444–450). New York: Oxford University Press.

Hannan, M. T., & Carroll, G. R. (1995). An introduction to organizational ecology. In G. R. Carroll & M. T. Hannan (Eds.), *Organizations in industry: Strategy, structure, and selection* (pp. 17–31). New York: Oxford University Press.

Hawley, A. H. (1950). *Human ecology: A theory of community structure.* New York: Ronald Press Company.

Hawley, A. H. (1986). *Human ecology: A theoretical essay. Chicago:* University of Chicago Press.

Jarvik, L. (1998). PBS: *Behind the screen.* Rocklin, CA: Prima/Forum.

McNeal, J. U. (1992). *Kids as customers: A handbook of marketing to children.* New York: Lexington Books.

Melody, W. (1973). Children's television: *The economics of exploitation.* New Haven, CT: Yale University Press.

Monge, P. R., & Contractor, N. S. (2003). *Theories of communication networks.* New York: Oxford University Press.

Pecora, N. O. (1998). *The business of children's entertainment.* New York: Guilford.

Polsky, R. M. (1974). *Getting to Sesame Street: Origins of the Children's Television Workshop.* New York: Praeger.

Ruef, M. (2000). The emergence of organizational forms: A community ecology approach. *American Journal of Sociology, 106*(3), 658–714.

Schneider, C. (1987). *Children's television: The art, the business, and how it works.* Lincolnwood, IL: NTC Business Books.

Turow, J. (1981). *Entertainment, education, and the hard sell: Three decades of network children's television.* New York: Praeger.

Wasserman, S., & Faust, K. (1994 /1998). *Social network analysis: Methods and application.* Cambridge, UK: Cambridge University Press.

3

The Economics of Children's Television

Alison Alexander
University of Georgia

James Owers
Georgia State University

The business of children's television is complex, profitable, and ever changing. The business synergies between production and distribution support media giants such as Time Warner, Disney, Viacom, and News Corp. Within the larger picture of media conglomerates, children's television is a very small piece of the pie, but, it is a highly profitable sector of the industry.

Children's television refers to programs targeted primarily to children and designed to attract a majority of viewers who are children. Children's television is only a small part of the total viewing of television by children. A popular primetime situation comedy may attract more child viewers than a "children's program" does, despite the fact that it is not targeted primarily to children and children are not a majority of the audience. As a result, many of the mostly highly viewed programs for children aged 5 to 17 are primetime programs. In industry parlance, children are divided into three major age groups: 2 to 5 years old, 6 to 11 years old, and 12 to 17 years old, although teens are frequently discussed separately from the younger age groups. Typically, when the industry talks about children's television, it is referring to the 2-to 11-year-old group.

This chapter focuses on the economics of the business, primarily on the internal factors of finance and operations as they accommodate national and international supply and demand. The goals are (a) to identify trends in content demand; (b) to trace the structure of children's television; (c) to identify patterns of program production, distribution, and promotion; and (d) to identify financial patterns within the industry.

MEETING DEMAND: ANALYZING TRENDS IN PROGRAMMING AND EXPOSURE FOR CHILDREN

Early children's shows were designed to sell TV sets by enhancing television's appeal to the entire family. Because most households in the 1950s had only one television set, programs appealing to children as well as adults were seen as a way of attracting families. Throughout the 1960s and 1970s, cartoons became synonymous with children's television. Reduced costs resulting from limited-action animation techniques and the appeal of cartoons to children transformed scheduling, and the institutionalization of the Saturday morning cartoon became complete—an unexpectedly lucrative timeslot for the networks. The 1980s brought a revolution to broadcast, as cable and VCR penetration began to erode the network audience and international co-ventures began to change the production process. Cartoons remained the standard children's fare, but cable networks that targeted children began to experiment with non-animation programming. For the cabled home, access to children's programming increased dramatically over the 1980s. (See Mitroff & Herr-Stephenson, chap. 1, this volume, for a detailed history of children's television programming.)

Based on the rationale that other outlets were adequately serving the child audience and that diversity of programming for the child was greater than ever before, many of the networks were getting out of the children's television business as the 1990s began. The legislative requirement of the 1990 Children's Television Act, as later interpreted for broadcast stations by the Federal Communications Commission (FCC), obliged the major networks to provide their affiliates with 3 hours of educational/informational (E/I) programming a week. In the past several years, networks have relied on synergies created by the rampant vertical and horizontal integration that has occurred in the media industry to provide children's programming. Currently, on Saturday morning you have ABC programming a 4-hour lineup of shows mainly from its parent Disney's studios; CBS is still using its Viacom sibling Nickelodeon to supply a 3-hour branded Nick and Nick Jr.; and NBC is using the synergy to its Discovery channels to offer 3 hours of Discovery Kids shows. The newer networks have an alternate strategy—courting the child audience in timeslots other than the traditional Saturday morning. These networks, such as FOX, the WB and UPN, have made children's programming central to their business strategies. Fox now leases its Saturday mornings to "4Kids" entertainment. The new CW network, combining WB and UPN, will rely for now on the Kids WB offerings.

But the biggest news of the 1990s was that networks are no longer the major players in children's programming. During the 1990s, children's viewing patterns changed dramatically from broadcast to cable. In the 1980s, children's viewing diet came almost exclusively (98%) from broadcasters (Petrozzello, 1998). Now only 15% of children's television viewing is to network fare; more than 77% of children's viewing is to cable, and 8% is to syndicated programs. Not only is children's viewing shifting, but it also appears to be diminishing. Children's advertisers (and consequently the networks) are concerned about an apparent drop in children's overall viewing, which has diminished by 3% in the past decade. A recent Kaiser Family Foundation study found that children's viewing is characterized by simultaneous consumption of multiple media: watching TV, playing video games, and listening to music at once (Whitney, 2005). They also noted that more than 60% of kids watched slightly more than 1 hour of television a day, but when video/ DVDs, prerecorded shows, and video games were added in, the total came to 3:51 hours of use per day.

This shift to cable has fragmented the child audience. In the United States, child-oriented fare accounts for more than 1,000 hours of airtime a week on network and cable channels, and viewing is widely distributed across that large set of offerings. Animation, though still predominant, is increasingly joined by live action and game/reality shows. Live action strengthened with the reaction to such hits as Disney Channel's *Lizzie McGuire* and *That's so Raven.* Preschool programming is the hot new area of program development with the Cartoon Network recently debuting a preschool block to join Nick Jr. and Playhouse Disney. Nickelodeon and the Cartoon Network garner more than 60% of child viewing, and the commercial-free Disney channel another 23% (McClellan & Tedesco, 1999).

These are percentages of total viewing and not to be confused with ratings, which show that the networks still predominate in amassing large audiences for single shows, despite a significant decrease over the decades. Saturday morning average ratings for major network children's shows ran between 2.2 and 2.4 in the four quarters of late 2004 and early 2005 (*Marketers Guide* to the media, 2004/2005). This can be compared to the average 6 or 7 ratings that network Saturday morning shows received in the 1960s and 1970s. These ratings indicate that, of the slightly more than 100 million television households, about 2.3 million households are watching. Despite the competition that cable provides for the young viewers, few cable programs reach the audience that a network show can.

Both those who purchase and those who produce children's programs operate with assumptions about the child audience that, although changing, remain important. They assume, for example, that there are gender differences in preference, with the important corollary that, although girls will watch boys' shows, boys will not watch girls' shows. They also assume that older children control the set, an assumption related to the axiom that younger children will watch "up" (in age appeal) but older children will not watch "down." Producers and purchasers also assume that children have a short attention span, that repetition is a key to education and entertainment, and that children prefer recognizable characters and stories.

ANALYZING THE INDUSTRY STRUCTURE

The children's network business differs in some significant ways from other network programming. In traditional programming, local affiliates air the shows provided by the networks and the networks, in turn, profit from affiliate viewers, who cumulatively provide the national mass audience that advertisers desire. In return, the networks offer compensation (payment) to affiliates for running programs and leave some advertising space available for local sales. For children's programming, however, no compensation from the networks is offered, because it is a regulatory requirement for broadcast stations. Local children's ads are also not particularly lucrative because of the relatively small audience. Costs for a Saturday morning ad in many markets may be only a few hundred dollars and, in smaller markets, could be significantly less than $100. At the local affiliate level, the program director oversees children's programming, in addition, generally, to managing all station production, community relations, and promotions. There is a long history of affiliates providing local origination children's programs.

Networks provide the programs that fill much of the affiliate schedule: primetime, network news, soaps, sports, quiz shows, talk shows, and children's shows. Vice presidents in charge of daytime or vice presidents for children's programs manage the network scheduling of children's programming. Promotion departments, research departments, and community relations departments become involved. In the current regulatory environment, the "Big Three" networks (CBS, NBC, and ABC) are successful in offering the required 3 hours of educational and informational programming for their affiliates. Their goals are threefold: to meet the regulation, to be able to point with pride to their program content, and to meet the competition within their timeslot. With the increased competition from smaller networks and cable, these programmers realize that regaining large numbers is unlikely. The smaller networks, which have made courting the fragmented child audience a specific objective, provide more than the 3 hours of required programming to their affiliates, and this has provided numbers that are satisfactory to them. In addition to this local/network affiliate relationship, it is also important to note that all networks have a certain number of owned and operated (O&O) stations, which, in turn, form station groups that often exert considerable pressure on the networks and act in concert in the purchase of nonnetwork syndicated fare. Other station groups include Tribune, Gannett, Hearst Argyle, and Cox.

Cable and satellite profit from a dual revenue stream in which advertising and subscriber fees are available. Cable TV involves distributing a number of television channels from a central location (called a *head end*) to subscribers in a community through a network of fiber or coaxial cable. Cable systems charge a monthly fee depending on the number and perceived quality of the channels ordered. Cable channels or networks fall generally into three categories: superstations, basic cable networks, and premium cable channels (HBO, Showtime). Cable systems typically "buy" channel programming for a per-subscriber fee, reversing the broadcast model. The most successful cable networks for children are Cartoon Network, Disney, and Nickelodeon. Disney reportedly costs $.78 per subscriber (Dempsey, 2005). Cable system operators are being gobbled up by conglomerates interested in owning the fiber link to the home for the delivery of multimedia services.

With the proliferation of cable and satellite offerings internationally, children's programming has developed a wide and lucrative international market. International co-ventures are increasingly an important part of program creation, as international licensing and co-venture capital are sought to both fund projected U.S. programming and to create programs for use in other countries. China has recently been an important market for co-ventures.

Economic Infrastructure: Industry Firms

Media conglomerates dominate media operations. Clearly, the majority of children's TV is produced and delivered by for-profit firms. For-profit firms seek to maximize profits (more specifically "value created") by efficiency-producing products and services that can be sold for more than cost. The examination of the economic infrastructure of children's

TV is somewhat complicated by the nature of the firms within which most of this activity occurs. These are either large conglomerates (such as The Walt Disney Company) or smaller private (such as DIC Entertainment) or public (4 Kids Entertainment) companies. When part of large companies, children's TV activities are typically a relatively small part of the total magnitudes. Even when large and diversified forms present "segment" or "Line of Business (LOB)" breakdowns, it is rare for the children's TV business to meet the threshold of relative scale to generate separate financial data pertaining only to those activities.

In free-market economies, it is widely considered that the best performing firms (in terms of Return of Assets [ROA] and consequentially share price) are "pure-plays" that undertake only one narrowly defined Line of Business (LOB). Diversified firms have generally fallen out of favor because investors don't like diversified firms, creating what is called the "diversification discount" in stock prices. This has led to the oft-expressed opinion that there is only one remaining successful conglomerate, namely General Electric. General Electric operates in approximately 20 different lines of business, one of which is media through its NBC network. The term *media conglomerate* thus refers to a very limited subset of "conglomerates." Some would argue for the use of the term *media cogeneric* rather than *media conglomerate* in that they are diversified but within a defined industry. This is in contrast to a conglomerate such as General Electric that operates in approximately 20 distinctly different industries. The major firms in children's TV are "media conglomerates" in that they are diversified communications enterprises with extensive horizontal and vertical integration. The Industrial Organzation (IO) of children's TV is such that much is housed within large communications and media firms and reflects the apparent advantages of vertical and horizontal integration in this business.

A major portion of children's TV programming is delivered by the "Big Four" media conglomerates. Although this is an industry with many participants, in terms of both the extent of broadcast, network, and cable ownership for the production and distribution of children's TV programming, there are the "Big Four." These are Time Warner Inc. (Ticker symbol TWX), Viacom Inc. (VIA), The Walt Disney Company (DIS), and News Corporation, Inc. (NWS), listed approximately in order of declining overall size as measured by total 2004 total corporate revenues. Reflecting concern regarding the "diversification discount" referenced above, in 2005 Viacom (CIA) split into two separate companies, Viacom (ticker symbol VIA-B) and CBS. Approximate 2005 revenues for CBS were $15.5 billion and for Viacom $10 billion. Thus, both parts of the former Viacom are now smaller than News Corp. as measured by annual revenues.

TABLE 3.1

Illustrative Media Operations of the "Majors" of the Media Conglomerates

Company	Broadcast Networks	Studios	Cable Networks	Cable Systems and TV Stations	Radio Stations	Other	Revenues (2004) (in Billions)
Time Warner (formerly AOL Time Warner)	WB TV network	Warner Bros.	CNN, HBO	TW Cable		AOL Publishing—TIME, excetra Professional sports	$42.089 (Subscript $21.8 Advert $7 Content $12 Other $2)
The Walt Disney Co.	ABC	Walt Disney Studios Buena Vista	ESPN (80%) A&E (38%)	10 broadcast stations	70	Parks & Resorts Internet Group	$30.87 (Network $11 Parks $7 Studio $8 Consumer $2)
Viacom Inc.	CBS UPN	Paramount Pictures	MTV, Nickelodeon, Noggin, Country, Music, BET	39 broadcast stations	Infinity Radio—183 stations	Publishing—Simon & Schuster Paramount Theme Parks Advertising—Viacom Outdoor	$22.5* (Cable $6.5 TV $8.5 Radio $2.0 Outdoor $1.8 Entertainment $4.0)

63

Table 3.1. (Continued)

Company	Broadcast Networks	Studios	Cable Networks	Cable Systems and TV Stations	Radio Stations	Other	Revenues (2004) (in Billions)
News Corp.	Fox	Twentieth-Century Fox	International Satellite, Sky,Direct TV	35 in United States		Newspapers — Many, Global Books — Harper Collins	$23.0 ($U.S.) (Films $5.7 TV $5.5 Cable $2.8 Sat. TV $1.8 Print $6.2 Other $0.9)

Note: Viacom had a tax-free split-off of its 81.5% interest in Blockbuster Inc. during 2004. This reduced corporate revenues from $26.6 billion in 2003 to the $22.5 billion in 2004. In addition, in 2005 it split into two public companies, VIA-B and CBS. Respective 2005 revenues were approximately $10 billion and $14.5 billion.

As previously noted, one of the challenges of examining the infrastructure of children's TV is that because these multinationals are so large, the children's TV activities are a relatively small portion of their total operations and are seldom reported in sufficient detail to evaluate their financial performance as separate lines of business. For the "majors," children's TV operations are part of the so-called "media conglomerate" total.

However, the limited information available indicates that children's TV operations are some of the more profitable, and fastest growing, segments of their media conglomerate totalities. Time Warner disclosed that its Cartoon network unit generates more profits than CNN. Viacom's Nickelodeon is the firm's fastest growing unit. That growth rate from 2002 to 2003 was 20%, significantly ahead of the aggregate corporate rate of approximately 10%. The "SpongeBob Squarepants" phenomenon is archetypal. It reflects the inherent synergy available to the media conglomerates by way of combining advertising revenues, pay-televisions sales and merchandising initiatives. There are both domestic and international dimensions to each of these sources of revenues and profits. Although these activities could be undertaken by separate entities, in practice there are additional benefits to be gained by all facets being in one corporate entity rather than complex contracting between several independent firms.

ECONOMIC PATTERNS OF PROGRAM DEVELOPMENT, DISTRIBUTION, AND PROMOTION

Program Development and Production

There are three basic ways in which a broadcast TV station can acquire programs: network, syndication, and local origination. As indicated previously, network programming refers to original programming funded by, produced for, and distributed by the networks. Syndication refers to TV programming sold by distribution companies to local TV stations, station groups, and cable networks. Local origination refers to programs produced by local TV stations for viewers in their own communities. Cable networks acquire programs through internal production, from independent production firms, and from syndicates.

The network programming process seems simple, but the work of program producers and distributors quickly becomes very complex. Some now-outdated rules shaped the original programming process. Under the financial interest and syndication rules (known as *fin-syn*), FCC rules limited network participation in the ownership of programs produced for them. Rather, networks paid license fees to production companies. After the network run, the shows were sold into syndication, with the networks barred from reaping any financial reward. Now the fin-syn rules have been abandoned, allowing networks to own their own shows and to sell them in syndication. Nonetheless, many programming practices that evolved under fin-syn remain.

The networks are now actively engaged in producing their own programs, as witnessed by the plethora of reality shows on primetime. Now it is much easier for media conglomerates to take advantage of vertical integration wherein they own movie and television production companies as well as cable and broadcast outlets (broadcast networks, television stations, cable channels, and cable systems).

As noted in Table 3.1, the production of children's programming is dominated by major studios, a few independents, and, increasingly, international producers and coproductions. Ironically, ongoing viable independents are hard to identify because, despite their number, a larger corporation quickly acquires the successful ones in a classic horizontal integration move. Small firms pitch ideas to networks or production companies and exchange some control over the production process in exchange for funding to produce their program content and production credit. Such a pattern of "joint venturing" is now widely recognized as an efficient organizational form for maximizing the synergy from combining the "comparative advantages" of large firms with extensive financial resources and the creativity of smaller entities with creative owners involved in operations. Increasingly, international programs and producers have gained entry into the U.S. market through these joint ventures. Nelvana, for example, is now part of the larger Corus, a Canadian media company, and once produced the entire Saturday morning line-up for CBS.

Most series begin with a program pitch to a production company or program distributor or to a network. Pitches begin with a concept or a short narrative known as a treatment and move to a storyboard or pilot. Unlike adult series, pilots are not commonly produced. If the program is chosen for further development, the network or studio will provide a licensing contract, in return for some measure of control over content. Thirty years ago, there were probably 26 episodes produced for a weekly show, rerun once during the year. Now a 13-show contract with three to four reruns yearly is common for a weekly show. This rerun practice is possible because younger audiences do not object and change quickly.

The barriers to program entry into the children's television market are enormous. One has only to prowl the aisles of the annual convention of the National Association of Television Program Executives (NATPE) to see the many creative children's program ideas out there.

NATPE is where companies without distribution outlets try to make deals and find financial support by selling to major U.S. networks, to the syndication market, or to put together international production and distribution deals. A company will use licensing and coproduction arrangements to fund the costs of production, and generally retain additional licensing right including rerun syndication rights. This is also the time when international revenues are sought to also funding the program production. Merchandising will be sought as well.

Networks usually require a measure of control on scripts, casting, and directing. Deep pockets are a necessity. Production companies retain ownership of the shows, although networks are now allowed to have some financial interest in the program. These business organizations operate on a near-term deficit-financing model, anticipating that aftermarket sales and merchandising agreements will create ultimate profitability. Networks pay a licensing fee to air the program, which is typically significantly less than the show costs to produce. The fragmentation of the current audience means less money to individual companies, so license fees, which for children's programs were once in the range of $250,000 to $500,000 per episode, have dropped significantly, to a low of $15,000 per episode (Jackson, 1999).

Networks, station groups, or individual stations want to buy from a reputable firm, someone they can trust to deliver what is promised. They would like to know that they are dealing with professionals who have been successful in similar endeavors in the past. But the children's television market is expanding with the new networks and cable services. How does it all come together in completed programs?

Patterns of Distribution

After network programming, the largest program providers are syndicators, the companies that sell directly to TV stations and cable services. Syndication companies sell two kinds of shows: off-network series (series that have appeared on broadcast and cable networks and are being rerun on cable or local broadcast stations) and first-run shows that are expressly produced for syndication. Off-network series are packaged so that stations pay for the right to play a certain number of episodes a specified number of times. For a children's show, the accumulation of 66 episodes allows for repeatability and makes the show saleable beyond its initial run to other outlets. Programs are frequently scheduled to run daily Monday through Friday, a process called *stripping*. Frequently, stations purchase syndicated programming on a barter basis. In barter syndication, the producer provides the pro-gramming free or at a reduced cost, but keeps some of the advertising slots in the show. The syndicator can place its own ads into the show or sell them to major advertisers. The key is market clearance. The more stations the syndicated program plays in, the larger the audience that can be offered to advertisers. First-run syndication, where syndicators sell shows expressly produced for syndication, is a bit murkier. Sometimes syndicators are acting as brokers for programming trying to find its way into the business, but other syndication companies are also part of conglomerates that are producing these programs, blurring the line between syndicators and producers.

Program distribution units with independent production firms or media conglomerates are increasingly taking the place of traditional syndication firms. With vertical integration and network consolidation, most major broadcast and television networks own production studios and prefer programming from that studio or purchase a block of programming from an independent. Thus, the majority of time devoted to children's television is produced by one studio or from studios under the same ownership as the network. Independent production companies can find it hard to place their programming

Advisory boards have become an important component of the production process. Developmental psychologists, educators, mass communication scholars, advocates, and others meet to discuss program acquisition and development. These boards offer advice on strategy and tactics within the network or production decision processes.

Nonprogram Content: Promotions and Public Service

Building a successful program or line-up does not end with program acquisition. The process of promotion is central to encouraging child audiences to sample, or indeed to eagerly anticipate, a new program. Networks use internal program promotions as well as cross-media promotions and website tie-ins. Nickelodeon shines at creating a kid's brand. With innovative promotions, games, magazines, and media tie-ins, Nickelodean uses an edgy approach. The Kid's Choice Awards offers kids the chance to vote for their favorites in movies, television, music, and sports, and are one example of a successful Nickelodean activity:

Part programming and part promotion, another popular strategy is a wraparound segment that has its own characters and interstitial material. These wraparounds include common characters, promote upcoming programs, and contain short sketches and may cover an entire morning or daypart segment. These themes link all the programs and help create branding and flow. These activities may be changing because the FCC is proposing to revise its definition of "commercial matter" to include promotions of television programs or other video programming services other than children's educational and informational programming. Thus, promotions previously exempted would count towards the "commercial matter" limits of 10.5 per hour on weekends and 12 minutes per hour on weekdays (Federal Communications Commission, 2004).

All the networks now have Web sites, and all the Web sites link to a children's programming page. Each of the networks offers a site for their child viewers or youth offerings. Most are interactive in some fashion, and some connect to other sites, some of which are educational in nature. Rarely can basic information such as production company, target age, educational objectives, or the E/I symbol be found. Most do include advertising, in some pages of the site.

An often-overlooked segment of nonprogram content is the public service announcement (PSA). The Advertising Council, which is an advertising industry group designed to provide social advocacy campaigns, provide, many of the PSAs that audiences see or hear. This group donates advertising space and creative talent to these campaigns, many of which are targeted to teens as well as the larger adult market. A recent publication of the Ad Council highlighted the availability for TV, radio, or print campaigns targeting children and young adults in the areas of antidiscrimination, crime prevention, fire safety, forest fire prevention, 4-H, math, and youth fitness. A major effort is now under way to address issues of school violence. Networks, however, also devote resources to their own campaigns. Recently, a number of V-Chip PSAs have been airing on the networks. One of the best known campaigns is the long-running NBC campaign called "The More You Know," which for the TNBC (teen NBC) segment features media celebrities talking about issues of interest to teens.

All of this is about branding. Branding is the process whereby a product or service is seen to stand for something and to be qualitatively different from similar products or services. Branding is an outgrowth of the integrated marketing perspective that advocates the integrated use of all marketing tools to produce a brand. Perhaps branding can best be understood by looking at the comments of some syndicators. Mort Marcus, president of Buena Vista Television, notes, "In this world of fragmentation, you need to be a little more consistent and you need to be branded. You need to be more of a destination, so kids can find you easier" (Schlosser, 1999, p. 28).

IDENTIFYING FINANCIAL PATTERNS

Inevitably, local station revenues come primarily from the sale of time to advertisers. Individual broadcast stations, particularly in large markets, can be very profitable, with annual profit margins in the 35% to 50% range. Networks, on the other hand, have not been particularly profitable business units in recent years, as audiences erode and program costs climb. However, media giants have been gobbling up available broadcast stations, resulting in the creation of more than three additional networks in the 1990s. Why this seeming contradiction? The answer lies in the amortization of program costs by program content creators (major studios, independents, and international firms) and networks in the ancillary and aftermarkets. Ancillary markets include, among other things, international sales and merchandise licensing. Aftermarkets, sometimes called the *back end*, refer to postfirst-run sales of the program.

The program costs vary widely, depending on longevity, stars, and quality. Nonetheless, children's programs are significantly less expensive to produce than primetime programs. A dramatic series averages between $2 and $4 million per week, a situation comedy between $1 and $2 million. Children's television programs tend to average $100,000 to $350,000 per half-hour animated episode (Jackson, 1999). Although the profit on children's programs is smaller than on adult series, their ancillary and aftermarket potential is vast. It seems clear that part of the pitch is a potential merchandizing link and international sales. Thus, the deficit per episode (the cost per episode minus the licensing fee paid by the network) to be made up in the ancillary and aftermarket. Licensing and merchandising for successful children's shows can be a multibillion dollar activity. Concurrently with the program run, the show can be marketing internationally. This internationalization is helping production companies weather decreasing ratings for children's shows in the U.S. market. An international co-production can take advantage of alternative sources of funding that might be available in some countries. For example, in some countries, government subsidies are available for programming production. Sometimes, in some countries, production costs are lower for "national" projects (even if they are co-ventures). And these co-ventures can overcome local quota restrictions (restricting non-native productions used on air).

It is this concentration that is the key to profitability. Chan-Olmsted (1996) concluded that the children's television market is moderately concentrated and on the verge of becoming highly concentrated as major players such as Disney and Fox consolidate their activities. She noted that network–syndication ownership is a critical combination for gaining market control.

Merchandise licensing refers to an agreement that allows the right to use a name or image in exchange for a royalty fee, generally 5% to 15% of the cost of the item (Pecora, 1998). Toys, games, clothing, lunchboxes, and the many other licensed products afford the manufacturer a recognizable character with ongoing "promotion" when the program airs, increasing product visibility and demand. The entertainment industry profits from the promotion of the product and the additional source of corporate revenue. Increasingly, production companies and product manufacturers have agents to manage these contractual negotiations.

The sale of licensed products is approximately a $60 billion industry. For the toy industry, these products help to introduce some stability to a volatile marketplace. For the entertainment industry, the royalties are an important source of income. Hanna-Barbera was grossing $40 to $50 million from licensed products in the 1970s; royalty fees for Mattel totaled $10 million in 1985 (Pecora, 1998). Toy makers are now intimately involved in producing kids' TV shows, either buying the master license on a packaged property or developing a show around an existing line (Schmuckler, 1995). Toymakers shoulder a large amount of the production tab, and Schmuckler even asserts that they pay television stations to clear shows by committing advertising dollars in exchange. These agreements seem to extend the life-cycle of both the toy and the program (See Tashjian & Campbell, chap. 9, this volume, for more information about licensing and merchandising.)

The toy/program tie-in can come at any time in the process. Children's films and merchandised products usually hit the market at about the same time. For television, licensed toys that can be purchased during the Christmas rush quickly follow the September premiere. Some programs evolve in popularity, and product lines emerge after that. For example, *Barney & Friends* products appeared after that show gained popularity. A few were popular toys before they become programs; *Strawberry Shortcake* and *My Little Pony* are two examples.

Despite the impact of program resale and merchandise licensing, the foundation of the children's television business is advertising. Sales for children's television ads passed the $1 billion mark in 1998, despite a trend that sees children watching less television. This can be compared to the $44.5 billion total advertising volume for television and cable together. Nationally, the children's television market is divided into two time periods. Upfront selling usually occurs in April, when advertisers make the bulk of their buys for the upcoming season, locking up the "prime" advertising real estate. What remains is bought up throughout the year on what is called the *scatter market*.

Whatever choices they make about when to buy, advertiser, buy gross ratings points (GRPs), the sum of all ratings for all programs in a schedule of buys. This is the most frequently used measure of audiences for the advertising community. Of course, these buys must be made at an appropriate CPM, which is the cost to reach 1,000 people or homes. Another frequently used measure is the Cost Per Rating Point

(CPP), which is the cost to deliver a single rating point. The *Marketer's Guide to Media* (1998/1999) reports an average CPM cost of network children's programming (cable and broadcast combined) of $5.92 in 1997–1998. This can be compared to a CPM cost in primetime of $ 11.93. One cable channel, Nickelodeon, controls 50% of the available children's gross ratings points (which is the same as saying that it accounts for 50% of all of children's viewing). Cable as a whole controls 80% of children's GRPs. However, these GRPs are very fragmented, and it is no longer easy to reach children efficiently.

The major advertisers on children's television are Hasbro, Mattel, Kraft, General Foods, and Kellogg, representing games, toys, and cereals and approximately 36% of total children's advertising dollars. The variety of companies spending on children's television is increasing. In 1994, toys and cereals accounted for 56% of total children's ad dollars; in 1998, that figure was only 36%. With children's programming proliferating, particularly on cable, some worry that a surplus of advertising time will be created, driving profits down. With more than 1,000 hours of children's programming a week on network and cable channels, the number of choices creates significant audience fragmentation and gives ad buyers more alternatives for where to place their ad dollars. Whatever the outcome, children's viewing has become a very fragmented demographic, raising serious questions about how to effectively reach them.

There are self-regulatory groups within the advertising industry that strive to oversee advertising. One of these is a part of the Better Business Bureau—the National Advertising Review Council's Children's Advertising Review Unit (CARU). Part of a comprehensive self-regulatory process of the NARC, CARU's goal is to work with the industry to ensure that advertising to children is truthful and fair. Like the larger review unit, CARU investigates complaints, recommends modifications or discontinuance of offending claims, and may refer the matter to appropriate government agencies. The major federal agency that deals with deceptive or untrue advertising is the Federal Trade Commission (FTC), which has in its time responded to numerous complaints about advertising practices to children, many filed by the former organization Action for Children's Television (ACT).

CONCLUSION

Due to its focus on children's television, this chapter only hints at the complexity of the children's media business. The increasingly integrated marketing of media products means that a "children's program" is almost never considered apart from concerns about merchandising and licensing; ancillary sales of videos, games, and music; book and movie tie-ins; international production and sales; creation of stars to be promoted; and branding of the network, to name only a few. The real profit in children's television is in the production/distribution arena, where ancillary marketing, aftermarkets, and international co-ventures and distribution are a multibillion dollar industry.

This profitable picture is threatened by fragmentation and technology. The proliferation of content in children's programming is significantly fragmenting the child audience. Less development money tends to be readily available for an individual program, particularly for independent production companies. Advertisers are justifiably worried that traditional television viewing is dwindling, and that mass child audiences are harder to reach. The erasure of ads with digital video recorders such as TiVo is only one aspect of the problem. Add in other components that attract children's attention like iPods, Internet, video games, video, and an increasing host of targeted electronic and nonelectronic media, and the competition for children's leisure time becomes intense. Many traditional advertisers are looking for alternate ways to reach viewers. One such alternative, product placement, is popular, but diverts attention from the development monies that may no longer be readily available. Production and distribution co-ventures, product tie-ins, and other ancillary markets have sustained the children's marketplace, but the segmentation of these markets could force a transformation in traditional models of programming.

The body of television content emerging from these economic and industrial practices has been a central component of childhood since the 1950s. Because children are seen as a special "group" of both citizens and viewers, great concerns for the role of television in the lives of children have accompanied the development of the medium. As a result, issues surrounding children and television have often been framed as "social problems," issues of central concern to numerous groups. Large-scale academic research enterprises have been mounted to monitor, analyze, and explain relationships between television and children. Congress, regulatory agencies, advocacy groups, and the television networks have struggled continuously over research findings, public responsibility, and popular response. The regulatory decisions of the 1990s transformed children's television. We are only beginning to assess the consequences of these transformations.

REFERENCES

Chan-Olmsted, S. (1996). From *Sesame Street* to Wall Street: An analysis of market competition in commercial competition in commercial children's television. *Journal of Broadcasting & Electronic Media, 40(1), 30–44.*

Cuneo, A. Z. (2004). Startup seeks to build $1B kids' food empire. *Advertising Age, 75,* (38), p. 18.

Dempsey, J. (2005, March 14–20). The rupe ripple effect. *Variety,* pp. 1, 65.

Federal Communications Commission (2004). Report and order and further notice of proposed rule making in the matter of children's television obligations of digital television broadcasters [Government document] MB Docket No. 00-167, FCC 04-221.

Jackson, W. (1999, April 12). Viewer's call. *Variety,* pp. 37, 46.

Marketer's Guide to Media. (1998/1999) Volume 21. New York: ASM Communications.

Marketer's Guide to Media. 2004/2005 Volume 28. New York: ASM Communications.

McClellan, S., & Tedesco, R. (1999, March 12). Children's TV market may be played out. *Broadcasting and Cable,* pp. 20–22.

Pecora, N. (1998). *The business of children's entertainment.* New York: Guilford.

Petrozzello, D. (1998, July 27). Cable competition for kids intensifies. *Broadcasting and Cable,* pp. 27–28.

Schlosser, J. (1999, March 1) Kids syndicators get squeezed. *Broadcasting and Cable,* pp. 26, 28.

Schmuckler, E. (1995). Toys & TV: An incestuous connection. *Brandweek. 36,* (25), p. 36.

Steinberg, D. (1998, July 19). What makes Nick tick: Nickelodeon is a sensibility, a world, an all-empowering club. It's CNN for children. *The Philadelphia Inquirer,* Sunday Magazine, p. 12.

Viveiros, B. N. (2005). Kids' clique: Television networks use the web to build relationships with children. *Catalog Age, 79–80.*

Whitney, D. (2005) For Kids TV, every day is Saturday. Advertising Age, *76,* (8), p. 10.

II

PRODUCING CHILDREN'S TELEVISION

4

Producing Children's Television

Robby London
Children's Television Writer–Producer–Executive

This chapter is divided into two sections. The first provides an overview of the basic process of creating and producing children's television programs. The second examines—from the producer's point of view—some specific issues, concerns, and challenges unique to producing television specifically geared for children.

The emphasis is, to a large degree, on animated programs. This medium constitutes the bulk of children's television. Not only are cartoons often more appealing to a younger audience for reasons related to the developmental and perceptual stages of childhood, but because such developmental stages are cross-cultural, cartoons for children are far more marketable *internationally* than are live-action programs. This is especially true in non-English-speaking territories because (a) the language redubbing is less apparent in animated mouths; (b) cartoons typically contain fewer obvious cultural and national signatures and cues than live action, and (c) cartoon characters often consist of animals or very unrealistic-looking humanoids of indeterminate ethnic or national origin. When it comes to children's programs, this marketplace reality of stronger *export potential* for cartoons creates a powerful business incentive favoring their production over live-action programs. And lastly, the emphasis on animation in this chapter results from the fact that it constitutes the majority of the author's experience. However, every attempt will be made to highlight key areas of divergence between animated and live-action children's programs, especially when they are relevant to the discussion at hand.

THE CREATIVE AND PRODUCTION PROCESS

Of course, it always starts with the idea. However, the sources and formats of an idea for a children's show can be as diverse as the ideas themselves. Often the ideas come from another medium, such as books, movies, video games, toys, or a celebrity persona—and children's television merely adapts such an existing property into a television series.

Original ideas that make their debut in the medium of children's television are often *creator-driven*. Series like *Bear in the Big Blue House, SpongeBob Square Pants*, and *Bill Nye the Science Guy*, were based on original ideas from individual creators (in the examples just cited, Mitchell Kriegman, Steve Hillenburg, and Bill Nye, respectively). These individuals came up with the ideas for their shows, "pitched" them to broadcasters, and once the show was selected for broadcast, these individuals became "show-runners," that is single individuals (or teams) responsible for realizing and maintaining their original "vision" throughout the production process.

In contrast, series like *Where on Earth is Carmen Sandiego?, Madeline,* and *Batman: The Animated Series*, are examples of more studio-driven productions. All were based on preexisting properties (a computer game, a series of children's books, and both a comic book and movie, respectively) that a studio identified as embodying the ingredients believed to have the potential to translate into a successful children's animated series. (Of course original ideas, too, can be generated from within a studio system or even by a network.)

In this latter category of "studio-driven" production, typically the studio acquires the production rights and develops them with hired personnel. The studio then assigns a story editor to be responsible for the scripts, a voice director to be responsible for the voices, a music supervisor to be responsible for the music, and a producer to be responsible for the animation itself—all as *employees* of the studio. The executives of the studio (sometimes in conjunction with the network and/or the original rights holders) serve as executive producers and the final creative arbiters of the production.

What are the ingredients that studios look for in acquiring properties for children's television? *Brand awareness* is always coveted because it helps to ensure a television program will at least be "sampled" by an audience that is already familiar with, and positively disposed towards, the title or characters. Of course, a brand alone will not create a hit series. Studios, broadcasters, and producers have learned that simply being well-sampled is *necessary* but not *sufficient* for success. Once attracted to the television screen at the appointed time and channel, the audience then has to love the show. The graveyard of children's programming failures is littered with big, well-known titles that got heavily sampled initially, but did not deliver a series that ultimately captured the minds and hearts of the audience.

Aside from brand awareness, interesting, well-developed, and *child-relatable characters* are an important asset. Properties like *The Archies*, *Dennis The Menace,* and *Garfield* (from comic strips and comic books) each had extremely entertaining, multidimensional and very kid-relatable characters and character relationships prior to becoming successful children's television programs. Of course, books and comic books are not the only place to find well-developed characters. *The Real Ghostbusters* (an animated series based on the hit movie *Ghostbusters*) had very well-developed characters with which to create a children's television series—and it was consequently a huge success over many years when it became one.

The Real Ghostbusters had another element going for it, which is particularly important in the medium of animation. It had a large *fantasy component*—a basic conflict and premise that was "larger-than-life." This is a particularly useful and desirable quality in television animation. Television animation, unlike theatrical-quality animation, is based largely on economies of scale and special techniques of "limited animation," pioneered by Bill Hanna and Joe Barbera in the 1960s and also employed to great success by Lou Scheimer, Norm Prescott, and Hal Sutherland, the founders of Filmation Studios, during the 1970s and early 1980s. (Hanna-Barbera and Filmation produced the bulk of children's television programs, both animated and live-action, during those decades.) Limited animation is effective at portraying *broad* action. It is often *not* effective at portraying subtlety, character nuance, or subtext. "Talking heads" are particularly unexciting to watch in limited animation because of the lack of visual sophistication or emotion. This is why it is more difficult to contemplate relationship-sit-com material in television animation and why, typically, producers seek out or create properties with very visually oriented gimmicks. Examples include *Inspector Gadget*'s endless bionic body parts and contraptions, the supernatural creatures and fantastical "ghost-busting" gear found in the aforementioned *The Real Ghostbusters,* and the larger-than-life capers and robberies orchestrated by *Carmen Sandiego.*

This observation helps to highlight the counterprogramming aspect of NBC's "radical" children'sprogramming strategy starting in the mid-1990s when they opted to abandon Saturday morning cartoons for a lineup of live-action sit-coms targeting "tweens" (the archetype and most successful of these series being *Saved By The Bell*). To an extent, Nickelodeon and The Disney Channel also employed a counterprogramming strategy in many of their early series, which were either live-action series or cartoons more akin to live-action sit-coms, such as *Hey Arnold!* and *Doug*.

One final element that has consistently produced hits in children's television is a story or character that embodies the concept of *empowerment*. The theory is that because kids experience such strong feelings of powerlessness in terms of an ability to control their *real* world, consequently their imaginations are particularly stimulated, captivated, and fulfilled by stories portraying normally "weak" or "powerless" characters being able to "transform" into a superhero. For example, consider the success of *Superman, Batman, He-Man, and the Masters of the Universe, Transformers, Mighty Morphin' Power Rangers, Captain Planet,* and literally dozens of other examples that no doubt come to the reader's mind. Of course superpowers are not the *only* means to empowerment. In series like *Sherlock Holmes in the 22nd Century, Stargate: Infinity,* or *Where on Earth is Carmen Sandiego?*, the protagonists (young people in the latter two examples) are empowered by means of their quick wit and intelligence. *Madeline* is empowered by her feistiness, competitiveness, and perseverance. But, still, there seems to be something about superheroes and/or magic (*Harry Potter*) that is instantly relatable and ultimately fulfilling to children in an immediate, visceral, and deeply resonant manner. For that reason, it is likely that this genre will always be a fixture in the children's entertainment landscape.

In addition to the elements just discussed that go into the decision to develop a property, there are many *common beliefs and assumptions* amongst producers and broadcasters that play a significant role in informing their decisions. These items of "conventional wisdom" have largely evolved from various qualitative interpretations, explanations, and theories of viewership trends over many years which are espoused by programmers. Of course, the reality is that there are virtually infinite explanations and variables to account for series popularity—and for why shows do and do not attract audiences; but nonetheless certain assumptions seem to have gained traction and remain prevalent. Many such assumptions are also reinforced by anecdotal experiences of children's television executives with their own children and their children's friends. In general, please note that, except where acknowledged specifically, the author has no scientific or empirical basis on which to comment on the *validity* of the beliefs and assumptions articulated in the following discussion, but rather is simply making the reader aware of their existence and influence on the decision-making process.

One such belief is that younger children (say in the 4- to 8-year-old age range) will watch "up"—meaning they will watch programs that are targeted to older kids or even adults. In addition, according to the popular wisdom, the converse is never true, that is older kids would *not* watch a show that they perceive to be targeted to someone younger. The theory behind this is the belief that kids always wish to envision themselves as older and never the reverse. This assumption was clearly in evidence in NBC's decision, referenced, earlier to target tweens. And indeed it *has* met with reasonable success in attracting younger kids as well.

Another assumption is that kids over the age of 6 or 7 do not want to watch programs that they perceive to be "educational"—the theory being that in watching television, they are seeking an escape from the 40-plus hours a week of school and homework that is forced on them. (For purposes of later discussion, it is critical to note that this belief only applies to children beyond age 6 or so—and that there is *not* the same perceived viewing dichotomy between "entertainment" and "education" in younger children.). Yet another belief is that there is far more advertising money targeting kids aged 6- to 11-years-old than 2- to 5-years-old, and this belief has been historically well supported with market realities. One final belief that prevailed for many years was that girls *would* watch series targeted at boys but that the converse was *not* true. However, in recent years, this assumption has been somewhat belied by several successful "girl-empowerment" series that were popular with both genders, including *Power Puff Girls, Sailor Moon,* and *Sabrina* (both the live and animated versions).

These assumptions, taken as a composite, would logically dictate that the greatest perceived likelihood of ratings success in the kids 6 to 11 demographic would be derived from a series targeting 11-year-old boys and, in fact, that generally *has* been the most likely category of series to attract the interest of broadcasters.

Once the creator or studio decides that a concept is worth developing, having taken all of what has just been discussed into consideration, the actual development process takes on a very consistent set of milestones. The first step is the creation of a series "bible." The bible is a written document, often illustrated, varying in length from as little as eight pages (this shorter version usually referred to as a *mini-bible*) to upwards of 40 pages. (For simplicity, henceforth we shall refer to both *mini-bibles* and *bibles* as bibles.) The bible's purpose is to define and describe the series, its characters, and their interrelationships, its tone, its underlying conflict, its settings, and to delineate sample stories and episodes. The idea is that the bible should contain virtually everything about the series that an executive would need to know to understand the series, and that a writer would need to know actually to write a script.

To digress briefly, it is valuable to note that in children's television, the choice of a writer in developing an idea is considered to be a very crucial creative decision.Writers are "cast," based on their perceived strengths or special sensibilities, specifically to match the genre and or special needs of a given project. Of course many writers object to such pigeon-holing and would assert that, as skilled professional writers, they can adapt their talents to a wide range of properties, genres, and styles.

In animation, bibles are *always* the first step and are considered *de rigueur*. In live action programs, that is not always the case. Some live-action series start with a pilot script, and the aspects and "rules" typically found in a "bible" presumably exist only in the mind of the writer-creator of the pilot script (who would normally become the show-runner should the series proceed to production). Sometimes during or after the first season of a live-action series, a bible of sorts is created by the writing staff to help new writers coming onto the series to understand what has come before. However, some live-action series are now following the process of animation development in terms of trying to create a definitive series bible early on in the process—and sometimes even prior to a pilot script being written—as is always the case in animation.

It is interesting to note that there can be two different versions of a bible coexisting simultaneously for the same series. The first is what is called a *sales bible* or *pitch bible* and its intended readers are potential broadcasters, merchandise licensees, and executives who are in a position to buy various rights to the series, *prior to the show even being produced.* (These are known as *pre-sales.*) Such a bible must be written in a very entertaining style and it is more important that the series *sound compelling* in this type of bible than it is to articulate all the information, details, and mechanics necessary actually to write scripts. Once a series is greenlighted and goes into production, often times the sales bible is revised and expanded into a *writer's bible,* which is less about making the series sound attractive and about being a zippy and entertaining read to a busy executive than it is about providing nuts-and-bolts and specifics so that different writers working on the series know as much as possible about it, ultimately resulting in a relative degree of uniformity in their script submissions.

One final note about bibles: It is virtually impossible to anticipate beforehand all the questions, quirks, and twists that a series of 26 or more episodes eventually will embody. (Currently, 26 half hours constitutes the standard minimum order for children's series.) As characters begin to emerge in the writing of actual scripts, and writers and artists generate new ideas for the series, invariably there will be changes and divergence—*sometimes substantial*—from the rules, descriptions, and details originally set out in the bible. So, in a sense, even the best, longest, and most comprehensive bibles are, in the end, really only basic blueprints.

In animation, not only is the writing set out on paper prior to production, but the entire look and feel of the series must be created from scratch. Thus, visualization is an aspect of the creation of a show that is nearly equally important to the conceptualization and writing. Consequently the design and visual creation will often start commensurate with, or immediately after, the writing of the bible. Although it is usually true that there are words on a page before an artist picks up a pencil (or a computer stylus),there are also occasions when an artist gets a visual idea for a set of characters or a world that is so compelling that it drives the written conceptualization—the veritable "picture worth a thousand words." In any case, in animation, the design and style are crucially important components, and a series is virtually never presold without a compelling set of illustrations to go along with the bible and verbal description of a series.

The next step is the creation of the *pilot*—or first script for an actual episode. This is usually assigned to the same writer(s) who wrote the bible. One question that often comes up is whether the pilot script should be an "origin story," which introduces the characters and initial set-up to an audience for the first time, (e.g., in *Superman,* telling the history of how Superman came to earth, was adopted by the Kents, etc.) as opposed to writing "Episode #7," a random episode that is not chronological and represents a typical episode that could occur interchangeably anywhere in the series and which does *not* divulge any unique or chronological background information. The advantage to the former is that it introduces everyone to the lore and back-story.(And, the advantage to the writers is that much of it has already been fleshed out in the bible.) The disadvantage is that because there usually is so much back-story, "origin" pilots tend to be overly story-heavy, requiring a lot exposition, and also often prove to be nonrepresentative of what a "typical" episode amongst the remaining 25 might be.

Once a series commences production, the story editor solicits written *premises* for episodes from freelance writers. In order to reduce overhead costs, the current studio trend is to dispense with the concept of "staff" writers to whom they must pay salaries and benefits and, instead, rely mostly on freelance independent contractors. In order to get an assignment, a freelance writer, after a thorough consultation with the story editor and exposure to the bible, is expected to submit a written premise containing a story idea for an episode. These premises, averaging about one page in length, are submitted on "spec" (that is, with no guarantee of payment), but the unwritten agreement is that *if* the production staff agrees that the premise will indeed make a good episode, then it is assigned to the writer who submitted it—and from that point forward the writer will be paid for her or his work.

The next step after a premise is an *outline,* which can be anywhere from 4 to 20 pages for a 21-minute episode, the approximate screen time required to fill a half-hour timeslot on commercial television, leaving time for the commercials. This wide variance in outline length is primarily a function of how much detail is requested by the story editor.

Then, after notes are given on the outline, the writer will commence the first draft *teleplay*. For animation scripts, the rule of thumb is typically one and a half pages per minute of screen time. For live action, the formula is one page per minute of screen time. Why the discrepancy? Because in writing animation scripts, writers are expected to do far more of what is called "directing on paper." This means spelling out *far* more detail about the camera shots, the physical action, and the environment. Because literally everything onscreen has to be drawn, animation writers are expected to provide very explicit instructions for the artists. In live action, less of the world is being created from scratch and more is left to the discretion of the director, production designer, and actors, hence the shorter teleplay length.

Once a teleplay for animation has been finalized and approved it goes on to be storyboarded, designed, and voice-recorded, usually in that order. (Sometimes the recording precedes the storyboard.) Think of a storyboard as being similar in format to a comic book but without color. Individual panels are drawn for each animation set-up (or "layout"), dialogue is indicated and action is described. Once the storyboard is complete, the script is essentially "thrown away" and the storyboard becomes the official blueprint for the remainder of the production process of that episode, a process which is now almost exclusively outsourced overseas. To wit, the main design, storyboard, timing, and colors are usually created by the domestic production studio, but the more labor-intensive drawing, coloring, and compositing is sent to territories with less expensive labor costs. The film or video is then returned and the originating production studio usually resumes full control and performs the postproduction, which consists of final color correction, assembling, and trimming the "picture" (video or film) and creating and mixing all the sounds including sound effects, music scoring and the voices (which were recorded earlier in the process).

It's important to note that this process goes on 26 consecutive times for 26 episodes, which ultimately must be delivered on a frequency of once a week. And equally important to bear in mind is that the two variables which have by *far* the most impact on animation quality are: time and money. In a typical television production, there is a paucity of both! In fact there is an old bromide in television production in which you draw a triangle and label each corner, respectively: "good," "fast," and "cheap." And then use the illustration to make the point that, unlike geometry, in the world of production, only two of these three descriptors can ever coexist simultaneously in a Euclidean universe!

We've discussed how ideas are generated and outlined the production process that occurs once a decision is made to go forward with a given idea. However, a vital link in the chain that has not yet been examined is the manner in which a series is sold and financed. Chronologically, this typically happens sometime after the bible is completed, and often even prior to the pilot script. To understand the dynamics of how a series is sold, it is important to take a brief historical look at the economics of children's television and how radically it has been impacted by the changing television landscape of the past decade.

Until the mid-1990s, U.S. networks paid license fees to producers for the right to broadcast children's series on Saturday morning for a limited number of years. These fees were typically high enough to cover the *entire* cost of production. During this era, as a result of the networks paying the full freight of production, they believed they were entitled to assert a tremendous amount of creative input and control on the content of the series. Producers, for the most part, were willing to go along and cede such control in return for these high domestic license fees. The pay-off was that all the revenues from *ancillary* sales, which included licensing and merchandise and international television, were pure profit for the producers. It was a very attractive business model.

All this started to change rapidly in the mid-1990s. With the emergence of the 24-hour a day, dedicated kids' channels on cable (e.g., Nickelodeon, Cartoon Network, Disney Channel, Discovery Kids, etc.) and the *total amount of advertiser dollars* directed at kids remaining relatively constant, the advertising revenues going to each network were substantially diluted. As a result, the license fees paid to producers by domestic broadcasters begin to drop precipitously—to the degree that within just a few years they were as little as *10%* of the fees a producer could expect just a few years prior! The economics shifted radically, and the ancillary areas that used to provide strictly *profit* were now suddenly crucial *simply to cover the costs* of production. Now, in order to get the money to finance shows, producers were required to piece together presales from many different international broadcast territories, in addition to a domestic broadcast as well as royalty advances from a wide array of merchandise categories.

This transferred a great deal more power and importance to international broadcasters, whose license fees were actually going up at the same time that U.S. fees were plummeting so steeply. It launched an era of coproductions between U.S. and international broadcasters and producers. Producing children's television became a *far* more economically challenged business model and the field of players who survived was substantially thinned. At the same time, the governmental revocation of the "financial interest syndication" rules (aka 'fin-syn')—a regulatory prohibition of broadcasters producing their own programs—and the resultant wave of media consolidation also served to reduce markedly the number of independent studios and producers. Most of the broadcast and cable outlets ended up either acquiring production companies—or starting their own—and subsequently programmed their own networks with their own product.

The few remaining independent companies, such as DIC Entertainment, Nelvanna, S. D. Productions, and Mike Young Productions, were forced to compete with vertically integrated behemoths in a marketplace of rapidly shrinking license fees. It had become (and remains as of this writing) a challenged environment for independents, to say the least.

So, in order to finance a series, producers were required to "pre-sell" it in all of the various markets and categories that, collectively, would barely finance its production. It meant that "pitching" the series with the basic materials of a bible, some artwork, occasionally a few brief snippets of sample animation (it is too expensive for most producers to produce an entire episode without the guarantee of presales) was the only way to get a series financed. It put tremendous pressure on the sales forces—or sales capabilities—of the producers, and it meant that a great pitch and great pitch materials were absolutely critical. In some respects, the simple reality that the "pitch must be king" dictated creative choices in terms of a producer ensuring that he or she developed and acquired properties that would "pitch well."(Once again explaining the previously mentioned desirability of a presold brand with which the prospective buyer was already familiar and had a demonstrable track record.)

MIP-TV and MIPCOM, the two largest worldwide television markets held each April and October, respectively, in Cannes, France, became must-attend events for producers, and their ability to go forward on a project was determined largely by the response to their pitches at these markets.

SPECIAL CONCERNS AND ISSUES IN CHILDREN'S PROGRAMMING

To quote from a pamphlet entitled *Special Considerations for Creators of Children's Media,*[1] "Young children ... represent a special audience

---

[1] A written set of content guidelines revised in 2000 by a working group assembled by DIC Entertainment and Mediascope and including participation from networks, producers, NEA (National Education Association), National PTA, UCLA and Stanford University, among others.

with special needs." Those of us who create television programs for children are faced with unique challenges and a massive degree of scrutiny. Moreover, it would be naïve not to acknowledge the reality that children's television makes an extremely attractive target for politicians, advocacy groups, and others who depend on the public goodwill (whether it takes the form of votes or financial contributions) for their survival.

Historically, when politicians have criticized or made an issue of children's television (and, not surprisingly, this has most often happened during an election campaign) they articulate and frame their positions in a manner that makes them virtually impossible to oppose or challenge without appearing to be, in fact, opposed to "improving" children's television or being opposed to "quality children's television." One tactic that has been particularly frustrating to children's television producers and broadcasters is the lack of differentiation by our critics between "children's television" (programs produced specifically for children) and "television children watch" (i.e., programs, movies, and commercials that target *adults*—but which kids see anyway). Critics would cite examples of inappropriate content on television that were not even *in* shows produced for children and then speak in generic terms about "violence," "sex," "language," etcetera, and lump it all under the label of "children's television." The reality is that few parents carefully monitor the content of children's shows and thus have no factual basis on which to evaluate such charges, and so, by and large, they simply accept these assertions at face value.

The initial outcry in support of a V-chip is a wonderful example of the extent of the rhetoric, as well as the power of using children's television as an issue to inflame popular opinion and rally parents. As politicians made hay over their support of this technology to "arm parents against the evils of Hollywood," there was an infamous "town hall meeting" in Peoria, Illinois in which outraged middle Americans decried the content of children's television and demanded a way to prevent their children from watching inappropriate material. According to polls, parents demanded the V-chip by huge margins. And yet, both research and anecdotal experience tells us that only a tiny fraction of parents actually *use* the V-chip now that it's virtually universally available (Kaiser Family Foundation, 2001).

The reality is that children's programs are—and always have been— very strongly self-policed by broadcasters and by producers themselves. Prior to 1983, virtually all children's programs were aired on one of the then three networks, NBC, CBS, or ABC. Each network has active and aggressive "program practices" departments that are separate and independent from the programming departments and whose responsibility it is to review all children's programs for inappropriate content. This includes not only violence, sex, language, or bad taste, but also things like ethnic stereotyping and anything deemed to be "imitable antisocial behavior." These departments are often staffed with people with a background in education or developmental psychology and they additionally consult with working experts in those fields in formulating and interpreting their policies (see Stipp, chap.6, this volume). All network programming is very carefully self-monitored. This is not to say that there are never complaints, nor that some questionable material never slips through. The reality is that with an audience as mass and diverse as is reached by television, it is virtually impossible to entertain such a huge audience and not offend *someone*.

In 1983, *He-Man and the Masters of the Universe* and *Inspector Gadget* launched a whole new television outlet for children's programs called "first-run syndication," which essentially bypassed the networks and in which producers sold programs directly to individual stations, local market by local market, and targeted weekday afternoons, which previously had not typically aired children's programs. Although there was no *formal* program standards mechanism in place for these syndicated series as had been the case at the networks, the reality was that the writers and producers of these syndicated series were the *same individuals and companies* who were working on network series. All of us had been extensively exposed to the "rules" and theories of what was and what was not acceptable for kids, and we had very much internalized these standards. So, at least in terms of inappropriate content, the syndicated marketplace had *de facto* broadcast standards similar to the networks.

When FOX came along as a network force, followed closely by the emergence of the dedicated kids' cable channels (Nickelodeon, Disney Channel, Cartoon Network, etc.) they all had program standards executives and sensitivities, as well. And although there were slight discrepancies between what the different networks would allow (FOX being typically more liberal and permissive), the rules were (and remain) mostly uniform and consistent. The bottom line is that the content of children's programs is—and always has been—self-regulated to great effect in terms of avoiding harmful content.

Of course, a working definition of what exactly constitutes "harmful content" is something that is extremely elusive. For one thing, there is a huge developmental range between the ages of 2 and 11. This range has always been the demographic of children's television as defined and measured by the all-important Nielsen ratings (with measured subsets of 2–5 and 6–11, which although narrower than 2 to 11, still represent ranges of childhood development that are typically too large accurately to target with the same content.). Remembering the earlier referenced belief that kids "watch up," what might be marginally acceptable for an 11-year-old, could be clearly inappropriate for a 5-year-old. But if you were to program only what was appropriate for a 5-year-old, the programs would simply not appeal to the older demographic. Of course, this analysis does not even take into account the vast range of mores, norms, and social values in childrearing which exists amongst parents in our culture.

Another huge challenge is defining "violence" and determining the degree to which *context* should come into play in deciding what is to be allowed. Is the so-called "squash-and-stretch cartoon violence" of *Bugs Bunny* or *Roadrunner,* in which there are extensive cues for children that the action is pure fantasy and wholly divorced from reality, to be evaluated equally with the more realistic "violence" of *Mighty Morphin' Power Rangers*? (At least one study, in fact, absolutely validates and encourages this distinction.)[2] Should verbal abuse be considered "violence," or is it a case of "sticks and stones?" One study[3] suggests that the lack of portraying accurately and viscerally the *consequences* of "violence" results in harmfully desensitizing viewers to the effects of violent acts. And yet, other developmental experts have suggested that such realistic and graphic portrayals are far too upsetting for children and thus inappropriate. Which is worse? Should violence in the service of *self-defense* be taught—or even condoned? And lastly, isn't there an inherent hypocrisy (which is typically something for which kids seem to have instant radar and which immediately destroys the credibility of both the message and the messenger) in a culture that preaches nonviolence in its television—while at the same time conducts an unpopular war frowned on by much of the world?

A thorough discussion of these and other such questions would take a book in itself. Suffice it to say that research and expert opinion has been contradictory and nonconclusive. The intent here is only to point out the kinds of questions and challenges with which creators of children's television are faced on a daily basis—and the reality that there are no unambiguous or unanimous expert points of view.

Because there *is* a cultural and market demand for children's television shows and since the essence of good drama is conflict and since much of what has been historically demonstrated to entertain our audience are story elements that some might deem inappropriate, it is a constant challenge for us to decide what to include and what must be

---

[2]The UCLA Television Violence Monitoring Report, UCLA Center For Communication Policy, 1995.

[3]National Television Violence Study, 1998.

censored. Most producers of children's programs basically apply the general guidelines originally dictated by the network program practices experts that have permeated the industry ever since. Probably the simplest, and most all-encompassing rule-of-thumb and key evaluative phrase followed when deciding what to censor, is "imitatable antisocial behavior." There is virtual universal agreement that, in theory, this should be avoided. However, there are always interpretive questions as to what is "imitatable" and what constitutes "antisocial." Some experts have argued that, to the degree the action is more fantastical, science fiction-based and noninjurious (e.g., unrealistic weapons that shoot "freeze rays") or the target of a physical action is inanimate (e.g. robots, or vehicles) or the action is simply too fantastical or difficult to be imitated (a triple somersault martial arts move), it may be less likely to foster violent or inappropriate behavior in young viewers. Along similar lines, others have suggested that cartoons, by their very nature, have more leeway than live-action, because of the more obvious cues that they are fantasy.

In addition to issues of inappropriate content, another challenge to children's program producers is the Children's Television Act of 1990 and subsequent Rules and Regulations of 1996, in which the Federal Communications Commission (FCC) attempted to clarify vagaries of the original Act (collectively referred to henceforth as "CTA"). This is the law that compels every local television station in the United States to broadcast 3 hours a week of "educational" children's television—as a requirement for maintaining their licenses to operate over the public airwaves (see Kunkel, chap. 11, this volume, for more details). The "rub" is this: What constitutes "educational" television and who gets to decide?

We noted earlier that there is consensus that kids under the age of 6-years-old seem to enjoy and be thoroughly engaged in the kinds of television that adults—both laypersons and educators—would agree to be wonderfully educational, for example. *Sesame Street, Dora the Explorer,* and *Mr. Rogers' Neighborhood,* etcetera. For producers of "educational series" that target this younger demographic, the mandate is clear and there is no controversy.

However, it is quite a different situation in trying to target 7- to 11-year-old kids with series containing educational content. These kids have free choice over what they watch and the ratings have demonstrated convincingly that most series that appear to have an obvious curriculum or educational agenda are not popular choices. Kids of this age range will instead gravitate to programs whose principal focus is to entertain with stories built around drama, conflict and comedy and *not* around perceived *curriculum.* (And this is certainly consistent with anecdotal observation of kids, not to mention being entirely consistent with adult viewing habits.)

Thus, it has been extremely challenging for producers of educational series targeting this older demographic. These producers believe that a great deal of leeway and flexibility is required in the types of curriculum such shows include and the manner in which they are portrayed. There have been but a handful of series targeting kids aged 7- to 11-years-olds which have been both unquestioned by educators *and* at the same time relatively successful ratings performers. Three examples are *Captain Planet and the Planeteers*, *Where on Earth is Carmen Sandiego?*, and *Bill Nye the Science Guy*. However, it is instructive to note that even the *most* successful of such "edutainment" series has not *begun* to approach the breakout success of true kids' hits such as *Mighty Morphin' Power Rangers*, *Teenage Mutant Ninja Turtles,* or *Pokémon*. Moreover, these educational series targeting 7- to 11-year-olds thus far have not driven the all-important merchandise—that, as detailed earlier, is now necessary to finance a program.

There are some experts in educational television who support a more liberal interpretation of what constitutes "educational" in the context of commercial television and who believe that life lessons that are more *story-based* will ultimately have more impact and resonance with viewers comprising this older demographic. Moreover, some educational experts acknowledge the demonstrated reality that the more "overt" the education seems to the viewers (of ages 7 and up), the fewer will actually watch it. An educational series which might meet the more demanding curriculum standards of the "narrow constructionists" could very likely have virtually nobody viewing it—becoming the veritable tree falling in the forest with no one to hear it!

The FCC itself, in its elaboration on the CTA in 1996, has supported this more broad-based point of view, liberalizing their wording from the original clause requiring education to be the "primary purpose" of such a show to the broader "significant purpose" (FCC, 1996). Moreover, it has noted specifically that "to serve children's needs as mandated by the CTA, educational and informational programming must also be entertaining and attractive to children" (FCC, 1996). Yet, despite this, as this chapter goes to press, stations that relied on the assurances of a superbly qualified and credentialed educational consultant that their programs met the educational criteria articulated in the CTA, are, in fact, having their license renewals challenged by advocacy groups alleging that that these series are not sufficiently educational.

In fact, producers are not typically experts in education. Thus, in order to ensure that series intended to qualify under terms of the CTA are indeed "educational," many producers have turned to educational consultants.

Although this topic is covered more extensively in other chapters in this volume (see chapters by Fisch and Stipp, chaps. 5 & 6 respectively), let it just be noted here that, from the producers' point of view, a key and very unique qualification for such a consultant is not only an expertise in child-hood development and childhood perception of media and education, but also an intrinsic understanding of *how a story works*. It is not sufficient merely to ensure that content is educational, it is critical that an educa-tional consultant also have a sense for, and a real-world acceptance of, what engages kids actually to choose to watch such a program when they have so many other alternatives (and not limited only to other television shows) competing for their limited leisure time. This skill involves a sense of craft and talent, not merely knowledge of research and child develop-ment. It is the reason that many consultants may have the academic cre-dentials but ultimately will not be effective in working with creative people to produce educational series that will be watched.

In closing, let us remind the reader of the essential nature of the U.S. broadcast landscape. When all is said and done (and with the partial exception of public television), free, over-the-air broadcast television is a purely advertiser-supported medium. Shows are made available to viewers without charge only because advertisers pay for them (albeit indirectly through the "brokerage" function of a network). Advertisers buy ratings points that they believe accurately measure the numbers of actual viewers for a given program (and the commercials attached to it). Kids beyond preschool age largely dictate their own choices in terms not only of which shows they watch, but, in fact, how they spend their leisure time in general. If producers wish to get their shows financed and broadcast, they *must deliver eyeballs,* so to speak. This is as true in children's television as it is in all of television. And this reality ultimately informs every creative decision made by a producer—otherwise they will cease to be producers.

However, one difference between children's programs and adult pro-grams is the perceived value of the audience to advertisers. Kids have less money to spend and are simply not as attractive to reach as adults. The number of advertisers targeting children is limited to fewer cate-gories (toys, fast foods, cereals, etc.) and the amount of dollars per program minute commanded by children's series and day parts is *sub-stantially less* than the rates collected for primetime series targeting adults and families. Moreover, in conjunction with the substantial down-ward pressures on fees paid from networks to producers (as outlined earlier), producers have been forced to lower their costs to remain viable. And one of the ways of lowering costs is to squeeze the produc-tion schedules into shorter increments so as to reduce labor costs.

One result of these economic realities and pressures is that there is simply less opportunity for the degree of intensive scrutiny, thought and attention to detail that producers would *prefer* to give to their projects, were it financially possible to do so. We *agree* with our critics in their stated expectations that we are obliged to make programs that are not only entertaining (which is necessary for the very survival of free children's television) but which also contain positive, educational, and prosocial content—and to come closer to approaching perfection in all of these respects. But there is often a sense amongst producers and creators that our critics operate under a utopian perception that we have unlimited resources and time with which to achieve such perfection.

The reality is that the nature of our free system of television tautologically dictates that most productions will be like a fast-moving locomotive *without* the luxury of the degree of attention to detail—or opportunity for improvement—that we would *all* prefer. All children's producers known to the author indeed take their special obligations to children very seriously and do their utmost to meet those obligations under extremely challenged circumstances. Our credo is to ensure that, at *worst*, our programs "do no harm," while at best, they enhance and enrich the lives and social development of our impressionable audience.

Until there is an alternate means of financing children's television, we would submit that it is crucial for those analyzing it, criticizing it, and trying to formulate policies that regulate it, accept the realities of how and why it exists in the first place. The system we have results in an abundance of programming for children that is free. As such, it is available to the most disenfranchised and disadvantaged amongst us. It seems problematic to assail this system without either offering an alternative or publicly acknowledging the inherent threat to the very existence of programs that most children enjoy and most parents are content to allow them to enjoy.

REFERENCES

DIC Entertainment and MediaScope. (2000). *Special considerations for creators of children's media.* Studio City, CA. Retrieved February 23, 2005, from http://www.mediascope.org/pubs/scccm.htm

Federal Communications Commission. (1996). *Report & order in the matter of policies and rules concerning children's television programming,* MM Docket No. 93-48. www.fcc.gov/Bureaus/mass_media/orders/1996/Fcc96335.htm#definition. Section IV, Nos. 81–86.

Kaiser Family Foundation. (2001). *Parents and the V-Chip 2001.* Menlo Park, CA. Retrieved February 23, 2005, from http://www.kff.org/entmedia/3158-index.cfm

National Television Violence Study. (1998). Joel Federman (Ed.). Thousand Oaks, CA: Sage.

UCLA Center For Communication Policy. (1995). *The UCLA Television Violence Monitoring Report.* Retrieved February 23, 2005, from http://www.ccp.ucla.edu/Webreport95/table.htm

5

Peeking Behind the Screen: Varied Approaches to the Production of Educational Television

Shalom M. Fisch
MediaKidz Research & Consulting

The history of children's television—and educational television—in the United States extends nearly as far back as the history of the medium itself. Informative and prosocial series such as *The Quiz Kids, Juvenile Jury, and Mr. I Magination* made their debuts as early as the late 1940s, and other series followed in their footsteps throughout the 1950s and 1960s. In 1951, for example, the broadcast networks were already airing 27 hours of family-friendly children's programming every week (Steyer, 2002).

Some of these early children's series were guided by a serious philosophy dedicated toward contributing to children's lives, or were intended to convey substantive academic content. For example, the producers of *Captain Kangaroo* intended to promote manners and the Golden Rule: "We were demonstrating that it takes strength to be gentle and to solve problems through thoughtfulness and kindness" (Keeshan, 1989, p. 113). The science experiments demonstrated on Mr. Wizard were gathered from a library of 1,000 science textbooks, encyclopedias, and other academic publications (Herbert, 1988).

Yet, although some series dealt with academic topics such as storytelling or science, these early series typically were not guided by any sort of formal educational curriculum or (apart from Nielsen ratings or

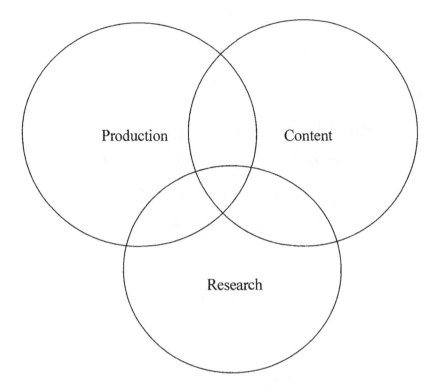

FIGURE 5.1.   The Sesame Workshop models.

letters from viewers) informed by research with children. It was not until the late 1960s that the Children's Television Workshop (now "Sesame Workshop") pioneered the integration of educational curriculum and empirical research into television production. In developing *Sesame Street*, the Workshop created what would eventually come to be called the *CTW Model* or *Sesame Workshop Model* (e.g., Fisch & Truglio, 2001; Mielke, 1990), an interdisciplinary approach to television production that brought together educational content experts, television producers, and developmental researchers, who would work hand-in-hand at every stage of production (Fig. 5.1). As *Sesame Street*'s first Executive Producer, David Connell, and Research Director, Edward Palmer, observed, "If *Sesame Street* was an experiment—and it very definitely continues to be one—this notion of broadcaster/researcher cooperation was the most bold experiment within it" (Connell & Palmer, 1971, p. 67). By all accounts, the experiment succeeded.

Today, the landscape of children's educational is far different than it was in 1969, when *Sesame Street* premiered. Although many children's television series continue to be noneducational, factors such as vast expansions in the number of available television channels, the commercial success of children's series such as *Barney & Friends*, and public policy initiatives such as the Children's Television Act of 1990 have given rise to significant increases in the number of educational television series available to children (e.g., Woodard, 1999). This proliferation of programming—and of producers who create it—has also brought a proliferation of models by which such material is created.

This chapter attempts to provide insight into the vast range of models by which educational television is currently produced in the United States: how educational content and empirical research are integrated into production, and some of the considerations that help to determine where the production of any particular series will fall along that spectrum.

INTEGRATING EDUCATIONAL CONTENT INTO PRODUCTION

For many educational television series, educational content is implemented through the services of one or more educational content specialists. In some cases, these specialists may have specific expertise in the subject matter that the series is designed to address (e.g., science, history). In other cases, specialists may have broader based expertise in informal education or child development, and in knowing how to implement various types of educational content effectively within the medium of television. Typically, the latter class of specialists draw specific content from the education literature in the relevant field and/or consultation with subject-matter experts; with that information as a foundation, the primary role of the specialist is then to translate the content into a form that will be educationally sound but also work well within the constraints of television (a point to which I return in the following section).

In general, although the extent of their involvement (and the manner in which their services are used) may vary, educational content specialists tend to serve fairly consistent functions across different television series. During early stages of development, content specialists define the educational goals or curriculum that guide the selection of topics to be addressed in the series, as well as the ways in which (from an educational perspective) those topics will be handled. Subsequently, content experts provide input to the production staff (e.g., writers, producers) to ensure that the content is presented in ways that are educationally valid. This input may be given at various stages of the production process—for example, through review of scripts, storyboards, or rough cuts of video.

In addition, experts serve a consultatory role by being on-call to answer content-related questions from the production staff as they arise.

Beyond these broadly stated commonalities, however, there is tremendous variability in the ways in which these functions are accomplished. On one end of the spectrum, of course, there are series that are produced with little or no involvement by content experts at all. Often, this is particularly true of prosocial programs, whose producers may feel that they already know how to create interpersonal stories that end happily and convey a moral (a perception that may or may not be fully accurate, as is discussed in the "Underlying Considerations" section that follows).

At the other end of the spectrum lies the full-blown Sesame Workshop Model, in which an in-house content director serves as an integral member of the core production team, collaborating closely with producers at all stages of production and reviewing all drafts of story premises, scripts, storyboards, and rough cuts of video. Typically, under this model, the in-house director is supplemented by a national board of advisors, which consists of several leading experts in the relevant field (e.g., literacy or science education). The board typically meets at the beginning of each season of production, to ensure that the educational approach of the series is consistent with the latest educational theory and practice in the field; input from the advisors informs broad educational directions for the coming season and provides feedback on the previous season. In addition, individual advisors also may be consulted as needed over the course of the season. (For detailed examples of the process, see, e.g., Lesser, 1974; Lesser & Schneider, 2001.)

Given the powerful expertise provided by the advisory board, one might wonder why it is necessary to include an in-house content director as well. After all, if the board consists of leaders in the field, wouldn't it be more effective to simply consult with these experts directly, on an ongoing basis? In fact, the answer is "no," because content directors and advisory board members typically bring different sorts of expertise to the table. As Stipp (chap. 6, this volume) has recounted with regard to NBC's Social Science Advisory Panel, advisors frequently have extensive knowledge about the educational content area under discussion, but little hands-on experience in implementing that content within the constraints of a television series. Without the aid of a content director who understands both worlds, collaboration among advisors and producers is likely to be far less effective; indeed, it may even be strained or combative. Thus, apart from providing his or her personal input, the content director is often responsible for taking the knowledge and opinions of the advisory board and translating them into concrete implications that can easily be implemented in production.

Between the extremes of the "no-involvement" model and Sesame Workshop Model lie numerous other methods for integrating content expertise into the production of educational television series. Variation among these models can be seen in several respects: the role played by content specialists, their level of involvement, and individual variation among content specialists.

A few television production companies employ one or more in-house staff people who are responsible for educational content (e.g., Sesame Workshop, Hit Entertainment, or some of the preschool television series produced by Nickelodeon). However, it is actually far more common for production companies to hire an outside educational consultant to oversee the educational content of a specific television series (as has been done at, e.g., Nelvana, Little Airplane, JP Kids, or Curious Pictures). These consultants serve a role that is analogous to that of an in-house content director (without the expense of a full-time salary or benefits), but their actual role within the series can vary greatly. For example, the mathematics series *Cyberchase*, produced by Thirteen/WNET and Nelvana, employs two content directors who work as out-of-house consultants, in addition to an in-house editorial director (who also has a background in education) and a national advisory board that consists of leaders in informal mathematics education. Even though the content directors are out-of-house consultants (and live in different parts of the country than the production team), their involvement in the series is as extensive as that of an in-house content director. They meet regularly with the production staff to select topics for episodes, to educate writers about the mathematical topic of each episode, and to review drafts of story premises, scripts, storyboards, and rough cuts, as well as *Cyberchase* ancillary material in other media.

By contrast, out-of-house educational consultants play much more narrowly defined roles on other television series. In many cases, an educational consultant creates educational goals and reviews story outlines and scripts (often one draft apiece), but not revised drafts, storyboards, or rough cuts. Thus, under this sort of model, the consultant has the opportunity to define the educational underpinnings of the series as a whole, and to strengthen the delivery of educational content during the initial development of each story. Indeed, at these stages of production, the consultant's impact can be substantial and result in significant changes to the plot and dialogue. However, this model does not involve consultants during subsequent iterations of the treatment of the content, so many production decisions must be made without their input as well.

Still, other series are produced under a model of production that limits the role of educational consultants even further. Under this type of model, a consultant is employed early on, to create the educational curriculum that guides the production of the series. However, once production begins, the consultant does not review outlines, scripts, or other materials. Thus, the consultant plays a central role in defining educational content but not in its implementation within the series.

Finally, apart from differences in the process used, it is worth noting that some degree of variability can also be found among educational consultants themselves. Educational consultants are people, and as such, they differ in their experience and inclinations. Some consultants are oriented primarily toward ensuring that harmful content (e.g., anti-social behavior, unsafe situations) is avoided. On the other hand, other consultants also flag harmful content, but devote greater attention to making sure that a program's positive, educational content is as strong as it can be. Depending on the type of series being produced, and the degree to which its educational content is substantive or "lite," either one type of consultant or the other may be more appropriate.

THE ROLE OF RESEARCH

The testing that researchers conduct in support of educational television production can be classified via two broad categories. *Formative research* is conducted while material is being produced—or even before production begins—to investigate questions that arise out of the production process (cf. Truglio, this volume). *Summative research* is conducted after the production of a television series is complete, and is intended to assess the impact of the series on its viewers, such as the degree to which sustained viewing influences children's knowledge, skills, or attitudes regarding subjects such as literacy or mathematics. (See Fisch, 2004, for a review of summative research on numerous educational television series.) Together, the results of formative and summative studies serve to gauge the effectiveness of the series and inform production decisions.

By nature, summative research is typically more in-depth than formative research, thus requiring greater time and resources. As a result, when resources do not suffice for both types of research, educational television series are more likely to employ formative than summative research—both because summative research is more expensive than formative research, and because it does not feed as directly into production.

Yet, even in the case of formative research, the degree to which research is integrated into production varies widely as well. At one extreme, many series are produced with no research at all, or perhaps with only a single test of a pilot program after it is produced. At the other end of the spectrum, formative research is used extensively to inform the production of series such as *Dora the Explorer,* or most of the series produced by Sesame Workshop. Such programs of research typically involve not only a significant number of formative studies, but a significant variety of *types* of research as well. Needs assessment research might evaluate children's prior knowledge and misconceptions about a topic, so that scripts can address these misconceptions directly. Potential character designs might be tested for appeal. Scripts or rough cuts might be tested for comprehensibility and appeal, so that improvements can be made before the final product reaches the air. And other types of studies might be used as well (e.g., Flagg, 1990).

One prominent example of this sort of model can be found in the production of the participatory series *Blue's Clues* (Anderson et al., 2000; Tracy, 2002). Particularly during its early seasons, every episode of *Blue's Clues* was tested at three stages: First, the script—along with the games and puzzles that comprised the heart of the episode—was tested with children to assess appeal and inform the treatment of the puzzles in the script. Subsequently, a rough version of the video (which included the host, but not animation) was tested to inform the creation of elements such as animation and voice-overs. Finally, the completed episode was tested to gauge its performance and inform any final refinements that might still be possible in postproduction. (For a parallel example of research conducted over the course of producing a school-age series, see Fisch, McCann, Jurist, & Cohen, 1995.)

Here too, many series fall somewhere between the extremes of these two approaches to integrating research into production. In these cases, a smaller number of formative studies may be conducted over the course of production. Because of the limited number of studies available, these studies must be chosen carefully, to map onto the issues and moments in production where they can have the greatest impact.[1] For example, because every episode of *Reading Rainbow* revolves around a featured children's book, these books must be chosen with great care. Formative research is conducted prior to production, to gather children's reactions to books that are being considered seriously for inclusion; only the ones that receive the most enthusiastic responses from children are then included in the series (Liggett & Benfield, 1994). Similarly, when WGBH planned to create a new version

---

[1]It should be noted that, in addition to making strategic choices about the type of studies that will be conducted, researchers must also make strategic decisions regarding which material to test (e.g., which segments in a magazine-format series will be tested). For a discussion of these issues and some of the considerations that feed into such decisions, see Fisch and Bernstein (2001).

of the school-age series *Zoom*, formative research was conducted early on, to identify the elements of the original *Zoom* that would be most appealing—and, thus, worth keeping—in the new version, 20 years later (Cohen, 2001).

Formative research was also front-loaded in producing the first season of *Cyberchase*, but it was research of a different kind. In this case, several preproduction formative research studies presented target-age children with hands-on problem-solving tasks so that scripts and dialogue could mirror the processes and language that real children used (e.g., Hypothesis, 2002). In subsequent seasons, this knowledge was already in hand, so the limited number of available formative studies could be devoted elsewhere instead (e.g.., to understanding children's use of *Cyberchase*'s online or outreach materials; e.g., Flagg, 2003).

Under any model of research, formative and summative research serve to bring the voice of the target audience into the production process. Naturally, though, that voice "speaks" loudest when research is used extensively and employed strategically during production to achieve its maximum impact on subsequent production decisions.

CHOOSING A MODEL OF PRODUCTION

Having described the wide range of models under which educational televisions series are produced, it is natural to ask why various series are produced in their respective ways. For any particular television series, the choice of model can be affected by numerous considerations, including: the culture of the production company, the level of resources that are available, producers' perceptions of the educational content, and requirements set by broadcasters or funding agencies. Let us consider each class of issues in turn.

Culture of the Production Company

On the most basic level, the prominence of content or research support within production depends on the degree to which the production company considers it to be an integral part of the process. For example, as noted in the introduction to this chapter, Sesame Workshop was built on the notion of close collaboration among producers, educators, and researchers. In the words of the Workshop's co-founder, Joan Ganz Cooney, "*We are talking about a marriage*—not researchers to work as consultants to producers. ... We were by then talking about a product that would come out of a marriage—living together, dealing together, drinking together, eating together until they all would absolutely understand what the product looked like" (quoted in Land, 1972, p. 34). With this philosophy serving as a cornerstone of the company from its inception, it is little wonder that research and educational content continue to play integral roles in the production of the Workshop's television series (and other media products) to this day.

This is not to say, of course, that Sesame Workshop implements its model in precisely the same way today as in 1969. Cumulative experience over time (and across various television series) has produced a body of knowledge that informs subsequent productions, so there is no need to reinvent the wheel in approaching each new television series or production season. Elsewhere, I have contrasted the initial development of *Sesame Street* (in the 1960s) and *Big Bag*, a preschool series that the Workshop produced for Cartoon Network in the 1990s. Both series operated under the Sesame Workshop Model, and employed in-house staff who were responsible for content and research, as well as a national educational board. However, *Big Bag*'s development process was streamlined greatly, thanks to the experience and knowledge that its producers and researchers had gained while working on other television series at the Workshop. As a result, input from *Big Bag*'s advisors and new formative studies with children could be applied at strategic points during production, to answer questions whose answers were not already known from past experience with *Sesame Street* and other series (Fisch, 1998).

Although research and educational content are probably most closely identified with the corporate culture of Sesame Workshop, other producers of educational television have also adopted content and/or research as important components of their process. For example, a core tenet of Nickelodeon's philosophy is "Nick is kids," so the network conducts an active, ongoing program of market and lifestyle research with children (in addition to the formative research that informs some of its programming) to maintain that position (e.g., Laybourne, 1993). Similarly, the educational cable channel Noggin has made use of both educational consultants and an in-house content director, as well as a comprehensive educational curriculum that guides all of its preschool programming.

Corporate cultures such as these provide a powerful impetus for employing production models that incorporate educational content and/or research. Production companies that do not share such cultures may also make use of research or content specialists, but they are less likely to do so automatically.

Available Resources

As with every aspect of television production, educational content and research cost money—money that, otherwise, could be applied to other aspects of production. When production budgets are limited, producers have a natural motivation to reduce or eliminate content and/or research support in the interest of keeping the production under budget.

The irony of this situation is that, typically, only a relatively small fraction of a television production budget is dedicated to research or educational content in the first place; it is usually far outweighed by other production costs. However, the fact remains that it is also possible to create and broadcast a television series without content and research support, even if the quality of the material may not be as strong in the absence of such support. Contrast that, for example, with the role of cameramen, without whom the series cannot be produced at all. Thus, in the absence of other compelling considerations (such as those discussed throughout this section), it is understandable that producers might look to content and research as one possible area in which they might conserve resources.

Perceptions of Educational Content

In establishing the role that educational content specialists will play in a given series, another influential factor is the degree to which producers feel they *need* support from a content expert, as opposed to trusting their own knowledge about the relevant area. If producers feel uncomfortable about their own expertise in a particular subject area (as often happens, e.g., with mathematics or science), they are likely to be more motivated to recruit the involvement of a content specialist. On the other hand, if producers believe that their own knowledge of the subject is sufficient for the sake of producing the series, they are less likely to feel that the expense of a content specialist is necessary.

As noted earlier, the latter situation is particularly likely to occur when the educational goals of the series are prosocial rather than academic. Even if they have not produced educational series before, experienced television producers may feel that they already know how to portray social situations among characters and do not need support from a content specialist to help them convey a prosocial moral.

In fact, however, my own experience in both academic and prosocial programming has shown that this belief is a misconception. Creating effective prosocial programs is actually at least as difficult as—if not more difficult than—creating academic series. This difficulty stems from two primary sources. First, because it is easier for writers to draw humor and action out of conflict and inappropriate behavior, it is easy to fall into the trap of what I refer to as the *standard sit-com model,* in which the vast majority of an episode is spent showing inappropriate behavior, with only a quickly stated prosocial message or resolution at the end (often accompanied by a hug). From an educational standpoint, this sort of approach is usually ineffective, because it often leaves young viewers recalling the entertaining and heavily emphasized inappropriate behavior instead of the intended prosocial message or behavior (Lovelace & Huston, 1983). Thus, one of the great challenges in creating effective prosocial programming is to spend relatively little time on negative behavior and find ways to make the desired prosocial behavior as engaging and memorable as (if not more memorable than) the negative behavior that precedes it.

Second, to convey prosocial messages effectively, stories and scripts often must negotiate a host of very subtle issues to ensure that the desired message comes through clearly for children and inadvertent negative messages are avoided. To illustrate this point, consider an example taken from *Mustard Pancakes*, an independently produced, prosocial PBS series for which I served as educational consultant. One early episode of the series was designed to celebrate the fact that everyone is different. In the first draft of the script, the plot ran as follows: One of the characters (Tiny Tina) was upset because she wanted to dance, but despite her repeated requests, the others were busy with their own individual activities (e.g., painting, doing a puzzle) and didn't want to join her. However, a heartfelt conversation with the series' lead character/parent figure helped the others understand that dancing was important to Tiny Tina, and the episode ended with everyone joining her for a dance.

At first glance, this appeared to be a perfectly good, prosocial story. However, on reflection, I pointed out to the production team that, in some ways, it inadvertently conveyed the *opposite* message than was intended. Ironically, the moment that was most consistent with the intended message about diversity came at the very beginning of the script, when each character was engaged in his or her own interests. Yet, instead of encouraging them, Tiny Tina was actually insisting that everyone do what *she* wanted, and she became upset when they didn't. The scripted resolution of the problem also worked against the intended message, because Tiny Tina's friends made her feel better by abandoning their own activities to join in the one she wanted them to do. Thus, although the first draft of the script included numerous instances of prosocial behavior (e.g., helping a friend feel better), it was unlikely to succeed in conveying its intended message about everyone being different.

To preserve the basic flow of the story but overcome this issue, I suggested a subtle but important change: As in the first draft, the story would open with the characters engaged in their individual activities.

This time, however each of them would be convinced that his or her activity was clearly the "best," and would be annoyed that Tiny Tina preferred to dance instead of joining in. Their negative reaction would upset her, until the parent figure would help the others see that everyone has their own favorite things to do—and it's all right for Tiny Tina's favorite activity to be different than theirs. By incorporating these recommendations into subsequent drafts of the script, the episode could follow a course that was very similar to that of the first draft, but the central message could be conveyed more clearly, without being muddied by any inadvertent, competing messages.

It is noteworthy that, on receiving such notes, the executive producer immediately appreciated their importance but remarked that he would not have noticed the issues on his own. This comment speaks to the fact that producers and content specialists approach material with different orientations, so each one is likely to notice different sorts of issues. (By the same token, producers' script notes frequently point to production issues that I have not noticed, despite 20 years' experience working in television and other media.) Thus, even when producers have experience with some type of educational content (be it academic or prosocial), there very well may be value to involving content specialists, in the same way that production teams typically include separate personnel to oversee lighting, sound, and set design. However, if producers believe—correctly or incorrectly—that their own expertise is sufficient, they are less likely to include a content specialist as part of the production team.

Broadcaster or Funder Expectations

All of the considerations discussed above center upon decisions that originate within a production company or the production team responsible for a particular series.[2] In addition, the involvement of educational content specialists and/or research may be mandated by the broadcaster that airs the series or the funding agency that supports its production. Such requirements are often intended to ensure the educational wherewithal of the series and to establish accountability—that is, to make sure that the money invested in the series has been well spent.

---

[2]Although the size of a production budget might depend on outside funders or broadcasters, the allocation of funds within that budget is typically determined within the production team or production company.

For example, content specialists are fairly standard members of production teams for educational television series broadcast by PBS or Noggin. Moreover, the informal science division of the National Science Foundation, which has funded the production of many television series about mathematics and science, requires substantive involvement by content specialists, as well as both formative and summative research, as part of every television-based proposal (e.g., National Science Foundation, 2004). Clearly, this provides a significant incentive for producers who wish to obtain funding from such sources or broadcast their programs through such outlets.

At the same time, outside funding makes larger production budgets possible, which makes it more feasible to incorporate educational content and research into production. Indeed, this is one of the reasons why some have lobbied for increased funding for PBS in the United States, or for the adoption of funding models that are similar to those used in Canada, Japan, or Great Britain (e.g., Palmer, 1988; Steyer, 2002).

CONCLUSION

As this discussion demonstrates, there are many models by which educational television is produced. The choice of a production model for any given series depends, not only on considerations concerning informal education itself, but also on practical considerations regarding issues such as corporate culture, available resources, and requirements set by funders or broadcasters.

Of course, not all educational television series are alike in their needs, goals, budget, or timeframe for production. As a result, the flexibility provided by multiple models of production is necessary in order to be responsive to the constraints of any particular series. By adopting the most appropriate model for any given television series, each series can receive the strongest support that is possible within the parameters of that series.

Under any model of production, however, the ultimate effectiveness of content and research support is a function of the people involved—the expertise and personalities of producers, content specialists, and researchers, and the chemistry among them (e.g., Fisch & Bernstein, 2001; Lesser, 1974). At its best, the collaboration becomes a true team effort, in which each member brings his or her own unique contribution to the table, so that the final product is something greater than any of them could have created alone. The results of such collaboration can only be beneficial for children.

REFERENCES

Anderson, D. R., Bryant, J., Wilder, A., Santomero, A., Williams, M., & Crawley, A. M. (2000). Researching *Blue's Clues*: Viewing behavior and impact. *Media Psychology, 2,* 179–194.

Cohen, M. (2001). The role of research in educational television. In D. G. Singer & J. L. Singer (Eds.), *Handbook of children and the media* (pp. 571–588). Thousand Oaks, CA: Sage.

Connell D. D., & Palmer, E. L. (1971). *Sesame Street*: A case study in J. D. Halloran & M. Gurevitch (Eds.), *Broadcaster/researcher cooperation in mass communication research* (pp. 65–85). Leeds, England: Kavanagh & Sons.

Fisch, S. M. (1998). The Children's Television Workshop: The experiment continues. In R. G. Noll & M. E. Price (Eds.), *A communications cornucopia: Markle Foundation essays on information policy* (pp. 297–336). Washington, DC: Brookings Institution Press.

Fisch, S. M. (2004). *Children's learning from educational television: Sesame Street and beyond.* Mahwah, NJ: Lawrence Erlbaum Associates.

Fisch, S. M., & Bernstein, L. (2001). Formative research revealed: Methodological and process issues in formative research. In S. M. Fisch & R. T. Truglio (Eds.), *"G" is for "growing": Thirty years of research on children and Sesame Street* (pp. 39–60). Mahwah, NJ: Lawrence Erlbaum Associates.

Fisch, S. M., McCann, S. K., Jurist, M. A., & Cohen, D. I. (1995). Integrating research into television production: *Square One TV* and the case of "Pauline." *Journal of Educational Television, 21,* 143–155.

Fisch, S. M., & Truglio, R. T. (Eds,). (2001). *"G" is for growing: Thirty years of research on children and Sesame Street.* Mahwah, NJ: Lawrence Erlbaum Associates.

Flagg, B. N. (1990). *Formative evaluation for educational technology.* Hillsdale, NJ: Lawrence Erlbaum Associates.

Flagg, B. N. (2003). *Cyberchase at home: Formative evaluation of outreach activities for parents and children* (unpublished research report). New York: Multimedia Research.

Herbert, D. (1988). Behind the scenes of *Mr. Wizard.* In M. Druger (Ed.), *Science for the fun of it: A guide to informal science education* (pp. 51–56). Washington, DC: National Science Teachers Association.

Hypothesis. (2002). *How fourth-grade kids approach, talk about, and solve math problems* (unpublished research report). New York: Author.

Keeshan, B. (1989). *Growing up happy: Captain Kangaroo tells yesterday's children how to nurture their own.* New York: Doubleday.

Land, H. W. (1972). *The Children's Television Workshop: How and why it works.* Jericho, NY: Nassau Board of Cooperative Educational Services.

Laybourne, G. (1993). The Nickelodeon experience. In G. L. Berry & J. K. Asamen (Eds.), *Children and television: Images in a changing sociocultural world* (pp. 303–307). Newbury Park, CA: Sage.

Lesser, G. S. (1974). *Children and television: Lessons from Sesame Street.* New York: Vintage Books/Random House.

Lesser, G. S., & Schneider, J. (2001). Creation and evolution of the *Sesame Street* curriculum. In S. M. Fisch & R. T. Truglio (Eds.), *"G" is for growing: Thirty years of research on children and Sesame Street* (pp. 25–38). Mahwah, NJ: Lawrence Erlbaum Associates.

Liggett, T. C., & Benfield, C. M. (1994). *Reading Rainbow guide to children's books: The 101 best titles.* New York: Citadel Press.

Lovelace, V. O., & Huston, A. C. (1983). Can television teach prosocial behavior? In J. Sprafkin, C. Swift, & R. Hess (Eds.), *Rx television: Enhancing the preventive effects of TV* (pp. 93–106). New York: The Haworth Press.

Mielke, K. W. (1990). Research and development at the Children's Television Workshop. *Educational Technology Research and Development, 38* (4), 7–16.

National Science Foundation. (2004). *Informal science education (ISE): Program solicitation* (NSF 04-579). Retrieved November 4, 2004 from: http://nsf.gov/pubs/2004/nsf04579/nsf04579.htm

Palmer, E. L. (1988). *Television and America's children: A crisis of neglect.* New York: Oxford University Press.

Steyer, J. P. (2002). *The other parent: The inside story of the media's effect on our children.* New York: Atria Books.

Tracy, D. (2002). *Blue's Clues for success: The 8 secrets behind a phenomenal business.* Chicago, IL: Dearborn Trade Publishing.

Woodard, E. (1999). *The 1999 state of children's television report: Programming for children over broadcast and cable television* (Rep. No. 28). Philadelphia, PA: Annenberg Public Policy Center, University of Pennsylvania.

6

The Role of Academic Advisors in Creating Children's Television Programs: The NBC Experience

Horst Stipp
Senior Vice President, Primary and Strategic Research
NBC Universal

This chapter describes the role of academic consultants in a self-regulatory process at the NBC television network that was designed to improve children's programming, primarily Saturday morning cartoons. The process relied largely on academic and other consultants with expertise in relevant fields who formed NBC's so-called "Social Science Advisory Panel." This analysis focuses on the role of the advisors during the 1980–1990 period when the panel was most active and the author was directly involved in the Panel's activities as NBC's Director, Social and Development Research.

NBC's use of academic advisors not only shaped children's programming during a time when that network often reached almost half of all children during the course of one Saturday morning, but it also impacted the use of advisors at other networks and the way writers, producers, and program executives approached the creative process of children's programming. This "Panel" process also influenced academic advisors, the way they thought about children and television, and their ability to impact programming in a competitive commercial television system.

Most of this chapter describes the panel process, but always with an eye towards its implications for the role of academics as consultants for commercial television in general, which is discussed at the end of the chapter. The process is described in specific detail, because those details are essential for understanding the role of the consultants as well as for providing actionable recommendations for making such consulting processes more effective.

THE ORIGINS OF NBC'S "SOCIAL SCIENCE ADVISORY" PROCESS

In 1975, NBC's head of Social Research, Ron Milavky, proposed that the network use consultants to provide a social science perspective regarding the content of its Saturday morning programs and the possible effects on children (Milavsky, 1975). The prevailing belief at NBC was that children are a special audience and that programming directed at them would benefit from a process designed to enhance understanding and consideration of their needs. As such, Milavsky suggested to management that they recruit a panel of consultants consisting of scholars with theoretical and research expertise about television and its effects on children. These consultants would meet a number of times a year to provide expert input in order to improve decisions about Saturday morning program content. The proposal was accepted and it was decided to recruit highly respected scholars. (For additional detail, see Stipp, Hill-Scott, & Door, 1987.)

Before the NBC panel process was established, the program development process did not involve any direct input from researchers. There was indirect input, because some broadcast standards editors had relevant academic training and tried to apply social science research learning to their work. The panel was designed to change that, and bring expert knowledge, but also judgment and opinion, directly to those involved in children's programs at NBC. The NBC executives, in turn, would work with the production companies to apply these inputs to the program development. Thus, the goal was a collaborative process that would to bring together research, child development theory, and creative expertise with the goal of producing entertaining children's programming with prosocial content.

Before describing the panel process, it is important to summarize the television environment at that time. The television market in the United States in general, and broadcast network TV, specifically, were, of course, very different from today, when most viewers have access to more than 100 channels. With regard to children's programming, three aspects appear most relevant: children's programming, regulation, and the use of consultants.

Children's Programming

A large portion of children's TV consisted of Saturday morning programs, primarily cartoons, aired concurrently on the three major networks: ABC, CBS, and NBC. The leading network often reached half of the child audience (defined as children aged 2- to 11–years-old) during the course of a Saturday morning. As advertisers, (primarily those selling toys and cereals) wanted to reach this audience, the networks were profitable during this daypart. In contrast, starting in the 1980s, in response to competition from local stations' afternoon programming and later from cable networks, Saturday Morning became a relatively small part of children's TV choices and viewing diet. As a result, the economics of Saturday morning programming changed for the networks (see also Kline, 1993).

Regulation

Prior to 1975, Congress, the Federal Communications Commission, (FCC), and the Federal Trade Commission (FTC) had addressed issues surrounding children's television, particularly violence on TV. NBC had responded by establishing a "Social Research" department that conducted a large panel study on the relationship between children's TV exposure and aggression (Milavsky et al., 1982). Regulatory pressure on the networks did play a role in the formation of the panel; however, it was deliberately designed to work without political pressure or publicity and was not a result of any mandate. In fact, the panel's role and scope of activities at the network actually increased during periods of lessening regulatory pressure.

Use of consultants

When NBC reviewed the self-regulation mechanism that the network employed for policy determination regarding Saturday morning program content, it was noted that the companies that produce Saturday morning programs rarely employed social scientists as consultants. (Scientists were more frequently used in connection with primetime programming.) Academic consultants were, of course, used in the development of programs for public television, specifically by Children's Television Workshop (Fisch & Truglio, 2001).

Furthermore, to understand how the panel mechanism was meant to operate and impact program decisions, it is important to outline how Saturday morning program schedules were created during this time at the major broadcast networks. Around the beginning of each year,

9 months before a new season started, independent production companies offered program ideas to the networks and the networks, in turn, suggested program ideas to production companies. (It is important to note that NBC did not own any of the shows.) Based on these discussions, so-called "bibles" were developed, containing short descriptions of a series concept and characters, some story ideas, and drawings of characters and settings (see London, chap. 4, this volume, for more on this topic). The new series were chosen and schedules were announced around April.

Once choices were made, the Children's Programming department at the networks worked with production companies to transform concepts into actual programs. During this development process, the "bible" was often changed to accommodate not only programmers' considerations, but also the considerations of the Broadcast Standards, until a framework for developing episodes, usually 13 per season, was achieved. Development proceeded from half page story premises to outlines to a complete script to a storyboard with rough drawings. Finally, the audio was recorded and the animation pictures were drawn. At each point, Children's Programming and Broadcast Standards could request changes and Broadcast Standards screened each episode for final clearance before airing. Needless to say, the production companies and writers did not always share the networks opinions regarding program changes. Broadcasting of the episodes usually began in October.

THE EVOLUTION OF THE "PANEL" PROCESS

The first meeting of what became known as the "Social Science Advisory Panel" was held December 17, 1975. During the following years, the frequency of Panel meetings, the scope of the Panel's work, and its influence on programming increased. It also became a model for other commercial broadcasters and for production companies, who increasingly employed social scientists' work on children's programs. This was not, however, a consequence of NBC actively promoting this new process. As mentioned, it had been decided not to publicize the Panel, and it was deliberately designed to work without political pressure and without publicity. This process was clearly different from some other uses of consultants (cf. "Calling in Consultant," 1985; Leconte, 1986; "Watching Out," 1985).

During the first 5 years, meetings were held several times a year with NBC staff, including vice presidents and/or staff from Social Research, Children's Programming, Broadcast Standards, and Program Research. Discussions focused on potential problems with series concepts being developed for the upcoming season and on recommendations for the next season of what were finished products for that year.

Starting around 1980, the process expanded due to increased interest by Children's Programming in using the Panel more regularly to address a broader range of issues. These included racial diversity among program characters, gender and racial stereotyping, social content, and child appropriateness of content and format. In addition, management wanted to impact the producer and writing community and, therefore, special meetings with advisors and those who supplied Saturday morning programs were organized. The Panel's input was also sought by Broadcast Standards editors who supervised commercials directed at children. The expanding role of the Panel reflected a learning process regarding the use of academic advisors in this kind of environment and an increasing recognition that such advisors could be useful not only from a regulatory and prosocial point of view, but also from a commercial perspective: The advisors and broadcasters learned how to make programs better and, at the same time, more popular.

In the beginning of the Panel process, it became apparent that some of those involved in children's programming at NBC, and most writers and producers at the production companies that developed the shows, had some reservations about outside advisors, especially with regard to their ability to make programs more prosocial without making them less entertaining and, therefore, less competitive. However, as the Panel evolved, these concerns were erased, especially within NBC. There are several reasons for this. First, Panel members' knowledge of child development, family life, and societal trends turned out to be very useful to programmers. Second, some of the programs chosen or modified along lines suggested by Panel members turned out to be very successful. *The Smurfs*, which ran from 1981 until 1990, and established NBC's Saturday morning dominance for several years, is an example. Third, the Panel members' sophistication and sensitivity in interacting with the network increased. Fourth, the network's staff learned the implications of social science for children's programs and started to apply that knowledge to their activities. Finally, Social Research management, which had originated and continued to supervise the process, learned how to conduct successful Panel meetings and improve the process. The Panel process evolved further in the 1990s when NBC changed its Saturday morning program schedule and started to focus on teens instead of 6- to 11-year-olds.

The Consultants and Their Role

The first Panel members were four social scientists who had published widely in areas related to children's television. They were:

- George Comstock, a social psychologist and communication scholar who had authored several books on television effects. In the 1980s, he was Professor at the S.I. Newhouse School for Public Communications, Syracuse University.
- William McGuire, a psychologist and a leading authority on attitude change and television effects. He was Professor of Psychology at Yale.
- Paul Mussen, a psychologist who specializes in child development, was Professor of Psychology at the University of California, Berkeley.
- Percy Tannenbaum, who had a PhD in communications, but considered himself a psychologist. He was Professor of Public Policy at the University of California, Berkeley.

In 1980, the Panel was expanded with the addition of Aimee Dorr, a psychologist who specialized in research on children and television. At the time, she taught at the University of California, Los Angeles' (UCLA) Graduate School of Education. In 1983, another woman became a Panel member and later played an increasingly important role in consulting: Karen Hill-Scott, Adjunct Associate Professor of Urban Planning at UCLA and Executive Director of Crystal Stairs, a private nonprofit child development agency in Los Angeles.

The addition of Karen Hill-Scott reflected NBC executives' preference for increased professional and personal diversity in the Panel and also a desire to become more flexible and tailor the Panel's composition to the issues at hand. As a result, the size and composition of the consultant group at meetings and working on scripts, excetra became more fluid, depending on the issues. Because the Panel was perceived as successful and beneficial, its role was expanding and an increasing portion of the consultants' work took place outside of formal Panel meetings. For example, there was more one-on-one consulting between an academic consultant and a programming executive. Also, additional consultants were invited to panel meetings and to special seminars where they presented to writers and programming executives, for example:

- Don Roberts, Professor of Communications and Director of the Institute for Communication Research at Stanford University. Don Roberts had become a consultant for *He-Man and the Masters of the Universe*, a popular syndicated cartoon series at that time, and was therefore of particular interest to NBC and our Panel consultants. His perspective and experiences provided valuable information for our Panel members—not only with regard to research issues, but also with regard to consulting issues in the area of children's programs in commercial television.

- Dan Anderson, Professor of Psychology, University of Massachusetts, Amherst, provided insights based on his extensive research in children's development. The Panel had identified this as an important area that, although central to public broadcasting's approach to children's TV, was sometimes neglected by producers of commercial TV programs for children. Anderson provided important insights on children's comprehension of TV content.
- Leo Estrada, Associate Professor at the Graduate School of Architecture and Urban Planning, UCLA, a specialist in demography who had worked extensively with the U.S. Census, provided insights on issues related to the changing ethnic composition of America's children.
- Felix Guiterrez, who was Professor of Journalism at University of Southern California and then became a vice president at the Gannett Foundation (Arlington, Va.) also addressed minority issues, an area of increasing concern at NBC starting in the early 1980s.

Minority issues were also addressed by the following consultants: Harry Kitano, Professor of Social Welfare and Sociology, Director of Asian American studies, and Chair of Japanese Studies, all at UCLA; and, Belinda Tucker, Director, Center for Afro-American Studies, UCLA. In addition to the consultants who took part in meetings, this author, as Director of Social research, had numerous meetings and correspondence with various academics who did research on relevant children's issues.

These choices reflected the learning that took place as the network gained more experience in the collaboration with academic advisors. For example, it became apparent that the academics' skill in translating abstract generalizations into ideas that the NBC staff could understand and apply to a specific program concept or episode were often more important than their theoretical insights. Also considered important was an ability to engage in successful "cross-cultural" interactions with creative people, in which the Panel member demonstrated respect towards the culture of broadcasting without giving up his or her own culture. Finally, on a very practical level, it turned out to be more convenient if those most actively involved in the Panel resided near Los Angeles, where most of the work on children's programming took place.

The Panel Process

During the first couple of years, Panel meetings focused on possibly harmful depictions in the programs, especially issues of violence. As outlined in the following section, the Panel members soon expressed interest in other issues and found a very receptive audience among NBC executives. By the end of the 1970s, the Panel operated on an expanded model.

Panel meetings took place when new programs were being developed, or when Social Research or programmers saw the need to have the Panel address an issue. New programs, development of programs on the schedule, and general issues about children and television were discussed at the meetings. When necessary, follow-up meetings were conducted that dealt with issues in specific shows. In 1985, for example, there were five Panel meetings. Almost all meetings took place in Los Angeles.

Moreover, because of the sensitivity surrounding requests for changes in scripts, excetra, the staff of Children's Programs usually communicated Panel comments to the productions company's producers and writers. Program creators sometimes participated in meetings with Panel members. Social Research and Panel members reviewed concepts, story premises, outlines, and the scripts for programs needing special care, completing reviews in a day or two and discussing reactions by telephone with Children's Programs and Broadcast Standards (e-mail had not yet been invented).

In some instances, Program Research was asked to explore children's understanding or perceptions of crucial program elements. Research was commissioned, under the direction of Social Research, to find out if programs were successful at communicating to children or to explore other issues directly related to programming. (Wurtzel, 1980, provides a good description of this type of research.).

Additional meetings were held to explore more general issues. Other researchers (e.g., Daniel Anderson, Donald Roberts) were invited to supplement the Panel's expertise and to share their research. In addition, interviews with experts that had been conducted by Social Research (e.g., Willard Hartup, Mavis Hetherington) were reported and discussed. Finally, a portion of most regular Panel meetings was given to a social scientist's presentation of his or her own research. This not only increased the base of participation in the Panel, but also kept those involved in children's programming up-to-date on research about children and television.

Challenges

As indicated, the Panel process turned out to be very successful. Nevertheless, there was a learning process and problems, which were mostly encountered during the first years, never disappeared completely. All participants in the Panel process agreed that children are a special audience who should be exposed to socially responsible programs. However, even with mutual agreement on this goal, there were continuing rough spots in the Panel process. (A discussion by Ettema, 1982, about similar problems at PBS suggests such difficulties may be a necessary part of this kind of mechanism.) Understanding their sources has helped develop attitudes and processes that appropriately minimize problems without removing the legitimate differences that cause them.

Differing Goals and Priorities. One source of difficulty was that the groups involved in the Panel process had some different goals and priorities. Panel members hoped to apply their scientific knowledge to improve the prosocial content of shows. Broadcast Standards staff members wanted to avoid program content that violated standards of taste and propriety or that may have negative effects. Programmers wanted to act responsibly, but they needed to entertain, attract large audiences, operate economically, and receive programming on schedule. Suppliers wanted creative freedom and financial success. These differing orientations were not necessarily incompatible, but they were often hard to achieve simultaneously. They required discussion and compromise—and that took time, which is in very short supply in the typical production schedule.

Differing Backgrounds. Another source of difficulty was the differing backgrounds and skills of social scientists, network staff, and the creative community. The advice of social scientists had to be implemented by members of the creative community and those at the network who knew how to conceptualize, develop, market, and schedule programming. They felt that they had delivered many entertaining, even prosocial shows to children, and it is not hard to imagine that they might resent someone telling them how to do their jobs or suggesting they had not done their jobs well (e.g., Dixon, 1985; Karp, 1984). The academics, on the other hand, were sometimes impatient with those who purported to understand children simply because they had provided programming attractive to children. Finally, advisors who had never been involved in the creative process were sometimes a bit naïve about the challenges involved in implementing their advice.

Collaboration. Since the Panel began, NBC and Panel members tried to develop mechanisms to minimize difficulties inherent in working together. There was an agreement that the Panel had an advisory function: Authority to adopt Panel suggestions rested with Children's Programs and/or Broadcast Standards. At the same time, it also was understood that Panel members were free to say whatever they like without influence or pressure and that they would clarify when they were speaking as social scientists, based on research, or when they expressed opinions as parents, citizens, or activists. Obviously, decisions about prosocial values involve value choices themselves, and in a pluralistic society, not everyone agrees on the same causes and sees the same priorities. Furthermore, on those occasions when the network made a programming decision that ran counter to Panel advice, members understood they needed to accept that decision and move on to the next matter at hand. It was important to make clear that the interests and goals of the various groups involved in the Panel process were to be recognized and respected.

Several mechanisms were developed to promote better interaction. Panel members usually met first with members of NBC's Social Research, who were themselves social scientists and researchers. This meeting provided a good opportunity for Panel members to debate issues and talk about research issues that might be a bit boring to others from the network or the creative community. When issues were particularly complex, the pre-meeting provided time to clarify them. As a result, it was made sure that that programmers would not be confused about an appropriate course of action. In general, comments about programming were given to network staff at a Panel meeting, over the telephone, or in writing. The staff then relayed these comments, with editorial license, to the production company. Meetings of Panel members with the creative community never occured without prior meetings of the Panel and network staff.

Issues in Children's Programs

Over the years, the Panel discussed and monitored a large number of issues during its work on NBC Saturday morning programs. Based on an analysis of corporate documents, including meetings, reports, memoranda, letters, papers, and written comments on program "bibles," concepts, premises, scripts, and storyboards, four major issues can be identified.

Violence.   Violent and aggressive program content was the first issue addressed by the Panel. It received much attention at that time and, as is well known, the issue has since been a recurring topic in policymaking as well as public debates. Also, it should be noted that NBC's Social Research department, which initiated the Panel process, was originally established to conduct a multiyear panel study on this issue (Milavsky, Kessler, Stipp, & Rubens, 1982). Thus, there was not only interest but also expertise at NBC on this topic.

In its first year, the Panel drew on existing research to formulate written suggestions about how to depict violence and aggression so as to decrease possible negative effects on child viewers. Based on research by Bandura (1977), it was recommended, for example, to use unrealistic settings, fantasy weapons, and show superhuman feats rather than fist fights to diminish the potential for imitation. By this process and others, programmers and Broadcast Standards editors were sensitized to the kinds of portrayals that are worrisome.

It should be noted that even before the Panel process started, NBC programmers had rejected program concepts they considered too violent. After a few years of the Panel, the network placed increasing emphasis on the development of "softer" program concepts. Thus, in the early 1980s, NBC's Saturday morning hits became *The Smurfs* and *Alvin and the Chipmunks*, two series that deemphasized action and aggressive interpersonal conflict themes. However, action programs were occasionally produced against Panel recommendations (e.g., *The Incredible Hulk, Lazer Tag*). In these instances, the Panel urged that natural catastrophe and jeopardy situations replace interpersonal conflicts as often as possible. At the same time, the Panel was wary of catastrophe and jeopardy, because their violence or threat of violence may frighten children. Another example, was when Broadcast Standards editors expressed concern about the jeopardy inherent in cliffhangers, The Panel felt that the majority of child viewers understand cliffhangers, but that young children could be frightened by those involving jeopardy for children or animals, separation from parents, or threatened death of parents. In general, these recommendations were accepted and acted on. Another time, programmers were interested in a contemporary live-action version of Dracula, but the Panel convinced them that the implied dangers would be much too frightening to younger viewers and that the concept lacked any redeeming aspects.

Panel members also had occasion to ask the network to reject script ideas for particular episodes or to change them substantially because of violence concerns. These recommendations were often accepted, although writers sometimes resisted, believing that aggressive interpersonal conflict is inherently interesting. However, violence soon became a rather infrequent serious concern of Panel members after scripts had been through the review process. In other words, after the process had been established and this issue had been addressed, violence became one issue among several, but it was not the Panel's top concern anymore.

Stereotyping.   Although violence was the predominant issue when the Panel began, stereotyping—especially of females and minorities—became the dominant issue. Panel members alerted NBC early on that the underrepresentation of females on Saturday morning could suggest to young viewers that women are not as important or interesting as men. In addition, the Panel felt that many programs depicted females according to negative stereotypes. They pointed out that a large portion of female characters in the programs was depicted as weak and in peril (to be rescued by a male character) or as coquettish flirts.

In this context, it is worth mentioning that practically every writer of Saturday morning programs in early 1980s was a young male. In contrast, NBC employed many women in Children's Programs, including the head of the department. NBC programmers were sympathetic to the Panel's concern not only for personal reasons, but because they also suspected that the girls watching Saturday morning programs would prefer female characters in a variety of roles. Thus, the Panel mechanism resulted in considerable progress in eliminating those images from NBC's Saturday morning schedule starting in the 1980s.

Changing the gender ratio among cartoon characters was not always easy. An interesting example: When NBC bought the concept for *The Smurfs* cartoon in 1981, programmers and the Panel agreed that having one Smurfette in a village of male Smurfs was another example of male overrepresentation. However, *The Smurfs'* creator, Peyo, could not be persuaded to change that, as he did not want a radical change to his creative concept. Peyo, however, did accept the Panel's recommendation to give the Smurfette a larger role and make her less coquettish and more active, resisting villains herself rather than always being rescued. Smurfette became one of the most popular characters on Saturday morning, and ratings data indicated that both boys and girls liked the program. This experience helped to increase the number and the status of female characters in Saturday morning programs and challenged the industry's conventional "wisdom" that "boys will only watch boys." (The fact that, by the end of that decade, production houses employed an increasing number of females, some in leading positions, also helped a lot.)

Concerns about the underrepresentation and stereotyping of ethnic, racial, and other (e.g., physically challenged) minorities were similar to those about women. This issue became a major concern when an African-American woman became NBC's Director of Children's Programming. She wanted to increase the number of nonstereotypical, ethnically diverse characters in Saturday morning programs and asked the Panel for information that would help achieve that goal. Again, it is worth noting that, to the best of my knowledge, the production companies who supplied Saturday morning programs did not employ any minorities, either as writers or in other management positions in the early 1980s. Therefore, to have a real impact, it was necessary to reach the producers and writers.

A special seminar was held, at which guest social scientists specializing in social attitudes, stereotyping, race relations, minority cultures, and minority child development shared their knowledge with Panel members and NBC staff. That meeting was a preparation for a second, similar symposium, which was held in December, 1982. It was attended by about 40 producers and writers who were involved in supplying programs to NBC, but who also created programs for the other networks. Among the many points emphasized at the symposia were that problems of stereotyping are greatly reduced when more than one representative of a minority group is included in a show and when writers and producers are knowledgeable about the variety of lifestyles and personal characteristics within minority groups. The network made a continuing effort to follow these recommendations, but putting them into practice has not always been easy (as detailed by Stipp, Hill-Scott, & Dorr, 1987). Another symposium took place 8 years later, in February, 1990. There had been relatively few management changes in Children's programming at NBC, but most of the audience at the 1982 symposium was no longer working on children's programs. Thus, it was the purpose of the 1990 symposium to impart these lessons to a new generation of writers and producers and increase their sensitivity towards these issues. (Research by Calvert, et al., 1997, indicates that NBC's work in this area had a continuing positive impact on diversity in children's programming.)

Developmental Appropriateness. Writers are understandably interested in stories they themselves find exciting or funny, and they sometimes lack awareness of children's developmental limits and needs. As a result, misunderstanding of programs or program elements by children was a recurring issue for the Panel. Members repeatedly identified instances where the language or plot seemed beyond the grasp of most 2- to 5-year-olds and even many 6- to 11-year-olds, the main audience for Saturday morning programs. This was not an issue that NBC and the Panel focused on initially, but it turned out to be of crucial importance. Social science researchers were able to make valuable contributions that, most participants believe, not only made programs better, but also more popular.

Pro-Social Program Content and Learning. This is an area where the Panel and programmers did not always agree. The gap was caused primarily by different emphases on entertainment versus prosocial content, even though both sides eventually agreed that the two goals are not incompatible. Panel members complained that NBC's Saturday morning schedule did not include the kind of prosocial, learning-oriented series one would find on PBS. The network responded that series originating from such a perspective had continually failed in the ratings in competition with more entertainment-oriented series shown on other networks at the same time. (As discussed by Entman & Wildman, 1992, this was not an issue that was limited to this consulting process; rather, it is typical of consulting in this field.)

Research, however, did help find ways to deal with the prosocial content versus ratings tension: They showed that children respond positively to messages about prosocial behaviors and themes embedded in series that were conceptualized with a primary emphasis on entertainment. This made the Panel members more comfortable working on entertainment-oriented programs and they routinely offered suggestions about possible prosocial content, and many scripts dealing with such sensitive issues as the death of a pet, disabilities, and child abduction turned out quite well, some well enough to win awards.

In addition, analyses indicated that children would watch short informational or prosocial messages sandwiched between programs, that such messages would not prompt them to change the channel. NBC decided to develop 1- to 2-minute long informational spots that were inserted in commercial breaks on Saturday mornings. (The other networks had similar spots at the time.) Panel members were initially quite skeptical and doubted their effectiveness. Still, they were closely involved in creating them and NBC commissioned research to test their effectiveness and provide guidance for future drop-ins (Dorr, Doubleday, Kovaric, & Kunkel, 1981).

Eventually, the Panel did accept the fact that these "drop-ins" were a good way to reach millions of children with social and educational messages, and that they reached many more children than the "educational" programs that NBC had on its schedule for a while and then cancelled because of poor ratings. At the same time, many Panel members continued to express frustration over the entertainment focus of Saturday morning programming and wondered if the main reason why informational programs had not been successful was simply an unwillingness to try again and learn how to get it right. They could not be completely convinced by the network's researchers who, in contrast, felt they had established beyond any doubt that most children over 6-or 7-years-old would not turn on the TV on a Saturday morning to learn more of what they were taught in school all week, and that they would only accept prosocial messages wrapped in "fun" content.

To meet the Panel's objectives and NBC's own desire to be innovative, several attempts to insert information into entertainment programs were made. However, this turned out to be another area where the academics' work on the Panel challenged their assumptions about how to best improve programming directed at children.

NBC agreed with Panel members who suggested to go beyond prosocial values and try to insert scientific facts that would be intriguing to children into programs. But on a practical level, this proved to be much harder than anticipated because of the nature of most children's programming, as exemplified in this 1982 report about a Spiderman cartoon:

> As discussed, Panel members have expressed their desire to see something informative in a series like that. For example, teaching facts of natural science rather than keeping everything on a pure fantasy level. Reading the concept and the new premises raised some doubts in my mind as to whether that is really possible in Spiderman. Discussions with Panel members Aimee Dorr and Bill McGuire resulted in the following:
>
> In order for children to learn something from the program, they have to be able to separate fact from fiction. Since Spiderman is essentially a science fiction fantasy, most children would probably not recognize true facts in the program if such information was inserted. Others might even assume that the facts are part of the fantasy plot. Thus, it seems difficult to add anything informative to a concept like Spiderman.
>
> Still, it may not be impossible. Spiderman contains sequences where the superheroes are in their normal "teen" identities, where they go to school, date, etc. According to the "bible," these sequences were supposed to show meaningful interaction between the characters. Useful information, including scientific facts, could be conveyed during those sequences since they are clearly separated from the superhero sequences. (NBC memo from March 2, 1982)

Most people involved in the Panel process, at NBC as well as the academic advisors, had not really thought about this when they first addressed this issue. Thus, it turned out that not only programmers, but also academics gained unanticipated insights from the consulting process.

LESSONS FROM NBC'S SOCIAL SCIENCE ADVISORY PROCESS

The consultancy process described here was one of the first of its kind and was clearly rooted in the circumstances of its time, but it contains important lessons, many of which are applicable today. Even though there have been dramatic changes in television during the last 25 years or so, there are also similarities in key areas: First, many aspects of the creative process regarding children's television programs have not changed dramatically since the 1980s. Second, the television market is still dominated commercial networks and has become even more competitive: Several networks, such as Nickelodeon and Disney, now air children's programming exclusively during daytime hours. Third, programming for children still has to consider the audience's special developmental needs in order to be successful. And, forth, academics and creative people still talk only rarely and must learn how to work together in order to be effective.

In sum, I consider the following key insights from the process described here:

1. It is clearly possible for academic advisors to have a positive impact on children's programs in a commercial environment and significant change can be achieved. However, such positive impact does not come automatically as result of providing information based on academic research to programmers. A series of obstacles need to be dealt with to achieve good results.
2. To be effective, buy-in from all stakeholders and a commitment to work together, respect each other, and overcome problems are necessary. The management of the network or production company should design a plan and a process to facilitate interaction and understanding, especially if programmers and consultants have not work together before.
3. Programmers and creative people also have to (gently) be made aware that academics know more about certain aspects of child development and children's understanding of television programs than they do.
4. At the same time, academics have to be made aware (as gently as possible) that programmers and creative people usually have expertise in certain areas that they don't have. Also, they have to recognize that academic theory and research do not always provide clear, unambiguous, and practical answers to a specific program issue. It is also helpful for the process, if academic consultants can assure programmers that they are conscious of the need to entertain children and that they share the goal of making popular programs with positive content and no unintended negative consequences.
5. Advisors also need to accept that program concepts and other circumstances may limit the amount of prosocial and factual or informational lessons that can be provided. Also, they will have little impact on the overall structure of the children's television business. Networks will always allocate air time, determine the basic parameters of the types of shows they will air, sell advertising

time, and schedule program and nonprogram content on the basis of the market conditions at the time. Advisors will be listened to, but they are not hired to design policy. In general, network people, apart from the constitutional issues they see in legislating program content, feel that a self-regulatory process that uses academics in an advisory capacity is in the best interests of all, especially in today's media environment. As said, they believe experience has shown that an entertainment schedule with prosocial content will bring more positive programming to more children than one built around messages and formal teaching. They also usually believe that current scheduling and advertising practices are necessary for the economic viability of children's programming.

REFERENCES

Bandura, A. (1977). *Social learning theory.* New York: General Learning Press.

Calling in consultants for children's programming. (1985, September 9). *Broadcasting,* pp. 100–103.

Calvert, S. L., Stolkin, A., & Lee, J. (1971, April). *Gender and ethnic portrayals in children's Saturday morning television programs.* Poster session presented at the biennial meeting of the Society for Research in Child Development, Washington, DC.

Dixon, B. (1985). Bam! Pow! Take this, Peggy Charren! *Emmy Magazine* (September/October), pp. 14–15.

Dorr, A., Doubleday, C., Kovaric, P., & Kunkel, D. (1981). *An evaluation of NBC's 1980–81 prosocial children's programming: Drawing power, play alongs, how to watch TV.* (Report to the National Broadcasting Company). [(ERIC) Document Reproduction Service No. ED 216 796)]. Los Angeles: University of Southern California, Annenberg School of Communications.

Entman, R. M., & Wildman, S. S. (1992). Reconciling economic and non-economic perspectives on media policy: Transcending the "marketplace of ideas." *Journal of Communication, 42(1),* 5–19.

Ettema, J. S. (1982). The organizational context of creativity: A case study from public television. In J. S. Ettema & D. C. Whitney (Eds.), *Individuals in mass media organizations: Creativity and constraint* (pp. 91–106). Beverly Hills: Sage.

Fisch, S. & Truglio, R. (2001). *"G" Is for growing: 30 Years of research on children and Sesame Street.* Mahwah, NJ: Lawrence Erlbaum associates.

Karp, W. (1984). Where the do-gooders went wrong. *Channels of Communications* (March/April), 41–47.

Kline, S. (1993). *Out of the garden: Toys, TV, and children's culture in the age of marketing.* Toronto: Garamond Press.

LeConte, P. (1986). The psychologist as TV guide. *Psychology Today* (August), 50–55.

Milavsky, J. R. (1975, December 11). Proposal—pilot project—social science consultants—Saturday morning programs. *Interdepartment correspondence to William S. Rubens, NBC.* New York: NBC Social Research Department Files.

Milavsky, J. R., Kessler, R. C., Stipp, H. H., & Rubens, W. S. (1982). *Television and aggression: A panel study.* New York: Academic Press.

Stipp, H., Hill-Scott, K., & Dorr, A. (1987). Using social science to improve children's television: An NBC case study. *Journal of Broadcasting and Electronic Media, 31*(4), 461–473.

Watching out for the programs children watch. (1985, September 23). *Broadcasting,* pp. 41–44.

Wurtzel, A. H. (1980) Academic research: A view from the industry. *Journal of Broadcasting, 24,* 479–486.

III

PROGRAMMING & SELLING
CHILDREN'S TELEVISION

7

Programming Children's Television: The PBS Model

Linda Simensky
PBS

Public television has its roots in education. In the early 1950s, the Federal Communications Commission (FCC) set aside 242 channels for educational television, mostly in the UHF band. These channels became the earliest noncommercial education television stations, and were mostly supported by the Ford Foundation, community groups, universities, and other educational institutions (Witherspoon, Kovitz, Avery, & Stavitsky, 2000). This grouping was known as National Educational Television and its main activities involved instructional programs for colleges.

In 1965, the Carnegie Commission on Educational Television laid the foundation for the current incarnation of public television. The Commission, under President Lyndon B. Johnson, made several recommendations based on two key ideas: increased federal support of public and educational television, and the creation of a Corporation for Public Broadcasting (CPB). The CPB was formed in 1968, and was uniquely positioned between the federal government and the rest of public broadcasting. The CPB's goals included interconnecting the public television system, managing the federal government's appropriations to public broadcasting, and making public broadcasting policy decisions. The promise of public broadcasting was always simply commercial-free, education-based quality entertainment, and an alternative to the mass sensibility of commercial programming.

Interestingly, through all the planning and visionary work that was done to define what public television would be, there was never in its history a satisfactory public policy about how to support "noncommercial educational broadcasting" (Witherspoon et al., 2000, p. 1). As Witherspoon et al. (2000) note in their book, *A History of Public Broadcasting*, public broadcasting today lives on an uneasy mix of audience subscriptions; local, state, and federal tax support; traditional philanthropy; sale of services and program-related products, and the increasingly enhanced underwriting that represents the system's compromise with advertising.

The Public Broadcasting Service, or PBS, was formed in November 1969 as a way to interconnect the stations that were checkerboarded across the United States. Although the architects of public television always felt that local public television stations should be able to acquire programming from a number of sources, PBS's mandate was to create a catalog of programs that local stations could choose from, and to suggest schedules as well as an overall vision for public broadcasting. PBS's main programming service is called the National Programming Service (NPS), and its goal is to provide to the local stations the highest quality documentaries, arts, children's, and news and public affairs programming.

A HISTORY OF CHILDREN'S PROGRAMMING ON PUBLIC TELEVISION

Public television has always seen children's programming as a major part of its mission since the 1950s. Because public television had the goal of serving the underserved, it was easy in the early years of television to see that children were an underserved audience. In the 1950s, the earliest shows for children were mostly puppet shows and locally produced hosted shows, which ran cartoons from major film studios that had run in theaters in earlier decades.

The educational shows produced with children in mind were not the strongest shows on television (according to Grossman, 1981):

> Public television has done the best job of presenting educational programs. Yet before Sesame Street premiered in 1969, PBS or then the children's National Educational Television shows hadn't gone beyond the first grade. Production was often shoddy, shows were slow. Dull hosts generally conveyed material in a manner so boring that most viewers might have felt they were being punished rather than stimulated. (p. 262)

Some of the puppet and live-action programs that were oriented toward kids, such as *Howdy Doody, Hopalong Cassidy, Davy Crockett,* and *The Lone Ranger,* spawned enormous lines of merchandised products which they blatantly promoted during their shows. Much of the programming was of dubious quality, and certainly the programs were much more concerned with selling ads and merchandise than with the well-being of their viewers. Outside of such shows as *Ding Dong School*, *Romper Room,* and *Captain Kangaroo*, there were few quality options for children viewers, particularly preschool viewers.

Meanwhile, in 1954, in Pittsburgh, Pennsylvania, a children's musical and variety puppet show called *The Children's Corner*, hosted by Josie Carey, began running on WQED in Pittsburgh, as well as on NBC affiliates. The program featured a newcomer, a producer and puppeteer named Fred Rogers, who eventually developed his own series for preschoolers, *Mister Rogers' Neighborhood*, which started in 1963. In 1966, the Eastern Education Network, an early public television regional network, began airing the program. By 1968, 120 public television stations were running *Mister Rogers' Neighborhood*. The show was in production until 2000 and still airs on many public television stations.

In 1969, along with the formation of PBS, came the show *Sesame Street*, produced by the Children's Television Workshop (CTW, now known as Sesame Workshop). The show focused on underserved audiences, namely the minority and inner-city youth, and was geared toward teaching kids aged 3 to 6 (at that time, an underserved segment of the television-viewing population) about letters and numbers. *Sesame Street* was instantly successful, and changed children's television in several ways. CTW's most important contribution to children's programming may be the integration of research and studio production, achieved by the focus group testing of each segment to determine if the segment will achieve its educational objectives. This sort of research resulted in a process of production, testing, feedback, and revised production (Witherspoon et al., 2000). *Sesame Street* was, in some ways, controversial at the time. Its detractors felt the show drew too much inspiration from the rapid-fire viewing of advertisements on television, and that the show was shortening children's attention spans. Nevertheless, the show, now it its 36th season, has many more supporters than detractors and remains one of PBS Kids' most successful programs.

In its earliest years, PBS added several children's shows to its roster. Soon after *Sesame Street* came CTW's *The Electric Company* in 1971. *The Electric Company* was similar to *Sesame Street*—educational, entertaining, and deeply influenced by popular culture. *The Electric Company's* logo was a brightly colored, Peter Max-inspired logo that spoke to the sensibilities of the era unlike any other show of the time. The show was geared toward post-*Sesame Street* viewers, with the goal of teaching underserved young audiences, (again mostly minorities and inner-city youth,) reading and math. Where *Sesame Street* focused on letters and numbers, *The Electric Company* added higher numbers, made letters into words, and phrases into sentences. Yet the show was also extremely funny, featuring comedy sketches and parodies, animated shorts, and such celebrities as Bill Cosby, Rita Moreno, and Morgan Freeman.

Other shows were added in as well over the next several years, including *Zoom, Big Blue Marble, Villa Allegre,* and *Vegetable Soup.* Although most children's shows on commercial television were animated, at this time, the shows on public television were mainly live action, puppets, documentaries or some combination of those. In the 1980s, several additional shows joined PBS children's schedule, including *3–2–1 Contact, Newton's Apple, Reading Rainbow, Sonrisas,* and *Wonderworks.* Notable additions in the late 1980s included *DeGrassi High, Ramona,* and *Square One.*

PBS IN THE 1990S

After a 40% decline in its child audience in the early 1990s, PBS engineered a comeback that it counts as one of its most successful programming initiatives. The audience declines at this time were mainly due to increasing competition from alternate sources of children's programming. Its main rivals were in cable; more specifically, the children's cable channel, Nickelodeon, and the Disney Channel (at that time, a premium cable channel.)

In the early 1990s, PBS added three new series to its children's offerings, *Barney & Friends, Lamb Chop's Play-Along* (with Shari Lewis), and *Shining Time Station* (which included Thomas the Tank Engine.) What made these series different from earlier PBS series was that, particularly in the case of Barney, these shows have all been merchandised, quite successfully.

Other shows added in this early 1990s period included *Bill Nye the Science Guy, Wishbone,* where in the world is *Carmen Sandiego? Ghostwriter, Puzzle Works,* and *The Magic School Bus.* PBS found particular success with several new shows in the mid-1990s: *Wishbone* in 1994; public television's first animated series, *Arthur,* in 1996; and *Teletubbies,* a show imported from Britain in 1998.

MAJOR CHANGES FOR CHILDREN'S PROGRAMMING AT PBS

Two major events changed the face of public television for children in the early half of the 1990s: *Barney & Friends* merchandising (and the politics of the 1990s) and the introduction of the *Ready To Learn* program. When *Barney & Friends* premiered in 1991, the show was not expected to be a hit until preschool audiences showed up in the millions. The merchandising program for the show began to grow, and shortly after that, stations began using Barney dolls, tapes, and other merchandise as incentives for pledge-drive donations. During a pledge drive in 1993, parents of young viewers complained that public television stations were being too aggressive in their use of Barney merchandise, accusing the stations of commercial manipulation and of violating the Children's Television Act. In response, a PBS task force suggested that fundraising adjacent to children's programming be directed to the parents only and that the fundraising be clearly separated from children's programming. This resulted in an examination of pledge practices and PBS decided not to repeat the program for the following drives (Witherspoon et al., 2000).

The next Barney-related accusation came shortly after, when critics of public television, largely from the political right, declared that public television was not being aggressive enough in making money from Barney. Conservative critics stated that public television was essentially providing free advertising for commercial programs and merchandise, which was allowing private companies to profit without any return to the tax-paying public that was paying broadcast costs and a portion of the program's production costs.

When questioned by the House Appropriations Subcommittee about this in 1995, executives from the CPB were able to show how the amount of money, after expenses and other merchandising costs, was not significant enough to replace CPB appropriations. Nevertheless, PBS began to reexamine their ancillary rights policies and began requiring larger shares of ancillary and back-end revenues from programs it funded or distributed (Witherspoon et al., 2000).

Shows such as *Sesame Street* and *Barney & Friends,* although extremely successful, are not the norm for any television station, public or commercial. It is relatively rare to have a hit show, and a show with a hugely successful merchandising program is even more atypical. Therefore, the idea that PBS could fund its own way if it just had a few huge hits and merchandising hits is a most unrealistic expectation. In addition, licensing a television show is no longer a guaranteed money-maker. Due to consolidation in the retail business, not as much shelf space is available, and most stores want to wait until a show is already a hit before launching merchandise.

In 1994, public television was once again in the public eye, as Speaker of the House Newt Gingrich and Senate Commerce Committee Chairman Larry Pressler (R-S.D.) led a charge against federal aid to the system. Although this was not the first time that this had happened, it became a huge national story. Republican leaders soon came to realize that ending federal aid to public broadcasting was not popular with voters. In some part, it was children's programming (*Sesame Street*, in particular) that brought out much of the support from the public.

With a slightly more dominant right wing, conservative think-tanks got busy instead trying to prove once again that PBS suffered from a left-wing bias. The CPB, at the time run by a Republican, funded several right-leaning projects, including a 1995 children's series, *Adventures from the Book of Virtues*, based on a book by former Education Secretary William F. Bennett. The need by conservative groups to end funds to public television has seemed to be more of a call for privatization or a call to move symbolically to the right, than a cost-cutting measure for federal aid. The amount of money that public television receives per taxpayer is not much more than $1 per year!

READY TO LEARN

The government in recent decades has not been completely opposed to public television. In the early 1990s, Congress, working with public television, came up with an innovative funding program to support a program designed to help preschoolers and school-aged children become more prepared for school. After an educational summit in 1989, state governors and politicians agreed that their first objective was to make sure all children entering school were "ready to learn." The developers of the *Ready To Learn* program ultimately determined they could help prepare children for success in school through television programming and related outreach programs. Today, the PBS *Ready to Learn Service,* which was started in 11 cities in 1994, now offers at least 6½ hours a day of nonviolent, commercial-free, educational children's programming through more than 140 stations covering 90% of the population, reaching 37 million children. The programs develop key school readiness skills in language, literacy, numeracy, and the social and emotional skills necessary for cognitive learning. Participating stations also offer outreach workshops to train adults who work with children to use television programs for their educational value. Built around the Learning Triangle concept of "View," "Do," and "Read," the workshops explain the curriculum within PBS Kids programs and show adults how to extend these lessons at home and in the classroom through children's books and hands-on activities. The service is designed to reflect the needs and circumstances of each community. Stations partner with local organizations such as schools, child-care providers, Head Start programs, and libraries to serve community needs. Shows that have been included in these workshops and programs include *Arthur, Between the Lions, Clifford the Big Red Dog, Dragon Tales, Reading*

Rainbow, Sesame Street, Maya and Miguel, and Postcards from Buster. More than 7 million children have benefited from the Ready To Learn training of more than 900,000 adults (Brantley, 2005). Recent research illustrates that children attending child-care centers where a teacher had attended a Ready To Learn workshop and the children viewed Sesame Street or Between the Lions as part of their curriculum showed greater change on a measure of emergent literacy than did children in comparison groups. Research also shows that parents and educators who attended Ready To Learn workshops were more likely to engage in a variety of literacy-related activities after workshop attendance than they were prior, including discussing the content of a program while watching with a child, talking about a program after it is finished, and reading books related to the topic or theme of a program (Horowitz et al., 2004).

THE CURRENT SITUATION AT PBS

It is quite a unique time in the history of children's programming at PBS, given the number of changes going on in the children's television industry. In 2000, PBS branded children's programming on air as "PBS Kids," complete with the familiar green kids logos designed by children's book illustrator Richard McGuire. PBS Kids has remained focused on its mission to be the number one purveyor of educational children's programming and the first choice of its viewers. Although commercial cable stations and networks tend to focus more on ratings and advertising dollars, PBS Kids has remained focused on children's best interests above all else. Due to its unusual structure and history, PBS has always had the ability to remain mission-based and focused on programming and education, rather than having to worry about ratings and advertising sales. PBS is not expected to be concerned with the commercial and merchandising aspects of its programs. However, as we discuss in this chapter, there have been many changes in the children's programming landscape, such as increased competition from well-funded cable networks, for example, that have already had or will ultimately have an impact on PBS Kids.

THE PBS KIDS PROCESS

Since its inception, PBS was designed to be a distributor, curator, and funder of programs, but not a producer. People often assume that PBS is structured like a cable network; however, PBS is a programming service, pulling together a catalog of programs for the benefit of its member stations, and offering scheduled feeds. Unlike its many competitors in the children's arena, PBS cannot own the shows it is running, and therefore has slightly less control over the shows it distributes and airs. Due to the changing nature of PBS's funding, shows are developed in many different ways to achieve a variety of goals. For instance, some shows are developed to accommodate specific mandates, such as *Ready To Learn* shows. Some shows are developed around specific topics or educational goals, in response to a Request for Proposals (RFP) that can be generated either by PBS, the CPB, or the Department of Education, for example.

PBS Kids is targeted to two different age groups. The first is what would be considered the standard preschool audience ranging, depending on the program, from ages 2- through 5- or 6-years of age. PBS also has an afternoon block called PBS Kids GO!, which is targeted to kids ages 5 through 9, with an emphasis on kids ages 6 to 8.

PBS's goal is to treat content not just as television programs and interstitial pieces, but as an online experience (with each show having its own Web site), and even as an interactive experience. The hope is to take a 360 degree approach to kids' lives, and to be wherever kids are utilizing media; with whatever new platforms are developed; bringing strong characters and stories, educational goals, and positive messages.

As with PBS's primetime programming, the goal is to serve the underserved, a term which changes depending on a variety of factors. In the case of targeting children ages 6 to 8, for example, PBS had assessed that viewers in this age group who were searching for educational or informative programming that was entertaining and developmentally appropriate were underserved. Thus, the PBS Kids GO! block was developed, so that there would be an option for kids looking for that sort of programming. PBS has also sensed that the focus of programming for preschool audiences has been slowly climbing to the older end of the audience, focusing on the 4- to 5-year-olds, leaving 2- and 3-year-olds with programming that is developmentally slightly advanced for them. This younger audience may ultimately be seen as an underserved audience. PBS has assessed in general that kids or parents looking for programming that is educational in a curriculum-oriented way and developmentally appropriate are underserved. Hence, PBS Kids' current mission is to develop programming that is entertaining, character- and story-driven, and clearly educational.

DEVELOPING NEW SHOWS

Shows are found and developed in a variety of ways. Several of the public television stations have development groups. Both WGBH in Boston and WNET in New York have specific departments that develop kids' shows for the PBS system. Shows such as *Arthur, Postcards from Buster, Zoom* and *Between the Lions* have been developed by WGBH. *Cyberchase* is WNET's contribution to the kids programming line-up. Stations in other cities have developed local shows that can be turned into national shows. Other stations have primetime development departments and, on occasion, develop and pitch series for kids.

PBS also has long-standing relationships with some existing production companies. Several of these companies, such as Sesame Workshop, are nonprofit companies, and have very similar missions and values to PBS's. Other companies, such as Scholastic and HIT, are publicly owned, but also have goals similar to PBS's. There are other independent production companies such as Nelvana, Cookie Jar, and Shadow Projects, which have developed and produced shows for PBS Kids. Often, international production companies and networks pitch children's series from other countries. Numerous individuals, both in and outside of the children's television industry, have presented shows to PBS for consideration, although in most cases the shows do not exhibit a strong enough understanding of PBS's needs. In some cases, creators or producers with shows that seem to have potential often connect with stations or with more established companies that can work closely to accommodate PBS's needs.

PBS produces anywhere from one to three new series a year, depending on the funding available and the needs of the stations. Currently, for example, PBS is looking for, and currently developing, shows for the 2- to 5-year old group, as well as the 6- to 8-year-old age blocks, particularly shows with literacy, math, science, technology, history, and the arts as their curriculum.

When a show is pitched to PBS, the producer or creator generally presents what is called a "mini-bible," which is the standard pitching tool across the industry. The mini-bible features an overview of what the series will be about, who the characters are (and what they will look like in the case of animated shows.) These pitches also feature four or five stories, as well as additional storylines and any other supplemental material that would help explain the show and its sensibility. A show developed for PBS would also have some elements not necessarily found in pitches for other networks. The presentation would include a curriculum for the show, as well as a list of at least four or five curriculum advisors with different backgrounds who are capable of helping to develop a sound curriculum for the show and of making sure the series remains faithful to that curriculum. The presentation would include the ideas for the series Web site. The pitch would also have suggestions for local outreach for stations. When PBS passes on a pitch, the producers can still bring a fully funded show to APT (American Public Television,) a smaller distributor that also focuses on public television stations, or even pitch to stations directly.

In the rare cases where the show being pitched turns out to be a fit for PBS, a deal is then made. PBS does not fund any series entirely. Rather, PBS will contribute roughly the equivalent of a license fee per episode, and that number is different for every series for a variety of reasons. Each series brings with it its own set of particular details. Some companies are able to raise the bulk of funding for a show through international sales or video sales and merchandising. Some rare shows come completely funded through other sources, such as completed international sales deals or merchandising deals. Other shows come with foundation funding (e.g., the National Science Foundation) although foundation grants rarely pay for the production of an entire series. As mentioned, it varies from show to show so greatly that it is virtually impossible to present a typical PBS series deal structure.

Some shows that are presented to PBS are well developed and interesting ideas, but they may not fulfill PBS's mission at that moment. Certain shows that are deemed to be strong shows and are fully funded, but are not the perfect fit for the national daily PBS schedule, are sometimes considered for a tier service that PBS offers, called "PBS Plus." Also, shows that do not have enough episodes to strip daily are considered for this tier. Programs such as *Thomas and Friends, Angelina Ballerina,* and *JayJay the Jet Plane* have found a home on PBS Plus, where they are considered by stations as supplemental material, to fill out a weekend schedule, for instance. Some cities have more than one public television station, and the stations counterschedule each other. For example, the cable system in Princeton, New Jersey, for example offers four different public television stations, NJN (NJ), WNET, WLIW (Long Island), and WHYY (Philadelphia.) In this case, a smaller station such as NJN may wish to differentiate its programming by running PBS Plus shows as well as shows from other sources.

BROADCASTING ON PBS

The goals of public television are different from the goals of commercial television in some ways, but not in all ways. As was mentioned earlier, commercial television tends to be, in general, more focused on ratings and advertising sales, whereas PBS has traditionally focused on achieving the mission of the show, on assessing the impact of the show (particularly if the show is part of the *Ready To Learn* initiative,) and on providing alternative, educational options to the commercial system, which, for kids at this time, is mostly cable channels, with a few broadcast options on Saturday mornings, or after school on weekdays.

This creates several advantages for producers and shows connected to PBS, as well as several hurdles. There are several reasons why a producer or creator may prefer to have a show on PBS. PBS, as a broadcast channel, has 99% penetration in U.S. households, according to Nielsen Media Research (Nielsen Media Research, 2005). With a larger possible audience, a show can get higher ratings or be available to more viewers than it could on some smaller cable channels with limited penetration and limited access to viewers. Also, because PBS is a broadcast channel, a show on PBS would be available to anyone with a television set, not just households with cable or satellite dishes.

When a producer or show creator makes a deal with PBS, the ownership rights will continue to reside with the producer or show creator. As mentioned, PBS is not a producer, and therefore cannot own shows. Although stations can have an ownership position on a show, PBS, as an entity, can only fund the show in some portion, and retain a back-end position guaranteeing ancillary income and other related fees. Cable stations often make deals that require an ownership position in the show if the show is not coming in with funding or as an acquisition (where it would be paid for with a license fee.)

Often, cable networks are parts of larger companies that task the networks with the job of building their programming libraries. In these cases, as with many shows on well-funded networks such as Nickelodeon, the Disney Channel, and Cartoon Network, the network is able to put up the entire budget for the show. In that situation, the show producer or creator accepts a back-end position, thus giving up ownership of the show they created. This would be considered an important consideration for most independent production companies, who are also in the business of building their own program libraries, and retaining ownership rights for the sake of greater royalty potential.

For producers, having a show on PBS also guarantees a greater amount of creative freedom for the producers. Because the show is not completely funded by PBS, PBS can offer feedback or "meaningful consultation," but for the most part, the production company is ultimately responsible for the content of the show, although they still must follow the specific requirements of all PBS Kids shows. Cable stations that produce children's shows tend to give a great deal of creative feedback (which, of course, is sometimes necessary.) Because the cable networks own the shows, or even because they have the staff to handle it, the cable networks often give more creative feedback and broadcast standards notes to the creatives working on the series.

Sometimes, show producers have to be concerned with issues such as how a show will be interpreted internationally. These shows, usually coproductions, often receive notes from several networks or production companies. This can often dull the creativity or uniqueness of a show, as when a show must appeal to several different sensibilities. PBS itself does not need to concern itself as much with how a show will play in other countries. Where PBS does weigh in is when a producer tries to cut back on educational content, maintaining that a show will not play as well on the BBC, for example, if it is too educational. Many series try to justify themselves as educational to get picked up by PBS, while positioning themselves as less educational for general entertainment networks in other countries. At PBS, this is cause for concern, as educational goals are a priority.

Generally, producers of a show on PBS have the benefit of overseeing the ancillary aspects of a show, from start to finish, including the Web site, the marketing of the show, the promotion of the show, the ancillary marketing and international sales of show, and the like. When producers contract to make a show with most other networks, they give up the control, because the cable stations handle all these ancillary and related aspects of the show, other than show production.

Another advantage to working within the PBS system is that the producers can focus on the mission of the program. When a show is educational, as well as entertaining, the goal is often to blend education with entertainment. Although ratings are important, they are never the only aspect by which to judge an educational show. Therefore, the producer is encouraged to focus on making the show work, both as an enjoyable show and as a successful educational tool. Often, being an educational show means that ratings may not be as high as other shows, but if the educational mission is successful, the show will be seen as a successful enterprise. Not having the pressure of generating ratings or selling toys can be liberating to producers, allowing them to focus on the program. Some producers have positioned their companies to be educational or mission-driven or even just creators of safe programming, and they may feel a sense of connection with PBS's mission and its designation as a safe and trusted haven, with no violent shows and no advertising (Harris Interactive, 2004; The Roper Center For Public Opinion Research, 2005).

And finally, there are local benefits, particularly for educational programs, to being part of a broadcasting system that is focused on the local stations. Stations in each city are often better equipped to handle localized outreach than a cable system might be. Thus, any programs that have events or traveling initiatives will benefit from the structure of the local stations or public broadcasting. For instance, local stations have worked with elementary schools in their communities to establish after-school *Cyberchase* math clubs.

SOME CONSIDERATIONS

For all the advantages of working with PBS, there are also distinct challenges that a producer might encounter when working with PBS. The advantages detailed in the preceding paragraphs are mainly advantages to larger and more established independent companies, who have access to the capital to fund their own shows and oversee their own initiatives. For creatives just starting out in the industry, the learning curve is quite steep, and not every young or less experienced creator is ready or willing to start their own company and deal with issues such as funding, marketing, ancillary merchandise, and promotion while trying to produce a program. The disadvantage for public television is that sometimes the most exciting creative experimentation, the newest ideas, and the most innovative uses of technologies, come from these less experienced creators, and PBS misses out on this when these creators go to the cable networks for funding. Often, these creators are not as committed to building a company or program library as they are to creating a unique show and building their own careers within the industry. For these creators, the PBS structure is a slightly more demanding scenario.

As mentioned earlier, there was never a truly successful funding plan put in place for PBS, so funding is often scarce, at both the national and local levels. Because there is no traditional advertising (commercials) on PBS, the system sells underwriting at both the local and national levels. Although this system worked quite well as an alternative in the days of three broadcast channels and few other options, it does not always work quite as well in the multichannel cable universe. These days, advertisers are often more focused on expanded reach and access to consumers than they are interested in positioning themselves to appear beneficent while receiving a 15-second acknowledgement by sponsoring a show on public television.

Public television stations must also compete with the plethora of cable channels, both new and old. Many of these networks are competing in the same arenas (kids, nature, science, history, culture) that PBS is in. But where these channels can brand themselves quite easily and focus on their target audiences, PBS remains more of a general interest entity with several different target audiences, so it is harder for PBS to compete with cable's process of branding (see Kalagian, chap. 8 this volume, for more on branding in the cable industry). Because the stations are free to run whichever shows they wish, and schedule them when they want, it is difficult for PBS to develop consistent messaging to target audiences (such as "tune in" or "coming up next" spots), as cable networks can do. Nevertheless, although PBS cannot restructure itself to be more similar to cable networks, it still must compete with them for viewers and for programs. Also, whereas cable networks can change their programming strategy or schedule in a matter of days, PBS, with its local stations and decentralized management, is not structured to move quickly at all.

Another consideration of working within the PBS system is that sometimes the system itself can be a bit unwieldy, and the different components within the structure, such as the local member stations and the production divisions within local stations, do not always have the same motives and goals as PBS or each other. Sometimes the local stations are focused more on ratings, and sometimes the stations or their production divisions develop shows that are not quite right for PBS. This can lead to strained relations, particularly when shows are involved.

Often, the system is confusing to outsiders wanting to sell their shows to PBS. Someone who is not involved within the system may not understand the difference between selling a show to a local PBS station and selling a show to PBS's National Program Service. And outsiders who are not part of the system at all, such as publishers, marketers, toy companies, or potential sponsors, often will have a limited sense of whom to contact for information regarding a particular program. Although this system allows for more options and possibilities for funding or for venues to air, this also can create confusion. Because there is no final authority—PBS is not always the final authority, and the stations are not always the final authority either—the end result is often a lack of clarity in terms of purpose or focus. A producer may pitch his show to the children's programming department at PBS headquarters, in hopes that they will acquire it for the National Programming Service, and the show may be rejected for any number of reasons. The same show can be picked up by APT and still end up on several PBS stations. That show can be marketed directly to stations, and get picked up by several of them, or get selected by just one or two local stations. Either way, the show producers can then tell toy companies or publishers that their show is on PBS and technically, it is. Hence, confusion can easily arise from this system.

In addition, PBS does sometimes encounter intense scrutiny, both from the public and from the government. By its very nature, PBS is "of the people," and ultimately, that means that it is open to quite a bit of criticism. Many viewers feel that it is PBS's responsibility to reflect their own personal views, and that anything else is wrong or an abomination. Other viewers demand that PBS must present differing and diverse points of view, as well as risk-taking subject matter and genres not covered on other networks. As mentioned, politically, both the right and left wings of political belief play into this argument. This has even impacted children's programming, as the government each year weighs in on appropriations and funding. The current administration has made it clear that if Department of Education funding is going into children's programming, they will expect to have their say about what they feel is appropriate and what they believe is "too diverse," (as was seen in the well-documented case of an episode of the show, *Postcards from Buster* that included two mothers) despite PBS's rule that funders have no say over the final content of programming.

There are also several other challenges that are impacting everyone in children's television across the board. The landscape in children's television is shifting rapidly. Twenty years ago, the networks owned Saturday morning viewing and syndication owned the afterschool market. Nickelodeon changed the landscape somewhat in the second half of the 1980s, and the addition of Cartoon Network in the early 1990s and the success of the Disney Channel in the late 1990s shifted the children's television dynamic even further. These channels have pursued the preschool audience, as well, and studies show that many parents seem to perceive all the networks that run preschool programming as equally safe, and equally educational (Sesame Workshop, 2005). Some of these shows are positioned as educational, and their researchers even segment research the way Sesame Workshop does. In turn, PBS has now had to keep an eye on its ratings, as Nick Jr.'s success in the area of preschool programming has particularly impacted PBS's domination in that audience. Preschool is no longer the underserved audience it once was. In fact, there has probably never been a better time for preschoolers in the history of children's television!

Furthermore, children's television itself must continue to compete with the Web, video on demand, digital video recording devices such as TIVO, video games, hand helds, and imminent additional platforms that do not yet exist. There are several approaches PBS can (and probably will) take to compete in this rapidly changing environment. PBS is uniquely positioned as the only public service entertainment-driven medium, and is committed to impacting the lives of children through curriculum-based multimedia that supports, challenges, and engages kids through every developmental stage of childhood. PBS needs to reestablish itself as the top choice for kids by improving its program offerings, differentiating itself by focusing on programming that is both more entertaining and educational than it currently is, and by having a greater presence in kids' lives through multiple platforms. PBS will need to keep its finger on the pulse of kids' television to determine where the underserved audiences are. Where PBS was able to identify the 5- to 8-year-old audience as underserved, it is also evident that as the other networks skew their preschool programming toward the older end of the preschool age group, there is room for more attention to the 2- and 3-year-olds.

In new distribution arenas, PBS has already had success with a digital PBS Kids channel on satellite. PBS will also extend further into cable, as both a way to expand the reach of its shows, but also to explore a greater digital future for PBS Kids. A new cable channel, PBS Kids Sprout, a joint venture between Comcast, HIT, Sesame Workshop, and PBS, with a focus on video on demand, is developing, and this initiative will hopefully allow PBS to start its exploration of new alternative revenue streams.

PBS, as a public entity, has endured constant studies and analyses, and each study ultimately points out that nearly all of PBS's challenges can be met with the infusion of additional capital. If the American public were to want a public television system as robust as the United Kingdom's BBC or Japan's NHK, then perhaps the real answer is figuring out a better funding structure to allow PBS to continue to nourish the minds of America's youth.

REFERENCES

Brantley, C. (2005). *Ready To Learn pamphlet.* Alexandria, VA: Public Broadcasting Service.

Grossman, G. H. (1981). *Saturday Morning TV.* New York: Arlington House, Inc.

Harris Interactive. (2004). *PBS Kids image tracking study.* Princeton, NJ.

Horowitz, J. E., Juffer, K., Davis, L., Lu Stout, J., Bojorquez, J. C., Dailey, K, et al., (2004). *Data collection of the federal performance indicators for PBS'* Ready To Learn*: Year four summary report.* Report submitted to PBS and the U.S. Department of Education. Washington, DC: WestEd.

Nielsen Media Research. *Special report to PBS on PBS Time Period, February 7–13.* New York, NY.

The Roper Center for Public Opinion Research. (2005). *Public opinion poll on PBS.* New York, NY.

Sesame Workshop. (2005). *Understanding the challenges facing PBS Kids.* Unpublished manuscript.

Witherspoon, J., Kovitz, R., Avery, R., & Stavitsky, A. G. (2000.) *A history of public broadcasting.* Washington, DC: Current.

8

Programming Children's Television: The Cable Model

Terry Kalagian
Cartoon Network

The decades between 1950 and 1970 saw the growth of broadcast from being a harbinger of the death of radio to being the main source of entertainment for America. The next two decades saw the growth of cable and satellite from being a rural occurrence to enhancing the overall experience of television everywhere. The question now is where do we go next? First, let's take a look at where we have been.

A LITTLE HISTORY

"Cable" officially started in the early 1970s when Ted Turner launched TBS as TBS Superstation and when Gerry Levin launched HBO. These networks were launched in the North- and Southeast and quickly spread across the United States. Soon after that, other cable networks came to the party, such as MTV, ESPN, and CNN. Cable was not necessarily a new idea, but was one that had been fairly limited to rural areas, areas that could not get television the "regular" way, with an antenna. About 15 years later, satellite companies were following in their footsteps. Today, the television marketplace has become exceedingly competitive with more than 90% of U.S. homes subscribing to either cable or satellite and about half of those homes wired for digital carriage (Nielsen Media Research, 2004); these are the households with the "500 channel universe" we've been hearing about for so long.

For the first few years, cable networks were trying to find their way as they experimented with different types of formats and programming. Meanwhile, there was not really any children-specific programming on cable. The kids' holy grail of Saturday morning TV was still left to the broadcast networks and kids generally did not watch cable TV. This world changed radically in 1985.

Nickelodeon

In 1985, Geraldine Laybourne, then an independent producer for Nickelodeon, was given the reins to the network that had launched 5 years earlier as a "good-for-kids" network. With a background as a schoolteacher and producer of children's programs, she was intimately aware of kids' media habits. Developmentally, children want and need different things from their media than do adults. The fact that children are drawn to animation and fantasy whereas most adults have grown out of it is evidence of this. Laybourne saw an opportunity here, realizing that children are not drawn to this type of content just on Saturday mornings or just before or after school. In "off-kid" times, they were forced to watch what their parents watched because it was the only programming on television for much of the day. Laybourne wanted to offer kids the choice of *kids,* programming *whenever* they were watching television, *every time* they were watching television (Jenkins, 2004).

Surprisingly, Nickelodeon (or Nick) in its initial days was not really popular with kids. In addition to kids' feel-good shows like *Reggie Jackson's World of Sports* and *Stand By: Lights, Camera, Action*, they aired prosocial or educational shows like *Against the Odds* and *Third Eye*. Kids were not buying it. And if kids were not buying it, neither was Laybourne. It was at this time that Nick went to an advertiser-supported model, so they needed to have large quantities of kids watching (B. Cohen, personal interview, December 6, 2004). Nick went back to the drawing board.

They conducted copious amonts of research asking kids what they wanted, what they liked, and what they wanted to watch. They had some successes after this "relaunch" with *The Ren & Stimpy Show, Double Dare*, and *You Can't Do That on Television*. But it was with *Rugrats* when they were able to really rock and roll! *Rugrats* launched in 1991 and within 3 years, it was an astonishing hit in all of kids' television, even beating popular shows on broadcast on Saturday mornings. Within 4 years, *Rugrats* was a tremendous overall cable hit, and not just when one considered the kids' channels. Within 6 years, it was regularly hitting the weekly top telecast lists for the top shows on all of television (including broadcast!). This included every child demographic rating as well as—and this was the most surprising part—with the general population. This one show really put Nickelodeon in the consciousness of kids and laid the foundation for Nickelodeon's string of hits since: *Fairly Odd Parents, Wild Thornberries, Hey Arnold*, and *SpongeBob SquarePants*.

The Disney Channel

Not long after Nickelodeon launched, another little network with a really big name entered the cable arena: the Disney Channel. Disney's strategy was very different to Nick's. Disney, purveyor of one of the world's megabrands, has always been about family entertainment— and, really, family entertainment at a premium. So under the management of James Jimirro in 1983, the Disney company launched the Disney Channel on cable, as a premium channel. This is a very important distinction.

In order to better understand this distinction, one must understand how "tiers," which is integral when you talk about the cable and satellite universe, work. This is one of the most important and substantial differences between cable/satellite and broadcast. With broadcast, every channel is free. As of October, 2004, Nielsen estimates there are 110 million U.S. homes that have at least one television that receives broadcast networks (Nielsen Media Research, 2004). With cable, not only do you pay for the service, but you are offered different packages. When Disney launched, consumers could choose just a basic package, which would generally include long standing networks like ESPN, CNN, TBS, TNT, and USA, as well as Nick. Or they could buy the basic package and upgrade with premium channels like HBO and Disney. This makes a difference because it greatly affects how many people can see the channel, which, in turn, affects how popular that channel becomes and, ultimately, how economically successful it is. The economics discussion will come up later. Table 8.1 provides the founding date and tier of most cable channels.

Up until 1995, the Disney Channel was seen in only 8 million homes in the United States. Although they were airing beloved Mickey Mouse cartoons and Disney classic movies, they were not thought of as a real competitor in the kids' television market by competitors or advertisers. In 1995, a new management team swept in and rocked the House of Mouse. Where did they come from? They came from Nick.

The new management team was led by none other than Geraldine Laybourne. One of the most important programming initiatives they instituted was to get the hit theatrical Disney titles on the Disney Channel, where they had not previously aired. When the Disney

TABLE 8.1
Select Networks—Dish Network, December, 2004

Launch Date	Network	Tier
1970	TBS	Basic
1977	ABC Family (launched as the Family Channel)	Basic
1979	Nickelodeon	Basic
1979	ESPN	Basic
1980	USA	Basic
1980	CNN	Basic
1981	Headline News	Basic
1981	MTV	Basic
1982	The Weather Channel	Basic
1983	Spike TV (formerly TNN)	Basic
1983	Disney Channel	Basic
1983	Country Music Television	Basic
1984	A&E	Basic
1985	Discovery	Basic
1985	VH1	Basic
1987	The Travel Channel	Basic
1988	TNT	Basic
1988	TV Guide Channel	Basic
1990	E!	Basic
1991	Comedy Central	Basic
1991	Court TV	Basic
1991	The Learning Channel	Basic
1992	Sci-Fi Channel	Basic
1992	Cartoon Network	Basic
1994	Home & Garden TV	Basic
1995	History	Basic
1996	TVLand	Basic
1998	Lifetime	Basic
1972	HBO	Premium
1976	Showtime	Premium
1980	Cinemax	Premium
1980	Bravo	Premium
1981	WGN Superstation	Premium
1984	AMC	Premium
1988	Hallmark Channel (was Odyssey Channel)	Premium
1994	FX	Premium
1994	TCM	Premium
1996	Game Show Network	Premium
1996	Fox News Channel	Premium

TABLE 8.1 (Continued)

Launch Date	Network	Tier
1996	MSNBC	Premium
1996	Animal Planet	Premium
1998	BBC America	Premium
1998	G4techTV	Premium
1998	Toon Disney	Premium
1999	Noggin	Premium
2000	Soapnet	Premium
2000	Boomerang	Premium

Channel was finally able to air their theatrical hits like *Toy Story*, *The Lion King*, and *Pocahontas*, they pulled huge kid *and* adult ratings and were finally viewed by their competition as players in the game. Disney was actually pulling viewers away from the other kids' channels.

During this time, another programming initiative in which Disney began "melting down" the tiers rolled out. (This initiative is now effectively complete.) This meant they started renegotiating their contracts with cable operators (cable affiliates) to move the Disney Channel from a premium (pay service) to a basic service. The Disney Channel, which had garnered a subscriber base of only 8 million homes in its first 12 years, quickly became a strong competitor and had a subscriber base of 85 million homes 9 years after Laybourne and her team stepped in (Nielsen Media Research, 2004).

Turner Networks

In 1991, Ted Turner, one of the true visionaries of television and a founding father of cable, bought the Hanna Barbera library. As he has said over the years, he bought it because "he just likes cartoons." Beyond that he also wanted to start a network that aired nothing but cartoons all day long. This library with 8,400 characters and 3,500 different cartoon titles is loved by people around the world and is more prolific than the Disney library. The Hanna Barbera library includes such beloved cartoons as *The Jetsons, The Flintstones: Yogi Bear: Scooby Doo, Where are You?: The Smurfs:* and *Josie and the Pussycats.* After Turner bought the library, these cartoons initially lived on a couple of Turner Networks (TBS and TNT). Then on October 1, 1992, Cartoon Network was launched as the main platform for airing this library. In addition to Hanna Barbera library, and when he bought the MGM library, Turner received all the MGM produced *Tom & Jerry* cartoons and the MGM produced (pre-1948) Looney Tunes at the same time; a nice complement to his Hanna Barbera collection.

The management team selected to roll out the network was a mix of Turner alumni and nontraditional talent. This team was led by Betty Cohen who was a Nick alumnus prior to her stint at Turner's TNT. She put in place a team of brand masterminds (Joshua Katz, Tom Cory and Stephen Croncota) as well as successful Turner veterans (Mike Lazzo, Dick Connell, and Shirley Powell) to break new ground that would lead this all cartoon channel to success.

The interesting thing about the team's mindset in the early days was that they did not consider Cartoon Network a kids' channel. Sure, they knew that kids would watch no matter what because of the nature of the content, but they also felt that the history of animation was not just about kids. It is about entertainment for a broad audience. The team wanted to establish a brand about the content rather than one based on a demographic and they were sure that if they did it right, it would be successful. And they were right.

Because the network was not just about kids per se, everything they did from production of the on-air look (promos and packaging) to how they "talked" to viewers, to how they would eventually develop original cartoons was seated in the notion that they needed to execute the creative ideas using the classic cartoon concept. The network differentiated itself, not to be different from Nick specifically, but to be unique in the overall television world. They did this by using the best and most beloved elements of classic cartoons in the way they did everything. It was about being edgy, irreverent, and, at the end of the day, funny. When Cartoon Network started producing original series under the leadership of Mike Lazzo (e.g., *Dexter's Laboratory* and *Powerpuff Girls*) the process was based on the way classic cartoons were created under Chuck Jones, Bob Clampett, and Tex Avery. The network was very selective about which projects they would greenlight, but once a project was greenlit, there was very little input from the network (B. Cohen, personal interview, December 6, 2004). This was a fairly risky proposition but Turner had always been about risky propositions, and Cartoon Network grew to be a top-rated cable network within a few short years.

WHERE THE CABLE MARKETPLACE IS NOW

Syndication

For a couple of different reasons (the economics of kids' advertising in local markets being the primary one), the kids' syndication market has dried up. Syndication is the process where local television stations buy shows for themselves (as opposed to receiving and broadcasting network programming like *American Idol* or *60 Minutes*). Up until about 1998 or so, many kids' television shows got their start through syndication. Before the Fox network launched, this is how most "before- and after-school" kids' programming made it on television. You might remember *He-Man* and *Strawberry Shortcake*—they got their start this way.

The demise of syndication can be tied back to the rise of the 24-hour availability of kids' programming on cable married with a local market-place where there are virtually no advertisers who target kids (almost all kid advertisers are national ones). The only exception is that local stations are required by the FCC to air 3 hours of educational programming per week to retain their license (a mandate brought about by the Children's Television Act, in 1990; see Montgomery, chap. 12, this volume). Oftentimes stations will buy kids' programming to fulfill this obligation.

Branding

Branding has become an integral part of the kids' cable world. Overall, branding is important because it influences children to turn on your channel, or at least that is the goal. Better branded networks tend to have a higher hit (show) ratio than unsuccessfully branded networks. Networks have been trying, mostly unsuccessfully, for years to establish brands. As the theory goes, if you have the most attractive brand to your target audience (the coolest network, the best shows, etc), you will be the "top-of-mind" network or the network with the most affinity and this will translate into more viewers, which means higher ratings, which means more dollars. Most networks have been either unsuccessful in establishing a brand identity (does "Must-See Thursday" on NBC make you want to watch NBC any other night?), transferring network brand equity to overall show success (MTV is a cool brand but only a few shows, like *Real World*, get really good ratings), or extending single-show success to overall network success (as in the case of *South Park* on Comedy Central). Kids' cable networks *have* been able to do this successfully and the three main players, Nickelodeon, Cartoon Network, and Disney, all have very defined brands.

Nick, with its anti-parent, "us versus them" message, together with shows like *Rugrats* that blatantly convey that parents were dumber than their babies, has created an exclusive "place" for kids. On Nick, it's "no grown-ups allowed." This remains the consistent (and very successful) thread that has run through Nick's entire image campaigns up to the present.

Unlike Nick's parent versus child branding, the Disney brand has always been about family entertainment. From its earliest days, Disney targeted their theme parks and Disney-labeled theatrical movies to families, and their cable channel is no different. From the Disney cartoons, which *are* targeted to kids, to their live-action shows like *Lizzie McGuire* and *That's So Raven,* to their made-for-TV movies, all have the Disney "family-friendly" hallmark tone.

Cartoon Network had decided not to focus on how to *talk* to an *audience*, but rather how to "live" and "be" on the air. In being true to their internal self-definition, they consistently communicated that "Cartoon Network loves cartoons" (and so do thousands of people of all ages). A key part of the mission statement for Cartoon Network is that this is a channel that is fun, funny, and irreverent. This is what classic cartoons were. If Cartoon Network can be the place for that, everyone who loves cartoons, no matter how old or young, will come to the network.

Alternatively, the kids' programming blocks on broadcast, namely on Saturday mornings, have either lost their brand identity or have been largely unsuccessful in establishing a brand with kids. Fox Kids for years had a strong hold as being the place for kids' action cartoons. *The Power Rangers* and *X-men* got their start there, and the block was a powerhouse for all action-based properties. Meanwhile, *Pokemon* was launched to success on KidsWB!. However, both Fox (which now has a Saturday morning kids' block called FoxBox) and KidsWB! are struggling to define a brand in the minds of their target audience.

This suggests that it takes the persistent presence of a 24-hour-a-day channel (or close to one) with consistently targeted programming and brand messaging, coupled with a target demographic that has fairly narrow tastes, to make practical branding successful. Of course, there is also the matter of a limited competitive set of preferred viewing outlets and of a viewer's limited hobbies and past times that affect viewership.

Cable versus Broadcast—Programming Strategies

Currently, broadcast networks and stations air very few hours of children's programming and Saturday morning is still the key viewing time for kids. On the other hand, there are numerous cable networks airing kids' programming in excess of 100 hours per week: Nickelodeon, Cartoon Network, Disney Channel, ABC Family, Boomerang, Nick Toons, Noggin, and Toon Disney. Table 8.2 shows the amount of monthly hours of kids' programming on kid channels and broadcasters.

Checkerboarding/Stripping. On broadcast today, the networks air kids' programming only on Saturday mornings with WB being the

TABLE 8.2
Number of Hours of Children's Programming—December, 2004

Network/Channel	Hours
Disney Channel	168*
Boomerang	168
Nick Toons	168
Toon Disney	168
Cartoon Network	126
Nick	107
Noggin	84
ABC Family	18
KidsWB!	14
FoxBox	4
ABC	4
NBC	3
CBS	3

Notes. Adapted from www.Nick.com, www.Cartoonnetwork.com, www.ABC.com, www.Noggin.com, www.KidsWB.com, www.4Kids.com, www.NBC.com, www.CBS.com.
*Some of the programming (i.e. Disney Movies) is coded "family" and not necessarily "Children's programming but have been included in this count.

exception. KidsWB! airs programming on Saturday morning and Monday through Friday after school (3:00p.m.—5:00p.m.). Currently only Fox and WB air kids' programming on broadcast that is primarily targeted at getting ratings for advertisers. The other broadcast networks air kids' programming mostly to fulfill their FCC educational requirement. Although due to consolidation within the industry—CBS airs Nick shows, ABC airs Disney shows, and NBC airs Discovery Kids Channel shows—none of the broadcast networks are getting very high ratings because kids do not see a difference between broadcast and cable. Cable continues to be their number one destination, and Saturday mornings are no longer necessarily their preferred time to watch television.

With the onset of 24-hour channels, programmers started programming the way kids (and most people) watch television. Mondays through Fridays, most people tend to have a schedule; they get up at about the same time every day, they go to school or work at the same time, they come home at the same time, and they watch television at about the same time. So, Monday through Friday, most cable channels *strip* programs, which means they air the same program (although not the same episode) at the same time every day across the week.

Many programmers experiment with *checkerboarding* but this tends to be more effective with adults than kids. Checkerboarding is the practice of airing something different every day in the same time slot and is most often done in primetime (Monday–Sunday 8:00 p.m.–11:00 p.m.). This tends to be a way broadcast networks program because of the limited time they have on the air. Most kids' cable networks do not program this way on a regular basis because they have a lot of time in which to air shows. Moreover, kids (and their parents) have said through research and exhibited through ratings that they like watching television as a habit. For kids, checkerboarding is hard because they are just figuring out how to remember things, so remembering what's playing on Mondays, which is different than what's playing on Tuesdays, which is different than what's playing on Thursdays makes watching harder. There are exceptions, of course, and we come to those shortly.

Franchises

Another thing happened with so many hours to program: the creation of *franchises*. In television, a franchise can be defined as a block of like programming (at least in the mind of the programmer) that will appeal to a specific audience. For example, to use NBC's "Must-See Thursday" example again, NBC has trained viewers with the multiyear placement of *Seinfeld* and *Friends* and promos (and packaging) that they will see NBC's best comedies on Thursday nights. NBC has a very successful franchise in "Must-See Thursday".

Franchises are useful for several reasons, especially to cable programmers:

1) *Easier to program.* It is easier to program 24 hours a day and makes sense to viewers if similar shows air together. People (including kids) very often tend to be in the mood to watch a certain kind of show (comedies, action, etc.). For example, Cartoon Network has a very successful franchise called *Toonami* (Saturday 7:00 p.m.–11:00 p.m.). It was created as a destination for viewers who like to watch action adventure cartoons. Although the rest of the network targets girls *and* boys, this block is specifically for boys who like action adventure. Many of these shows are imported cartoons from Japan (also known as anime).

2) *Follows audience viewing patterns.* The majority of American kids leave for school between 8:00 am and 9:00 am Mondays through Fridays. Those who stay home tend to be preschoolers, so it makes sense that the kids' programming on television during

this time is preschool. Most of us grew up with *Mister Rogers' Neighborhood* and *Captain Kangaroo* and, of course, the beloved *Sesame Street*. It was quality programming at a time with no competition and no pressure. In today's viewing world, the environment is so much more competitive, especially in the preschool world. Again, Nickelodeon has made great strides to be at the top of the heap by creating their preschool franchise, Nick Jr. PBS, the first network to have preschool programming, still has quality programming, of course, and still gets high ratings for preschool kids but they have a disadvantage. Because they are public broadcasting, the viewer often finds it difficult to know the times when certain programs air. Also, because the broadcaster is a local affiliate, they may or may not choose to air the program. The power of a national message is undermined when local markets do not follow national messages that tell viewers when the shows air. Meanwhile, in 1994, Nick really focused on Nick Jr, which currently airs Monday through Friday, 9:00 a.m.–2:00 p.m. nationwide (Jenkins, 2004). Parents view this franchise as a safe, educational, consistent "place" for their young kids.

3) *Easier to promote.* It is difficult to promote every show on a 24-hour network. There are too many messages and not enough time. If a programmer can congregate similar shows together and viewers become used to and then look for certain programs to be inside of a franchise, the programmer can very often promote just the franchise (i.e., "Come watch 'Cartoon Cartoon Fridays' on Cartoon Network!!!"). Especially if the franchise is able to incorporate a large number of shows or a certain genre, it makes promoting to those shows much more effective for the network.

4) *More efficient to sell.* One of the struggles of the media age is the one between advertiser and programmer, where the advertiser says "I only want to buy your top show," and the programmer says "Have I got a package [of multiple shows] for you!" At the core, advertiser-supported networks (Disney is not because it does not accept ads), are only able to be profitable if they sell ads in all their shows, not just the highest rated ones. Meanwhile, advertisers want to buy ads in only the highest rated shows because it gives them more bang for their buck. In many ways, franchises are the compromise. Programmers are able to sell a "package" of multiple shows and, if the franchise is successful, it averages a good rating and brings in a sought-after viewer demographic. On the other hand, because the franchise averages a good

rating and brings in the demographic, the advertiser is willing to trust the programmer and will buy the franchise package, or if a programmer has been extremely successful, an advertiser will ask to be a part of the sought-after franchise from the get-go, and the show-specific conversation does not happen at all.

Franchises do not have to have a "title" per se (Toonami, Nick Jr, "Must-See Thursday"); however, titles often make franchises easier to define. Examples of common and other kid franchises are Saturday morning (as a daypart on every kid programmer), Miguzi (Cartoon Network), Snick (Nick), Playhouse Disney (Disney), The N (Noggin), Teen Nick (Nick), and Jetix (ABC Family, Toon Disney).

Seasonality

Another way that cable kid programmers have become more relevant to kids' lives than broadcast is that they are able to program according to the seasonality of those kids' lives. Because broadcast is mostly targeted at adults, it follows the seasonality of adult lives which equals *No Summer!* Because the majority of American kids are out of school for the summer, cable kid programmers can (and do) adjust their programming so it makes sense for the majority of kids who are home. For example, because older kids (aged 6 to 11 years) sleep in, stay up later, and watch television during the day in the summertime, programmers make sure there are more shows available during these times for these kids (see Fig. 8.1).

THE ECONOMICS OF CABLE

The kids' television world has become increasingly competitive. In the 1960s, PBS started offering kids' programming; then in the 1970s, the broadcast networks came along on Saturday mornings; then came Nick, Disney, and Cartoon Network. Over the past 5 years, there are more that 10 cable networks that have either launched as a kids' channel or added kids' programming to their line-up. Much of this expansion is due to the expansion of cable but much of it is also due to mergers of media conglomerates.

Most broadcast television networks are advertising-supported, meaning that they make their money by selling ads. The exception of course is PBS, which is funded by corporate donations, individual donations, and grants. Meanwhile most cable networks have two revenue streams—advertising and subscription fees.

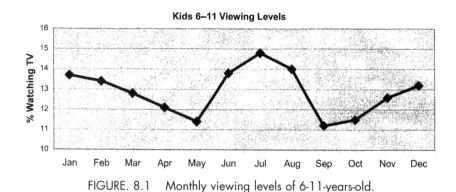

FIGURE. 8.1   Monthly viewing levels of 6-11-years-old.

Adapted from annual aged 6–11 viewing levels (puts), by Nelson Media Research 2003. Copyright © 2003 by Nelson Media Research.

Generally, cable and satellite companies have to pay programmers to be able to carry their programming and they normally pay a certain amount per subscriber. The following is an example of how much programmers are paid per subscriber (see Table 8.3).

Proof of Performance—Ratings

Broadcasters are tied to sweeps, the months when all television viewership is surveyed. This has to do with the fact that among the 210 U.S. local markets or Nielsen-defined Designated Market Areas (DMAs), the majority uses a diary system for measuring viewership. And because it is so costly, Nielsen usually only surveys these markets at certain times of the year; the major sweeps occur in February, May, July, and November. Secondary sweeps are conducted every other month of the year.

Most cable networks do not tie performance to just sweeps. Because cable is difficult to track through diaries, most markets that have the overnight meter system (an electronic device attached to the television set that monitors viewing habits) are able to track viewership every day so they do not limit tracking ratings to just certain months of the year. They tend to look at ratings every month, every week, every day. Sweeps are largely irrelevant to cable networks.

In the cable world, how a network generates most of its revenue most often influences how they program. For example, if a cable network is *not* advertisement-supported (e.g., HBO), they will focus on offering the best programming for their cable affiliates who say they need the highest quality of programming for their viewers. Because most non-advertisement-supported cable networks are in a limited

TABLE 8.3
Estimated Subscriber Fees per Month (2002)

	MTV	VH1	Nickelodeon	Disney
Average Sub Fee/month	$0.21	$0.10	$0.30	$0.68

Note: adapted from Subscriber Reports (Morgan Stanley, 2002)

number of homes (HBO is only in about 30 million homes compared to the 95 million homes that subscribe to cable [Nielsen Media Research, 2004]), they are less concerned about the total number of people seeing their programming and more concerned that the ones who do will continue to subscribe to their service and be vocal about wanting their cable operator to continue to carry the service. This absence of ratings pressure allows these networks to incubate shows for a longer period of time, which often times allows them to accumulate an audience. And, because the goal is not necessarily generating the highest ratings all the time, but having quality programming, they can make do with lower ratings.

For kid networks that are not advertisement-supported (i.e., Nick in the early days and Disney Channel more recently) the main goal is to please the person who is paying for the cable, the parent. To refer to earlier in the chapter, there is no coincidence that Nick focused on getting kid ratings at the same time they went advertisement-supported (B. Cohen personal communication, December 6, 2004).

For those cable networks that generate most of their revenue from advertising, generating the highest ratings, or attracting the most eyes to the channel, is of utmost importance. This is why advertisement-supported networks do everything they can to increase carriage, in other words, get more subscribers. And the only way of getting more subscribers is to be in those cable packages that cost less or be as close to the basic package as they possibly can. It also means that most cable networks; like broadcast networks, cannot or will not allow a program that is not performing to a minimum ratings level to stay on the air for an extended period of time. The cable network just cannot afford to have advertisers complaining about (and not paying for) low ratings.

Fragmentation

Several years ago at a National Association of Television Program Executives (NATPE) conference, John Hendricks, founder and Chairman of the Discovery networks talked about his prediction of the cable world. He said that as the cable world fragments into the digital world of 500 or more channels, he predicted that his established brand (Discovery Channel) was going to have to offer many services. These services, in turn, would have to aggregate their shares into one pot to be able to get the share that his one channel was getting earlier. This prediction has come true and his strategy has been adopted by most companies in the cable space. Children's television is no different. Another extension of that fragmentation (and consolidation of audience share) is the strategic relationships that have been bartered between the cable and broadcast channels. As previously mentioned, most broadcast networks are airing children's programming that can also be currently seen on cable in a noncompeting time period. Those shares are being aggregated to reflect the strength of certain brands or to maximize advertising dollars (see Table 8.4).

CONCLUSION

A child's world is much more integrated today than it ever has been, with television as just part of the experience of living. There is no distinction between broadcast and cable. Every day, something else adds to kids' media experiences, whether it's a new Web site, a new video game, a new platform to see a favorite show, a DVD with a favorite show that is packaged with a toy from that favorite show, etcetera. The lines are blurred between these categories because kids see no lines. It is not about the differences between broadcast and cable anymore; it is about the evolution of television for the next generation. The leaps we, as an industry, have had to make over just the last 5 years make the next 5 years an amazing proposition. The industry is going to have to figure out how to program to a world with the schedule-negating TIVO; a world that is watching actual shows on cell phones and other portable devices; a world where kids have Internet-like interactivity inside television shows—truly a world with no boundaries. That's what the TV world today is for kids, a TV world with no boundaries. The exciting question is: "Where will we go from here?"

ACKNOWLEDGMENTS

I would like to thank Betty Cohen, Tom Ziangas, Daniel Wineman and Alice Cahn for participating in this project with me.

TABLE 8.4
Select Cable Networks and their Kids Network Expansion

Nickelodeon	Cartoon Network	Disney	Discovery	Showtime	PBS	HBO
→	→	→	→	→	→	→
Nick Toons	Toon Disney	Boomerang	Discovery Kids	WAM	PBS Kids	HBO Family
→	→		→			
	ABC Family		TLC			
	→		→			
Noggin	ABC Sat. A.M		NBC Sat. A.M			
→						
GAS (Games and Sports)						
→						
CBS Sat. A.M.						
→						
Nick Games						
→						
Nick 2						

REFERENCES

Dish Network. (2004). *Title*. Retrieved December 2004, from, http://www.dish-network.com

Jenkins, H. (2004). Interview with Geraldine Laybourne. In H. Hendershot (Ed.), *Nickelodeon Nation* (pp. 134–152). New York: New York University Press.

Morgan Stanley. (2002). *Subscriber reports*.

Nielsen Media Research. (2003). *Annual kids aged 6–11 viewing levels (PUTs)*.

Nielsen Media Research. (2004, October). *Universe estimates*.

9

Licensing and Merchandising in Children's Television and Media

Joy Tashjian
Joy Tashjian Marketing Group, LLC.

Jamie Campbell Naidoo
University of Alabama

Talking sponges! Fruit-scented dolls! Bilingual backpacks! Cuddly blue dogs! Sentiment-savvy bears! Take a trip to your local Target or Wal-Mart, and you will be bombarded by a plethora of products featuring Dora the Explorer, SpongeBob SquarePants, Blue's Clues, Bob the Builder, Thomas the Tank Engine, Strawberry Shortcake, Care Bears, and all of their character friends. From toys, clothing, books, and video games to toothbrushes, bubble bath, cereal, and snack foods, store shelves are overflowing with products prominently featuring children's television and cartoon characters. "It's true," Linn acknowledges, "that books, films, and television programs have ... always generated toys ... But it has been only since 1984, when the Federal Trade Commission deregulated children's television, that licensed products have dominated the market so completely" (pp. 72–73). This character invasion is not a coincidence. By June 2004, just 4 years after the character's product launch, SpongeBob SquarePants products had generated more than $3 billion in retail sales (Drug Store News, 2004) of merchandise ranging from bandages, blankets, and bottles to toys, toilet tissue, and t-shirts. As retailers had strategically planned, SpongeBob could be found anywhere and on most any consumer product imaginable. Yet, this SpongeBob surge did not happen instantly. Licensing character merchandise is well orchestrated, carefully prepared and planned years in advance. It is specifically timed to coordinate at least 12 to 18 months after the launch of a children's television series.

When considering the licensing and merchandising process, several questions arise. Are all licenses the same? What are the benefits of licensing to the producers of children's programs? Do all children's television shows have licensed products? How do producers ensure merchandising success? This chapter considers these questions along with the complexities of quality children's programming versus successful children's product retail sales. In addition, using the context of licensed book publishing, we examine the exploitation of licensed characters across all children's media.

ENTERTAINMENT VERSUS BRAND LICENSING

According to Allen , "licensing is a contractual arrangement that allows copyright holders to loan out their intellectual property for another company to use" (p. 479). Currently, the Consumer Product Licensing Industry, an aggregate of sports, fashion, corporate trademarks, and all types of entertainment licensing, represents an industry exceeding $172.7 billion annually (Licensel, 2004). Of this total, $39.3 billion represents the character licensing business, $19.7 billion represents the entertainment licensing business, and $34.2 billion represents brand and trademark licensing Licensel, 2004). In 2004, with profits ranging from $4 to 15 billion, the five leading licensing companies—Disney Consumer Products Worldwide, Warner Bros. Consumer Products, Nickelodeon, & Viacom Consumer Products, Marvel Enterprises, and Sanrio—all had stakes in the children's entertainment industry (Wilensky, 2005). The licenses held by these companies comprise both entertainment/character licenses and brand licenses.

Entertainment and character licensing includes "television-related properties, in addition to merchandising programs based on films, classic characters (Mickey Mouse, Looney Tunes, Peanuts, etc.), and comic book characters" (Raugust, 1996a, p. 10). Similarly, brand licensing includes logos, trademarks, and brand "names" such as Nestlé, The Cartoon Network, Nickelodeon, Coca-Cola, Mary Kate & Ashley, and Sanrio. In theory, brand licensing features products and names, used in our everyday lifestyles, which we *cannot* live without. Essentially, entertainment/character and brand licensing are agreements that allow the purchaser of the license (publisher, toy company, clothing manufacturer, etc.) the right to use a name or image in exchange for a royalty fee—generally 5% to 15% of the wholesale cost of an item (Allen, 2001; Pecora, 1998). However, despite the same goals, Raugust (2000) asserts that, "traditional entertainment licenses still account for most of the bestselling [sic] tie-ins ... [even with] the current popularity of brand licenses" (p. 24).

Historically speaking, entertainment/character licenses have always been successful. A peak in total sales of entertainment/character-licensed merchandise—books, toys, apparel, food products, etcetera—occurred in the late 1970s with Star Wars; the mid-1980s with The Smurfs, Cabbage Patch Kid dolls, Masters of the Universe, and Strawberry Shortcake; and in the early 1990s with The Simpsons, the Ninja Turtles, and New Kids On The Block (Raugust, 1996a). Our current decade is exemplified by tremendous sales of character-licensed merchandise featuring new characters such as Dora the Explorer, Blue's Clues, Barney, SpongeBob, Harry Potter, and Bob the Builder; and nostalgic characters such as Rainbow Brite, Strawberry Shortcake, and the Care Bears.

PRODUCTION COSTS AND LICENSING

After being inundated by the vast array of children's-entertainment licensed products associated with a new children's program, most consumers incorrectly assume that the producer is making millions of dollars. Yet, financing a children's television show is extremely costly. The average animated 22 minute episode with an estimated 26 half-hour episode production schedule has a low end cost of $200,000 per episode and can increase greatly in cost contingent on whether the animation is 2-D or computer graphic imaging. Labor costs, talent costs, celebrity voices, award winning writers, and the program's country of origin can all significantly drive up the cost of an episode.

In the children's television world, children's productions require a minimum of 26 half-hour shows. This provides the broadcaster with enough episodes to minimize reruns, and to have sufficient international appeal to support the merchandising program. Ideally, the more episodes of a program produced, the greater the potential for international merchandising. Unfortunately, if the number of episodes produced is less than 26 half hours, the cost of production increases because economies of scale cannot be leveraged. In other words, the unit cost for producing each episode proportionately decreases when more episodes are produced.

With all these factors increasing the cost of program production, revenues are minimized forcing producers to turn to licenses for ancillary revenue streams. Pecora (1998) quoting Kesler (1987) states, the goals of brand licensing are to "increase name recognition, create a secondary income source, and protect trade names from illegal use" (p. 56). Additionally, entertainment/character licensing provides children's television producers with advertising income and endorsements that often add significant revenue to the production. However, simply owning a license does not ensure increased cash flow. Similar to the dramatic changes in primetime television—with the growth in cable channels, video, and TiVO—children's television has experienced an enormous expansion. Long gone are the days of children's programs appearing on select channels only on Saturday mornings. Now, impressionable child audiences have numerous channels from which to select, making it very difficult for broadcasters to reach critical audience numbers in children's ratings. With this fragmentation of viewership, ratings have splintered, causing the price for television advertising spots to decrease. This directly affects the episode license fee a broadcaster can justify to purchase a new series. With the decline in license fees, producers must secure alternate revenue streams such as merchandising to cover the cost of production. Regrettably, many children's programs have a short life-span and do not remain on the air long enough to see the merchandising windfall that the producers hope to generate. Nonetheless, a successful merchandising and licensing program can be a tremendous asset to a producers' bottomline and thus help fund the costs of producing new episodes.

BROADCASTING AND MERCHANDISING

The most important feature of a good children's television program is the creative aspect. Without interesting characters with diverse personalities, captivating scripts and a premise that has longevity, the consumer product value of the program will never survive. Therefore, first and foremost, a producer must focus on creating the best children's program possible and then evaluate merchandising opportunities. Characters that endure over time and provide years of enjoyment usually end up generating meaningful merchandising revenue.

However, a highly rated successful television show and licensed product does not necessarily equal merchandising success. A strategically orchestrated product release is essential but there are many variables influencing this success. For instance, although broadcasting and merchandising are both focused on numbers, they each consider other factors that do not often coincide. Broadcasters and retailers do not share the same timelines or business concerns. Whereas broadcasters are driven by viewership, ratings, and advertising dollars, retailers are concerned about product sell-through. Retailers will examine unit sales on licensed properties; if these sales are falling weekly, they will pull the product from the shelves and reduce the price of the merchandise for immediate sale.

Further, although merchandising is important to all parties, the broadcaster is most concerned about quality and uniqueness. Broadcasters are extremely dedicated to building their network, creating a brand, and protecting the integrity of their viewership. They have a challenging job that requires tremendous balance between acquiring the best shows and an advantageous license fee and maintaining high ratings. At the same time, a broadcaster must build a following for ever-green programs.

Another factor influencing merchandising success is the potential for licensed product. Many children's programs currently on the air do not have any merchandise in store. This is largely attributable to the fact that they do not lend themselves to potential children's products, or the licensing phase has ended even though the show remains on the air. For example, *Fairly Odd Parents* on Nickelodeon is one of the highest rated shows in children's television, but has had limited success with licensed product sales.

Also, with the number of hours programmed for kids today, many animated series are on the air, but they are not in the best timeslots, nor are their ratings meaningful enough to generate licensing agreements. They are quality programs that kids watch, but they do not necessarily translate to product or consumables. The converse is also true. There are many well-recognized licensed children's characters on products at retail that do not have current television series. Instead, these characters are tied into brands, toys, video games, DVDs, books, excetra. Such examples are the globally recognized Mickey Mouse, Barbie, Cabbage Patch Kids, GI Joe, and Bratz.

DEMOGRAPHIC AUDIENCE

So what does this all mean? As a producer you have successfully sold your show to a top children's broadcaster and you need to generate merchandising income—what do you do? Licensing children's products based on a television series requires a blueprint and 5-year business plan at minimum. This plan must include careful analysis of your demographic target audience. Is the television series targeted to preschoolers, boys, girls, or 'tweens? Certainly, your timeslot and key characters all provide indicators as to your core consumer. A broadcaster may view the demographics far more broadly than a retailer. Retail, in the children's business, is somewhat gender-specific. Generally, a retail buyer is defined by category and gender, that is girls, small doll buyer; boys, action figure buyer; excetra. Coincidentally, creating a television series that appeals to both boys and girls is acceptable because they are both viewers, but from a product standpoint, generally boys and girls do not purchase the same products in toy, interactive, and apparel categories.

Thus, for merchandising success it is crucial to outline what products are appropriate for the age group and gender. Children are sensitive to products that are not true to their favorite character. It is now an expectation of these young consumers that products are creative and have play value. The latter is essential considering that products today are far more sophisticated than they were years ago. Interestingly, Raugust (2004), quoting Ben Ferguson of Bendon Publishing International, which published the Brainy Baby series, notes parents and grandparents of very young children will purchase licensed products if they are tied to an educational program. "It's more about content than popularity. Kids aren't going to ask for it. But parents and grandparents will pick education over entertainment every time" (p. 19). In light of this difference between child and adult consumer expectations, products must have a fair balance between play and educational value.

PRODUCT LAUNCH TIMELINE

In today's highly cluttered children's programming environment, there are many children's programs competing for the young viewer's attention. For instance, in 1999, children—with access to both broadcast television and cable stations—had 29 different child-oriented channels from which to choose 1,324 shows (279 unique titles; Woodard, 1999). Certainly, the number of children's programs available today is quite comparable. Considering this vast number of children's programs, producers must consequently find innovative outlets for promoting their licensed characters. Television-based character merchandise at toy stores, book stores, grocery stores, video stores and quick service restaurants provide the property with additional visibility at alternate channels of retail. This strategically placed product encourages children to remain loyal to their favorite television programs by purchasing merchandise featuring their favorite television characters.

However, most licensors today agree that releasing massive amounts of children's product on a new series is very dangerous. It takes time for children to establish a viewing commitment with a new series and even longer to consent to purchase character merchandise from that program. Currently, there are numerous characters vying for the young consumer's attention. An upsurge in reintroducing nostalgic characters has created longevity problems for characters from new children's series. Rainbow Brite and Teenage Mutant Ninja Turtles are all taking up the precious shelf space of would-be rising characters. Tashjian, quoted in Jenkins (2005), comments, "Because shelf space is jammed due to so many characters being launched, retailers will not give up the real estate until the new character has a proven track record" (p. 28). Also, children usually have a specified dollar amount to spend; so even though they may watch several programs, they can only commit to product from a few of these programs. More and more, children's licensing programs are following the series launch by anywhere from 6 months to 18 months after initial airdate with the optimism that the characters will be established by then.

Retailers and licensing executives have found that flooding the retail shelves prematurely prior to establishing a strong viewing audience will result in slow product sales forcing the retailers to reduce the prices and place the product on clearance. This can adversely affect the show in numerous ways. The retailer will discontinue carrying the merchandise, and the consumer may perceive the marked down product as a statement that the show is not performing. In addition, there may be critical damage to both the program and the licensed product if a time-line is not adhered to. Yet, Woolf, quoted in Jenkins (2005), notes, "Globally, we are seeing shorter windows, and quicker turnarounds, so properties have much less time in which to establish themselves" (p. 30). As a result, cross marketing is utilized to bolster character recognition among the targeted demographic audiences.

CROSS MARKETING AND CROSS MEDIA EXPOSURE

Uniquely positioning and marketing a new children's series has become essential. Television programming in itself is not sufficient enough to break away and capture kids; it is thus critical to explore many types of cross-marketing exposure that are consistent with the demographics. Some examples of promotions are online, in-store and cross-media promotions. As Raugust points out, individual licensed characters are "increasingly exploited across all media—television, film, video games, home video, books, magazines, and so on—in order to lengthen their life spans ... Thus, the line between a television property versus a film property versus a video-game property, and so forth, is increasingly fuzzy" (p. 34).

Examining and implementing alternate methods of exposure to support programming maximizes the property's importance and helps to secure retail and broadcast continued interest. There are virtually innumerable avenues to consider—food, apparel, toys, books, video games, household products, stationary, and school supplies, to name a few. Each property must be examined in order to make a compelling statement to the consumer. A perfect example of the power of cross marketing to increase exposure to support product success is Disney's *W.I.T.C.H.*. "Created after two years of sociocultural studies on 'tween girls," *W.I.T.C.H.* was "launched as a comic magazine in Italy in 2001" and as a book series in the United States in 2004 (Grala, 2005b, pp. 17–18). Within the first year, Disney's creation had sold more than 6 million copies in Europe, and more than 1 million copies in the United States. In 2003, after only a few weeks on European shelves, *W.I.T.C.H.* licensed products (toys, stationary, and apparel) experienced a 70% sell-through. By the end of 2004, magazine sales had reached $15 million, making *W.I.T.C.H.* the "fourth largest magazine in terms of distribution and the largest children's comic book" (Grala, 2005b, pp. 18, 20). In January 2005, *W.I.T.C.H.* was launched in the United States as a half-hour animated series on ABC with the potential for numerous licensed products to hit shelves in 2006. According to Mooney, the chairman of Disney Consumer Products Worldwide:

> Once the show gets on-air and establishes firm ratings, the licensing community will see the strength of the ratings and the property, and get on board. ... The beautiful thing about children's cable television in the UnitedStates is its widespread reach. Having a successful TV show is our marketing strategy and our way of supporting W.I.T.C.H.'s presence at retail. (Grala, 2005b, p. 20)

As *W.I.T.C.H.*'s cross-marketing success suggests, children's licensed book publishing provides a natural frame for examining the exploitation of licensed characters across all media types to reap lucrative financial rewards. The remainder of the chapter provides a brief history of licensed children's books and examines the cross-media extensions of this form of children's media.

LICENSING AND CHILDREN'S BOOK PUBLISHING

"The importance of licensing within the publishing industry rises and falls periodically along with the number of licensed titles—as well as retailers' and consumers' interest in them" (Raugust, 2004c, p. 18). Increased sales of products featuring licensed characters or brands significantly influence the sales of books featuring the same characters and brands. For instance, if Barbie videos, dolls, clothing, and games experience an influx in sales, then books featuring Barbie will also exemplify financial success. Prompted by sales of Barbie product, the increased saliency of the Barbie brand encourages consumers to seek out additional products—including books—featuring the doll.

According to Masters (1988a), "Tie-ins with popular licensed charac-ters ... are helping to reposition children's books as part of the broader entertainment industry, a development that's driving sales gains at retail" (p. 125). Roback (1999) observed that in 1998, more than 60% of the top children's hardcover frontlist books (selling 300,000 or more copies) featured licensed characters. Blue's Clues was "top dog" on the list filling the first two slots. That same year, more than 90% of the top children's paperback frontlist books (selling 300,000 or more copies) featured licensed characters as well. The most recent sales of children's books with licensed characters are quite comparable, maintaining a large percentage of both frontlist paper- and hardback book sales. According to Roback (2004), "movie tie-ins dominated the paperback frontlist [in 2003]" (p. 593) with more than 66% of the bestselling children's paperback books (selling 500,000 or more copies) featuring licensed characters or relating to children's movies. In fact, children's books that tie into licensed characters or brands are so popular that *Publisher's Weekly*, the magazine responsible for the sales statistics in publishing, added a tie-in category to their Children's Bestseller list in August 1998. That same year, Rick Richter, president and publisher of Simon & Schuster's children's books department, noted, "children's books are becoming an entertainment business" (Masters, 1988b, p. 39). A few years later, Hade (2001) echoed Richter's sentiments and asserted that the Big Media (Viacom, News Corporation, Pearson Ltd., Bertelsmann, Von Holtzbrink, Reed Elseveir, and Scholastic) own children's book publishing and "are looking for stories that transcend the medium of the book and become a recognizable brand that can be licensed to and integrated across a wide range of products" (p. 20).

Certainly, the same can be said of children's books today. Holt (2004) indicates that, "though they're hardly new, two interrelated trends are on the upswing [in children's publishing]—an emphasis on licensed charac-ters and the power of marketing for other media properties to move books" (p. 33). She explains that movie and television promotions are lucrative to the book industry, and quotes Susan Katz, president and pub-lisher of HarperCollins Children's Books, "what kids want is what they see—either it's marketed to them on TV or it's marketed to them in the movies" (p. 33). Presently, there are numerous books with licensed char-acters slotted for release in Summer/Fall, 2005 and Winter, 2006. Some of these licenses include the ATOMIC BETTY, Marvel Comics, Transformers, My Little Pony, Candy Land, and Build-A-Bear Workshop (Grala, 2005a). Publications International is a prime example of the current revenue asso-ciated with creating books that feature licensed characters. The com-pany's "Story Reader" books—which retail from $10 to $30 and feature licensed characters and brands such as Scooby Doo, Dora the Explorer,

My Little Pony, Barbie, and Barney—have sold more than 7.5 million copies since their creation in 2003 (Desjardins, 2005).

Although licensed tie-in books are a very profitable business venture, they also serve other important purposes for the owners of the license. Licensed tie-in books "generate awareness with the target audience; provide a means to extend story lines, backstory, environments, and character development beyond the core entertainment property; and enhance the brand's image, in some cases, by strengthening its association with literacy and education" (Raugust, 2004a, p. 105). As a result, it is very important to acquire the right license.

Acquiring Licenses

"The link between the entertainment industry and children's books is growing stronger, as publishers look for ways beyond traditional licensing agreements to increase exposure for their own brands and tap into Hollywood's resources" (Raugust, 1998a, p. 26). In fact, many publishers have begun to seek out licenses with entertainment companies rather than waiting to be approached by the licensing executives. In 1998, Scholastic and Penguin Putnam announced long-term deals with studios that guaranteed them first choice of rights to licensed productions. Scholastic's alliance with Warner Bros. provided the publishing company access to children's licensed properties to be exploited in a variety of book formats (Raugust, 1998a, p. 26). Likewise, two publishers have launched imprints devoted to licensed titles: S&S's Simon Spotlight, started in July 1997, and HarperActive started in 1997 with titles debuting March, 1998 (Lodge, 1998; Raugust, 1998a). According to Steven Chudney, director of product development and licensing for S&S Children's Publishing, about "60% of Simon Spotlight's list is based on licenses from the Viacom family, with Nickelodeon accounting for the majority" (Raugust, 1998a, p. 26). HarperActive's books are based on licenses from Fox's Anastasia and Saban Entertainment productions. Interestingly, HarperActive merged with HarperEntertainment just a few years later, combining children and adult content in order to make licensing agreements simpler. Further, HarperCollins has another children's imprint partially devoted to licensed characters. According to the publisher's Web site, HarperFestival is "home to books, novelties, and merchandise for ... children 0–6 ... Festival boasts a wide range of novelty and holiday titles as well as character-based programs such as *Biscuit*, *Little Critter* and the *Berenstain Bears*" (Harper Collins, 2004, p. 1).

Another publisher with licensed imprints is Random House. In 2001, Random House launched its Disney Books for Young Readers, "an imprint featuring books based on Disney live-action and feature films and classic characters such as Mickey Mouse and Cinderella" (Johnson, 2003, p. 36). Also, Johnston (2003) notes that the publisher acquired its chief competitor, Golden Books, in 2001 along with a substantial list of licensed characters including Nickelodeon characters, Bob the Builder, Precious Moments, and Barbie. As a result, in 2003, 40% of Random House/Golden Book Group's titles were licensed. However, Kate Klimo, vice president and publisher for Random House/Golden Books Young Readers Group, reflects:

> At Random House, we never let licenses take over our program. ... They were a key component, but we were always careful to build our backlist— the bread and butter. The licenses are the candy. You can't make money off the candy unless you have the bread and butter to tide you over when licensing is in its down years. (Johnson, 2003, p. 36)

Once publishers have acquired licenses, they are ready to produce tie-ins to all types of media including television, movies, comic books, and video games. The following section describes various types of licensed books for children, and provides a brief historical look at each tie-in's conception.

TYPES OF LICENSED TIE-IN BOOKS FOR CHILDREN

Current tie-in books for children contain licensed characters from a variety of media formats: comic strips/books, movie/television, toys, greeting cards, video games, "recycled" book-to-screen programs, and product brands. However, the first licensed characters originated from children's radio programs and pre-television motion pictures.

Radio/Motion Picture (Pre-Television) Tie-Ins

The very first media tie-in title for children featuring a licensed character was published more than 80 years ago, and was a direct tie-in to cinema motion pictures. In 1919, Felix the Cat began his silent career in animated shorts entitled *Feline Follies*, and by 1923 appeared in his own bound annual (Hunt, 1995; Lowery, 2004). Felix's debut was quickly shadowed in 1930 by the appearance of Mickey Mouse in Disney's *Mickey Mouse Annual*.

In 1932, Whitman Publishing Company published the first Big Little Book, *The Adventures of Dick Tracy*, based on the 1931 comic strip that later became a radio show in 1935 (Lowery, 2004). The material for Whitman's Big Little Book series was "drawn mostly from radio, comic, strips, and motion pictures" (Lowery, 2004, p. 3). The character Betty

Boop, created in 1930 by Grim Natwick, made her appearance in the Big Little Book series in the book *Betty Boop in Snow White* (1934), an adaptation from the 1933 Max Fleisher-Paramount Studios' Talkartoon of the same title (Lowery, 2004; Markstein, 2004). Other popular characters in the Big Little Book series included Bugs Bunny, Mickey Mouse, Donald Duck, Popeye, Buck Rodgers, Mighty Mouse, and The Lone Ranger.

Comic Strip Tie-Ins

Also around this same time period, numerous books were tie-ins from various comic strips. Little Orphan Annie, a comic strip character created in 1924 by Harold Gray, first emerged into radio programs in 1930 and into her own book in 1933 (Lowery, 2004). The book, *Little Orphan Annie*, coincidentally was one of the Whitman's Big Little Books previously mentioned. Just a few years after the appearance of Little Orphan Annie, Popeye debuted on July 17, 1929 in Elzie Segar's comic strip *Thimple Theatre*. In 1933, he appeared in a cartoon with Betty Boop, and in the early 1930s, he unsuccessfully aired in radio shows (Markstein, 2004). In 1936, Popeye finally appeared in his first book, *Popeye Sees The Sea*.

On February 23, 1935, Little Lulu—created by Marjorie Buell—made her first appearance in the *Saturday Evening Post* as a comic strip character, and was depicted in children's books as early as 1936 (Buell, 1992). Two of the first Little Lulu books emerging in 1936 were *Little Lulu*, published by Rand McNally, and *Laughs With Little Lulu*, published by David McKay Company. In 1938, two teenagers, Jerry Siegel and Joe Shuster, created Superman for *Action Comics* (Hunt et al., 1995). Since his inception, Superman has found his way into bound comics, cartoons, and tie-in books. Other more recent licensed characters that originated from comics, made it to television, and later appeared in children's books, include: *The Smurfs*, created in 1958 by Belgian cartoonist Peyo; *Garfield*, created in 1978 by Jim Davis; and *Teenage Mutant Ninja Turtles*, created in 1984 by Kevin Eastman and Peter Laird (Markstein, 2004).

Movie/Television Tie-Ins

Perhaps the most popular type of tie-ins for children's books is the category of movie/television tie-ins. Yet Larson (1995) alleges that film novelizations or movie tie-ins are the most "misunderstood species of contemporary popular literature" (p. 3). He describes three distinct kinds of movie tie-ins. The first is a reissue of a previous novel, which was adapted into a film, and is repackaged with a cover from the movie. In this kind of tie-in, no change takes place in the original content of the book. The second kind of movie tie-in is a novelization of a film or television screenplay in which the screenplay is specifically adapted for the book. The final kind of movie tie-in, and the most popular, is an original novel based on the existing characters of movie or TV series. This type of movie tie-in can evolve into a totally different creation than the original source. In some rare instances, the third type of movie tie-in has outlived the originally syndicated movie or TV series from whence it was adapted. Raugust (1988b) mentions the television series *Full House* as a case in point. The last original show of the series was aired in early 1997 with reruns continuing on several television stations today; yet, the books are still popular. It seems that reruns of the series are creating demand for tie-in books. The first tie-in to *Full House* was published in 1993 and the most recent tie-in was published March 2004.

According to Raugust (1996a) "merchandise licensing is not a new phenomenon in the television industry. *Howdy Doody* in the 1950s, *Star Trek* in the 1960s, and *The Six-Million Dollar Man* in the 1970s are just a few of the television-based properties" responsible for many consumer products including children's books (p. 11). In fact, many publishers in the 1950s and 1960s published books with characters that tied into movies, television shows, and cartoons. Some of the most notable publishers were Golden Book, Wonder Books, Jolly Books, Treasure Books, Bonnie Books, and Elf Books (Jones, 1987). However, the most influential of these publishers was Golden Book, an imprint of Western Publishing Company. Duke (1979) maintains that, for many years, Western Publishing was one of the primary publishers of licensed books for children. The company's affiliation with Disney, since its first contract of a Big Little Book of Mickey Mouse in 1933, was very successful with nearly 2 billion Disney items produced by 1979. In September 1944, Western Publishing Company's Golden Book imprint published the first Disney Studios tie-ins: *Walt Disney's Through the Picture Frame,* an Disney adaptation of the Hans Christian Andersen story *Ole Lukoi,* and *The Cold-Blooded Penguin,* an adaptation of Disney's "The Three Caballeros" (Jones, 1987). Other TV/movie tie-ins published by Golden Book throughout the years have integrated characters from various children's programs including *Lassie, Captain Kangaroo, Bozo, Sesame Street, Benji,* and *Bugs Bunny.* Another imprint of Western Publishing, Whitman was equally involved in printing TV tie-ins. As Peer (1997) mentions, Western Publishing's Whitman imprint expanded their standard-size line of children's hardbacks to include TV tie-ins in the early 1950s. Around the same time period, Western Publishing Company based many of its tie-in children's storybooks on the cartoons of William Hanna and Joe Barbera. As Raugust (1996a) affirms, "many of the major Hanna-Barbera characters attracted significant licensing activity in the 1960s and 1970s, including Ruff and Reddy, the Flintstones, the Jetsons, Huckleberry

Hound, Quick Draw McGraw, Scooby Doo, Wacky Races, Magilla Gorilla, and Peter Potamus" (p. 95).

Scholastic, Inc. is another example of a successful children's publisher of movie/TV tie-ins. In 1946, the company began with the formation of the Teen Age Book Club by Pocket Books, and in 1950, bought out Pocket Books, thus becoming one of the largest producers of paperback books for children (Duke, 1979). By the late 1970s, Schloastic was distributing "80 million paperbacks a year to 80% of U.S. elementary schools and 50% of the high schools" (Duke, 1979, p. 224). More than 50% of the books sold in its book fairs and book clubs contain licensed characters from movies, televisions, and cartoons. Some of Scholastic's tie-ins have included characters from *The Karate Kid*; *Star Wars*; Disney's *Herbie, The Love Bug*; and *The Addams Family*. More recent tie-ins to television programs and movies are *Fear Factor, SpongeBob SquarePants, Kimpossible, Scooby Doo, Dora the Explorer, Rubbadubbers*, and *Rugrats*.

Many other publishers have become attracted to the entertainment market of licensed characters. Unfortunately, there is not enough space to include information about all of them. Certainly, Western Publishing and Scholastic are good representative examples of publishers of TV/movie tie-in books for children.

Toy Tie-Ins

Children's books tied into toys are probably the second most popular category of licensed tie-in books for children. At the same time, they are probably the hardest category to determine the origin of the licensed characters. Many tie-in books relate to a toy that originated as something else but did not reach popularity until it was produced as a toy. Examples of the origin-blurring problem abound. For instance, it appeared that the tie-in books with the Care Bears originated from the toy. Yet, closer examination confirmed that the Care Bears were the prodigy of the greeting card company American Greetings (Raugust, 1996a).

Perhaps the oldest toy to have tie-in books is the Raggedy Ann doll. According to Hall (2001), Raggedy Ann was created and patented in 1915 by Johnny Gruelle. The doll appeared in her first book *Raggedy Ann Stories* in 1918 and her brother's book, *Raggedy Andy Stories* was published in 1920. Tie-in books to Raggedy Ann and Andy were very popular in the 1960s and 1970s. Her popularity waned in the 1980s but regained strength in the late 1990s with Simon & Schuster's adaptations for young children by Jan Palmer.

Through the 1940s to the late 1960s, most of the tie-in books for children were based on cartoon and television series. Consequently, there are few examples of toy tie-in books during this time period. Mattel's

Liddle Kiddles, however, would be an example of a popular toy in the 1960s with numerous tie-in books. In 1979, Mattel, Inc., acquired Western Publishing as a subsidiary through a $120 million transaction (McCormick, 1981). Resulting from this contract would be numerous tie-in books to popular toys such as Barbie and Hot Wheels. A classic example of the generated rewards is Mattel's He-Man and Masters of the Universe. The toy line, as indicated by Raugust (2003), "premiered in 1982, followed by a television series the next year. From 1982 to 1991, the brand generated more than $2 billion at retail in toy and licensed merchandise sales [which included books published by Western]" (p. 32). At this same time during the early 1980s, Western received comparable rewards from licensing with 4Kids Entertainment for Coleco's Cabbage Patch Kid dolls.

Similarly, Random House joined Western Publishing in developing titles based on toys. Random House had a licensing contract with Hasbro that enabled the publisher to issue tie-in books based on the My Little Pony toys. Ballantine and Marvel Books also had a contract with Hasbro in the 1980s that gave them rights to publish tie-ins to the Transformers. During the 1990s, Dutton Children's Books licensed the Playskool line of toys from Hasbro and published tie-in books to Mr. Potato Head, Easy-Bake Oven, and Playdoh (Raugust, 1996b). Likewise, Raugust (1996b) states that Modern Publishing licensed Fisher Price's toy line and had tie-in children's books with toys such as Little People. As mentioned earlier, many of the toys from the 1980s are currently being reintroduced, and naturally so are books that tie-in with them. These "relaunched" toys include My Little Pony, He-Man and the Masters of the Universe, Cabbage Patch Kids, and Transformers. Interestingly, Random House has decided not to carry the license for these toys, and instead, is allowing HarperCollins, Running Press Kids, Reader's Digest, and Bendon access to the nostalgic characters.

Another interesting toy tie-in that has proved very profitable is Pleasant Company's American Girl books. These books are included in this section because sales and popularity of the dolls have spurred the mass interest in the American Girl books. In actuality, both American Girl dolls and books were simultaneously released in 1986 by Pleasant T. Rowland, the founder of Pleasant Company (Acosta-Alzuru & Kreshel, 2002). Initially, both products were only offered via mail-order catalog, but surprising popularity brought a Web site and retail stores in the late 1990s. By 2004, more than 100 million American Girl books had been sold along with more than 10 million American Girl dolls (American Girl, 2004). In 2004, American Girl produced a television movie on the Warner Brother's Television Network. The movie, entitled *Samantha: An American Girl Holiday,* was broadcasted on November 23, 2004, and of course had numerous tie-ins including new spin-off books and dolls (Jevens, 2004).

Greeting card Tie-Ins

Another type of media that capitalized on the success of character licensing was the greeting card industry. In 1967, the character Holly Hobbie was created; by 1977, she was one of the most sought-after licensed characters in the world (Carlton, Cards, 2003). In the early 1980s, Those Kids From Cleveland, the licensing group for American Greetings, created several characters that they licensed as both pro-grams and merchandise, including tie-in books for children (Pecora, 1998). Some of these characters were Care Bears, Strawberry Shortcake, Popples, The Get Along Gang, and Herself the Elf. Care Bears and Strawberry Shortcake were by far the most successful characters created by American Greetings. As noted by Raugust (2003), "con-sumers purchased more that $1.5 billion worth of merchandise from licenses [for Care Bears], including Random House and Parker Bros. Publishing" (p. 32). Comparatively, Strawberry Shortcake generated $1.2 billion in sales of licensed products, including books, in just 5 years (Raugust, 2003). Both Care Bears and Strawberry Shortcake were reli-censed with books and other merchandise that hit the shelves in early 2003 followed by an added surge of licensed products in 2004.

An additional greeting card company took advantage of American Greetings' success, and developed its own licensed character. Markstein (2004) asserts that in 1983, Rainbow Brite made her debut on Hallmark's greeting cards. That same year, as a result of Hallmark's only cross-media phenomenon, Rainbow Brite and her friends appeared in toys by Mattel and in her own movie. By 1985, DC Comics adapted one of her movies, *Rainbow Brite & the Star Stealer*, into a comic book of the same title. Rainbow Brite later became a weekly cartoon series in 1986, and was followed by a plethora of licensed merchandise. According to Raugust (2003), "retail sales of [Rainbow Brite] dolls and other [tie-in] products topped $1 billion in the 1980s" (p. 32).

Video/Computer Game Tie-Ins

One of the fastest growing trends in tie-in publishing for children is the extension of video and computer games into book formats. Raugust (1999) maintains:

> While interactive properties, particularly video games, have made a splash in licensing over the years, most have been supported by popular television series that boosted awareness and drove sales of books and other licensed goods. In contrast, many recent interactive licenses are being merchandised on the strength of the software alone. (p. 26)

Publishers find video and computer game properties attractive because they appeal to a very hard demographic to reach—teenage boys. Random House's theory for obtaining licenses to attract teen males is very simple, "that guy in the dorm room down the hall may not be buying William Styron now, but if we get him used to reading for pleasure, he'll be a lot more likely to buy that kind of book 10 years from now" (Zeitchik, 2003, p. 27). However, to attract the coveted male audience, publishers have to be selective in how they construct video and computer tie-ins. The Ballantine imprint of Del Rey, according to Zeitchik (2003), works closely with software developers to locate and develop a backstory that will complement the game. "It's a tricky goal—incorporate the game too much, and gamers will grow impatient (why read about characters when you can shoot them?); but stray too far, and gamers will wonder why they need to read a book about it" (Zeitchik, 2003, p. 27). Nancy Cushing-Jones, president of Universal Studios Publishing Rights and executive Vice President of Universal Studios Consumer Products, agrees that creating game tie-ins can be an editorial challenge. She remarks that the game player and the reader of a tie-in novel may not be the same person. Consequently, Cushing-Jones, as noted by Raugust (1999), affirms, "you need to create the same kind of excitement in the book world that exists in the game world" (p. 26.) If publishers successfully create the appropriate game tie-in book, then the rewards can be overwhelming. Maas (2003) comments that a good title can sell over a million copies. One of the most profitable game tie-in novels created is *Halo: The Fall of Reach*, published in 2001 by Del Rey, and selling more than 150,000 copies by the beginning of 2003. Another equally successful title, *Resident Evil* was published in 1998, and exhibited continuous gains in sales through 2003 (Maas, 2003). Pokémon is also an example of a successful game tie-in with a long "shelf life." The video game originated in the mid-1990s, and still enjoys success in 2005. Other game tie-ins with licensed characters include Pac-Man, Ms. Pac-Man, and Q-Bert which all originated as video games in the 1980s, and supported tie-in storybooks throughout the early 1980s.

Whereas most all video and computer game tie-ins are directed at boys, there was a failed attempt to establish games for girls with Brenda Laurel's *Purple Moon*, which was founded and ended in the late 1990s. Purple moon was "part of a movement toward 'pink games'— titles and activities aimed specifically at young girls and women" (Rafan, 2003, p. 2). In 1999, Scholastic launched a book series based on Purple Moon's character Rockett Mavado. The computer game tie-in series was entitled *Rockett's World* (Raugust, 1999). Unfortunately, both the books and the game were unsuccessful.

"Recycled" Tie-Ins

The category of "recycled" tie-ins reflects children's books that were adapted into movies or television series and resulted in tie-in books utilizing the licensed characters that were originally in the book. This type of media tie-in actually includes most of the licensed characters currently available in children's television programs. Franklin was created in 1986 by author Paulette Bourgeois, and appeared in his animated series in 1997. Shrek starred in his own movie in 2001, but was originally a book character created by Willam Steig in 1986. Arthur was introduced in 1976 as a book character created by Marc Brown, and emerged on screen in 1997 as a cartoon character on the PBS television series *Arthur*. Ludwig Bemelmans created Madeline in 1939, and the character starred in her own movie in 1998. Clifford's PBS series started in 2000, but Norman Bridwell developed him in 1961. The list of these "recycled" characters continues with many other licensed figures including The Cat in the Hat, Berenstain Bears, Bozo The Clown, Winnie-the-Pooh, Corduroy Bear, James and the Giant Peach, Stuart Little, Harry Potter, and Rolie Polie Olie. A recent example of a "recycled" character is Curious George. Originally appearing in 1941 as a book character created by H. A. and Margaret Rey, Curious George has appeared in numerous animated children's programs over the years and will appear in his own movie in 2006. PBS is scheduled to run an animated series of George's adventures after the release of the movie. Numerous book tie-ins and other licensed merchandise featuring Curious George are sure to follow (Raugust, 2005).

The popularity of "recycled" characters has several roots. First, by using a book character, entertainment producers start out with a fully developed character instead of having to create one from scratch. Second, librarians—large purchasers and promoters of children's literature—are more accepting of these "recycled" friends because the characters originate from quality literature. Likewise, publishers are drawn to this type of licensed book because it attracts reluctant readers and affords the publishers an opportunity to entice children back to the original books. Also, parents believe that if their children watch the cartoon, then perhaps they will also read the book. Most importantly, children like the "recycled characters" because they are easily accessible in book and animated formats, becoming familiar to the children and assuming the role as friends.

Lifestyle Brand Tie-Ins

Although all of the aforementioned types of tie-in books feature entertainment licensing, children's publishers are increasingly turning to brands and lifestyles licensing. Raugust (2000) observes that "opinions differ on whether corporate brands should have a place in children's publishing, but there is no doubt that brand licensors and publishers are teaming more often for licensed children's books" (p. 24).

Perhaps one of the earliest media tie-in books for children, based on a "lifestyle" or everyday product, is the storybook published in 1926 by Bon Ami. Pecora (1998) quotes Davey who reminisces, "the story of *The Chick That Never Grew Up* featured the Princess Bon Ami and was dedicated to 'the millions of children whose mothers find Bon Ami a good friend'"(p. 24). In 1932, Wonder Bread also created a tie-in children's book entitled *Happy Wonder Sandwich Book* (Pecora, 1998). Further, in 1951 Little Golden Book's *Dr. Dan, the Bandage Man*–written by Gaspard with illustrations by Malvern–successfully tied into Johnson & Johnson's Band-Aids . According to Jones (1987):

> The publisher reached an agreement with Johnson & Johnson, makers of Band-Aids, in which … eighteen million Band-Aids would be … given away with books sold. The first printing of 1,600,000 was the largest first edition of a Little Golden Book ever produced at this time. … Johnson & Johnson advertised Dr. Dan on their television programs and purchased 400,000 copies to be sold in drugstores. The book was issued … with 'what the publishers believe to be unquestionably the most extensive advertising and promotional campaign ever staged for a low-priced book.' (1987, xvi)

Jones (1987) also mentions that Simon & Schuster soon surpassed this promotion with their largest promotional campaign ever. On May 1, 1954, *Little LuLu and Her Magic Tricks* was released with more than 2 million copies in print. The book contained a packet of Kleenex tissues along with instructions on how to make a doll, a flower, and a bunny. As part of the promotion, a demonstration of tricks from the book was presented on the "Arthur Godfrey Show," reaching an estimated 7 million families, and full-page ads ran in several magazines including *Life*, *Woman's Day*, and *Family Circle*. Likewise, Little Golden produced 400,000 copies of a promotional record to accompany the book.

In the past 10 years, there has been a surge of obvious tie-ins to branded products. Many of the books, published by HarperCollins and Simon & Schuster, are marketed as educational books intended to strengthen children's math skills. Some of these books have included *The M&M's Brand Chocolate Candies Counting Book, Sun-Maid Raisin Play Book,* and *The Cheerios Counting Book.* In spring 2004, Simon & Schuster's Little Simon imprint released *Crayola Rainbow Colors.* Cindy Alvarez, vice-president and editorial director at Little Simon, indicates that the book teaches children about colors and is "as close to the brand as you can possibly get without being crayons" (Raugust, 2004b, p. 29).

One final type of brand-licensed books for children involves entertainment artists writing books for children. Essentially, the name of the artist or song becomes the brand to entice children into reading the book. The most common of these tie-ins are no more than illustrated versions of the artist's songs. Dolly Parton's *Coat of Many Colors*, Woody Guthrie's *This Land is Your Land*, and Steve Seskin's *Don't Laugh at Me* are but a few examples of this genre. Another form of these branded-artist tie-in books exists, and is increasing in popularity. This form simply involves entertainment artists writing original stories for children. Again, these books sell because of the brand name of the artist. Two recent books of this form, published in 2003, are Madonna's *Mr. Peabody's Apples* and Vince Gill's *The Emperor's New Clothes: A Country Story*. That same year, Madonna's *The English Roses* and *Mr. Peabody's Apples* sold more than 1 million copies, grossing over $14 million in sales (Roback, 2004).

Interestingly, one of the first artists to have tie-in books was Ross Bagdasarian. In 1958, Bagdasarian (under the name David Seville) created Alvin & The Chipmunks, whose first song, "The Chipmunk Song," was a huge success (Markstein, 2004). According to Markstein, Bagdasarian was the voice for Alvin and his two brothers, Theodore and Simon. In 1959, Dell Comics published a series of the Chipmunks adventures; but it wasn't until 1961, when CBS aired the animated *The Alvin Show,* that Alvin & the Chipmunks became popular as cartoons. Soon, many tie-in books were being published featuring episodes from *The Alvin Show*.

SUMMARY AND CONCLUDING REMARKS

The next time you take your weekly trip down the aisles of Target or Wal-Mart and become overwhelmed by the plethora of licensed characters, remember that you are actually the recipient of a strategically planned business strategy implemented by the product licensing industry to seize every disposable dollar from your family. When successfully executed, the business of licensing in children's television and media can be quite profitable for both program producers and retail merchants. Timing is crucial for merchandising and licensing success. Producers and retailers must carefully select the right licensed character for the right products, releasing them at the right time for the right demographic of consumers. Although releasing too much licensed product too soon has the potential for merchandising failure, releasing licensed merchandise too late can be equally disastrous. To capitalize on all licensing and merchandising dollars, cross-marketing and cross media strategies must be planned to reach the largest number of consumers using as many outlets as possible. Licensed characters can be exploited across all types of media including television, video games, movies, books, greeting cards, comic books, DVDs, and toys. This media blending to produce the largest revenue is evident in children's licensed book publishing. Increasingly more licensing agreements are being forged in the publishing world, thus providing ancillary revenue to children's program producers and other license holders. At the same time, licensed books for children have increased in popularity and incurred large profits for many publishing houses. Consequently, when carefully planned, licensing of children's media can equate to huge financial success for all parties involved.[1]

REFERENCES

Acosta-Alzuru, C., & Kreshel, P. (2002). 'I'm an American Girl ... whatever that means": Girls consuming Pleasant Company's American Girl identity. *Journal of Communication, 52*(1), 139–161.

Allen, J. C. (2001). The economic structure of the commercial electronic children's media industries. In D. G. Singer & J. L. Singer (Eds.), *Handbook of children and the media* (pp. 477–493). Thousand Oaks, CA: Sage.

American_Girl. (2004). *Fast facts.* Retrieved August 28, 2004, from http://www.americangirl.com/corp/media/fastfacts.html

Buell, M. (1992). A Little Lulu chronology. In B. Hamilton & L. Clark (Eds.), *The Little Lulu library* (Set I). Scottsdale, AZ: Another Rainbow Publishing.

Carlton_Cards. (2003). *Corporate history.* Retrieved April 1, 2004, from http://www.carltoncards.ca/english/corp.html

Desjardins, D. (2005, April 11). Networks partner with publishers to grow brands. *DSNRetailing Today, 44,* 19.

Drug Store News. (2004, June 21). Can SpongeBob soak up more dollars in drug? *Drug Store News, 26,* 90.

Duke, J. (1979). *Children's books and magazines: A market study.* White Plains, NY: Knowledge Industry Publications.

Grala, A. (2005a, March). Titles for tykes. *License!, 8,* 38.

Grala, A. (2005b, March). W.I.T.C.H.ing. *License!, 8,* 16–20.

Hade, D. (2001). Short primer on children's books in the global economy. *The Looking Glass, 5*(1/2), Retrieved September 19, 2004, from http://www.the-looking-glass.net/rabbit/2005.2001/illume.html

---

[1]For further information on the proliferation and business of character and brand licensing of children's media, we suggest consulting *Out of the Garden: Toys, TV, and Children's Culture in the Age of Marketing* (Kline, 1993), *Consuming Kids: The Hostile Takeover of Childhood* (Linnm 2004), *Sold Separately: Children and Parents in Consumer Culture, Merchandise Licensing in the Television Industry* (Raugust, 1996a), and *Animation Business Handbook* (Raugust, 2004a).

Hall, P. (2001). *Raggedy Ann & Andy: A retrospective celebrating 85 years of storybook friends.* New York: Simon & Schuster.

HarperCollins. (2004). *HarperFestival.* Retrieved March 31, 2004, from http://www.harperchildrens.com/hch/aboutus/imprints/festival.asp

Holt, K. (2004). Children's books: The great balancing act. *Publisher's Weekly, 251*(1), 31–34.

Hunt, P. (1995). Retreatism and advance: 1914–1945. In P. Hunt (Ed.), *Children's literature: An illustrated history* (pp. 192–224). New York: Oxford University Press.

Hunt, P., Butts, D., Heins, E., Kinnell, M., Watkins, T., Avery, G., et al. (1995). Children's literature in America: 1870–1945. In P. Hunt (Ed.), *Children's literature: An illustrated history* (pp. 225–251). New York: Oxford University Press.

Jenkins, B. (2005, March). The space age. *License!, 8,* 28–30.

Jevens, S. (2004). American Girl's *Samantha character comes to life in a life-action television movie on the WB.* Middleton, WN: American Girl.

Johnston, C. (2003, June). Book marks. *License!, 6,* 36–38.

Jones, D. (1987). *Bibliography of the Little Golden Books.* Westport, CT: Greenwood Press.

Kline, S. (1993). *Out of the garden: Toys, TV, and children's culture in the age of marketing.* New York: Verso.

Larson, R. (1995). *Films into books: An analytical bibliography of film novelizations, movie, and TV tie-ins.* Metuchen, NJ: Scarecrow Press.

License! (2004, December). 2004 Annual report: Licensed products estimated retail sales 1999–2003. *License!, 7,* 10–13.

Linn, S. (2004). *Consuming kids: The hostile takeover of childhood.* New York: The New Press.

Lodge, S. (1998, March 2). HarperCollins rolls out mass-market line. *Publisher's Weekly, 245,* 26.

Lowery, L. (2004). Learning about big little books. Retrieved March 30, 2004, from http://www.biglittlebooks.com/

Maas, J. (2003, February 10). Publishers get game. Publisher's Weekly, 250, 61–62.

Markstein, D. (2004). *Toonpedia: A vast repository of toonological knowledge.* Retrieved April 10, 2004, from http://www.toonopedia.com/

Masters, G. (1998a, September). Going Hollywood. *Supermarket Business, 53,* 125.

Masters, G. (1998b). Lights, camera, read. *Discount Merchandiser, 38,* 38–40.

McCormick, E. (1981). *"Librarians hate us":* But the public loves Golden books. *American Libraries, 12*(5), 251–257.

Pecora, N. (1998). *The business of children's entertainment.* New York: Guilford Press.

Peer, K. (1997). *TV tie-ins: A bibliography of American TV tie-in paperbacks.* New York: TV Books.

Ratan, S. (2003). Game makers aren't chasing women. *Wired News, 1–2,* Retrieved April 2, 2004, from http://www.wired.com/news/games/2000,2101, 59620,59600.html.

Raugust, K. (1996a). *Merchandise licensing in the television industry.* Boston: Focal Press.

Raugust, K. (1996b, December). New toy-related imprints experience growing pains: publishers face challenges to bookstores and consumers. *Publisher's Weekly, 243,* 30–31.

Raugust, K. (1998a, March 16). Creative alliances attract publishers: TV and movie production, long-term licensing deals and co-marketing efforts present multiple opportunities. *Publisher's Weekly, 245,* 26–27.

Raugust, K. (1998b, January 19). TV tie-ins target teen and preteen girls. *Publisher's Weekly, 245,* 243–244.

Raugust, K. (1999, October 25). Getting wired: Characters from licensed interactive products become book characters. *Publisher's Weekly, 246,* 26.

Raugust, K. (2000, June 5). Talking trends. *Publisher's Weekly, 247,* 24–26.

Raugust, K. (2003, August 18). Selected 1980s relaunches: Here are some of the licensed properties that are being introduced. *Publisher's Weekly, 250,* 32.

Raugust, K. (2004a). *Animation business handbook.* New York: St. Martin's.

Raugust, K. (2004b, March 8). Color me Crayola. *Publisher's Weekly, 251,* 29.

Raugust, K. (2004c, July 26). Trends in the licensing world. *Publisher's Weekly, 251,* 18–19.

Raugust, K. (2005, February 28). Technology is top trend at toy fair. *Publisher's Weekly, 252,* 16.

Roback, D. (1999, March 29). Licensed tie-ins make registers ring. *Publisher's Weekly, 246,* 46–52.

Roback, D. (2004). Children's bestsellers: Big year for Harry, Lemony, cat in hat. In D. Bogart (Ed.), *Bowker Annual Library and Book Trade Almanac* (49th ed., pp. 593–613). Medford, NJ: Information Today, Inc.

Seiter, E. (1993). *Sold separately: Children and parents in consumer culture.* New Brunswick, NJ: Rutgers University.

Wilensky, D. (2005, April). Are you on the list? *License!, 8,* 16–39.

Woodard, E. H. (1999). *The 1999 state of children's television report: Programming for children over broadcast and cable television* (No. 28). Philadelphia, PA: Annenberg Public Policy Center of the University of Pennsylvania.

Zeitchik, S. (2003, January 6). Have joystick, will read? new readers, the DVD and Xbox way. *Publisher's Weekly, 250,* 27.

10

Networked Kids: The Digital Future of Children's Video Distribution

Steven C. Rockwell
University of South Alabama

Children today have a dizzying array of media options. From the Internet, DVD and video releases, digital cable and satellite systems, to traditional broadcasting, children are awash in a sea of choice. As the digital age continues to mature, even more innovations are being planned and developed, aimed at increasing both ubiquity of media access and options in media selections. But, in this environment, what choices will our children and their parents make when selecting from the promised superabundance of media content? What options will truly be available for them? These questions must be addressed to ensure that quality children's programming thrives in the new media landscape.

Relatively recent technological advances in digital video allow for unprecedented control of how, when, and where children access video programming. Increasingly, children can watch what they want, when they want, and where they want (Kaiser Family Foundation, 2005). The development of digital compression techniques has greatly expanded the ability to offer a number of channels via cable systems, the Internet, and through digital broadcast and satellite systems. In fact, choices on an interactive, bidirectional network are fully scalable and almost limitless.

Along with the increase into the home of the number of delivery channels, digital compression and digital storage technologies allow for the easy recording of material for later playback. Many of these devices utilize "smart" technologies (e.g., Tivo and Replay TV) allow for unprecedented control over how content is selected for recording. They are

189

able to download program guide information and choose content that is either selected by the consumer or determined by the device, based on past consumer behavior, to be something the consumer might want to watch.

Additionally, an increasing number of portable, hand-held video devices (e.g., Sony's PS2 Play Station Portable system), combining video game play, digital video viewing, and MP3 audio playback are being marketed to young consumers. The portability of these devices allows for control of not only what digital video content is being viewed but unprecedented levels of control over where this content will be viewed.

Although this technology certainly will provide numerous choices to the consumer, how will it be used to benefit children? In his book *Life after Television*, George Gilder (1990) suggests that the conversion from analog to digital media delivery systems combined with high-speed, bidirectional networks to the home will radically alter the media landscape. Gilder writes: "Television is a tool of tyrants. Its overthrow will be a major force for freedom and individuality, culture and morality. That overthrow is at hand" (p. 20). According to this view, access to this digital stream will put everyone on the same level with regards to content distribution. Monolithic broadcasting outlets will face competition from anyone desiring to distribute content over the digital network. As a result, their once-dominant voices will be drowned out by the countless content streams available at any given time. Anyone with access to such a digital stream will be able to be a producer as well as a consumer. In this type of environment, boundless opportunities exist for the producer of children's digital video.

Stipp (1999) counters that far from disappearing, traditional broadcast networks will continue to thrive in this new arena. He suggests that whereas there will be some convergence between broadcast television models and interactive networks like the Internet, the appliances used to deliver these different media streams will remain separate. Consumers will prefer to be entertained via television and turn to the more interactive networks when actively seeking information. Chan-Olmsted and Ha (2003) echo this view by suggesting that current trends indicate that television programmers are using the Internet to "complement" their core programming products, rather than seeking a new model of content delivery.

This view does have some merit. The psychological processes and motivations of watching television are usually different than when using a computer. We tend to watch television from across a room, usually sitting in a chair or sofa, whereas most computer use finds the user situated about 12 inches from the monitor. Also, television viewing is seen as a more passive entertainment experience, whereas using a computer is a more interactive, goal-oriented behavior (van Dijk, 1999). Also, television viewing can involve groups, such as families, watching and commenting on the same content, whereas computer use tends to be more of singular activity. This would suggest that the television and the computer might not converge into a singular, multipurpose "information appliance."

However, Stipp (1999), in contrasting the differing uses of the information appliances themselves—the television versus the computer— appears to ignore the digital similarities of the underlying means for delivering information to these appliances. In fact he seems to suggest that traditional broadcasters are the only means for providing more "passive" entertainment on large-screened appliances. In reality, digital content can be displayed on any type of device that is able to decode the signal. Even if separate information appliances are utilized for separate functions, in the era of digital networks, competing digital streams will feed these appliances. The transmission of digital forms of video, regardless of the system used to transmit the signal to the end-user, could be displayed on any appliance capable of decoding the signal. With sufficient bandwidth to the home, broadcast "stations" could easily be streamed "on demand" via a two-way network like the Internet and displayed on the terminal of choice, thus offering competition to traditional broadcasters.

Chan-Olmstead and Kang (2003) suggest that broadband networks to the home offer an advantage over the broadcast model. By allowing the consumer to access digitally stored video on demand, these networks allow greater flexibility in the both amount of, and access to, programming than that afforded by a traditional broadcast model. In this type of environment, the consumer will not only be able to display what they want, when they want, but, also on the appliance of their choice.

In this type of environment, digital content could be displayed on any type of video terminal, from a large-screen plasma terminal to a personal, hand-held display device, including mobile phones that are already beginning to offer this type of content. In fact, the recent developments in the area of personal, hand-held digital video players will allow for a more singular viewing experience. In a true broadband-delivered, video-on-demand environment, gaining group consensus over what to watch will become increasingly problematic. Faced with a near unlimited menu of content to choose from, finding content that is mutually agreeable for any sized family or group of people will become increasingly difficult. This might make the new breed of personal, portable video terminals (e.g., the Sony PSP) attractive to many adopters. Children might find these devices particularly appealing. They will have the ability to go where they want and watch what they want. The portability of these devices could have profound implications regarding parental control and input of what video content children are consuming.

VIDEO PACKAGERS AND GATEWAYS

Chan-Olmstead and Kang (2003) also suggest that due to the on-demand nature of the new networks, traditional media broadcasters will be less important in this environment. By allowing for control of not only the choice of content, but also when and where the content is being viewed, these broadband networks will render obsolete traditional broadcast scheduling and delivery, giving way to a new breed of media packagers competing for consumers' attention on whichever video appliance is chosen by the consumer.

These packagers will compete with one another to attract viewers, thus generating revenue either through advertising support or some type of pay-per-view or subscription model. Traditional media outlets, with huge budgets for program acquisition, will most likely emerge as early favorites. It is unrealistic to assume that large media corporations, faced with massive amounts of competition delivered via high-speed networks will be forced into bankruptcy. With the current heavy infrastructure deployment by television broadcasters in converting to an all digital television system, it is likely that they will remain a major provider of video content for the foreseeable future. Although these corporations might no longer have a stranglehold on channels of delivery, other marketing forces will come to bear to attempt to keep their voices heard over that of their numerous competitors.

However, other companies will have room for success as well. By fundamentally changing the methods of delivery from highly regulated wireless and analog cable to a true digital broadband environment, any one with sufficient access to the network will be able to offer digital video content. But the consumer has to be able to filter out the content that they find appealing and useful. The media packager and media marketer will play crucial roles here. Faced with an overwhelming amount of content, consumers will gravitate toward video gateways hosted by trusted content packagers. Successful marketing of these gateways to build brand awareness and trust will be crucial in creating a sustainable environment for these new businesses. This is where much can be done to increase the quality of digital video targeted towards children. By capitalizing on integrated marketing concepts such as brand awareness and trust, some organizations will be able to emerge as leaders in the delivery of children's content.

This sense of trust will become increasingly important if video consumption, aided by the successful adoption of personal video devices, becomes a more personal experience. Parents will need ways to ensure that their children are only consuming age-appropriate material and, if able to limit their children's choices to a few gateways, should opt for the ones that they trust the most to deliver quality, age-appropriate content without the need for constant supervision. Obviously, brands that have this reputation in the more traditional media environment of today, brands like PBS Kids, Nickelodeon and Nick Jr., Disney, etc., will have an early advantage in this area but can be challenged by other creative packaging companies.

The marketing of these packagers and gateways will be crucial to their success. With a superabundance of choice, creative marketing of products will become increasingly important to drive content consumption. Whether this is accomplished via direct marketing or through techniques such as promotional tie-ins, content providers with larger budgets will create more demand for their products and likely make it difficult for smaller companies to compete. Thus, by controlling the market, these companies might eventually serve to limit the amount of digital content available. These successful marketers, would, in essence, emerge as entities similar to today's networks. However, there would be one major difference in these networks of the future. Although they might control the lion's share of a particular market, they, unlike today's cable and broadcasting giants, would not control the channels of distribution. This would make this market much more fluid, always open to change if an innovative content provider were able to capture audience attention.

This new environment will also allow for local and regional groups to get involved in the packaging process. Organizations like schools, PTAs, churches, excetra, will be able to establish their own gateways that promise to deliver appropriate, prosocial content to children. These organizations will have to work out mutually agreeable deals with content packagers and providers, but this should be a relatively small obstacle as the benefits that these groups can offer in terms of trust and awareness will be attractive to many of the packagers and producers. By focusing on quality content and brand recognition, these groups can distinguish their products from the countless content that will be available via the digital network and offer an easier means for parents to control their children's media consumption. If parents trust these gateways and are satisfied that the content offered is appropriate for their children, they are more likely to allow their children to use these portals as a gateway to video content. These gateways might be successful, then, even when competing with established giants. Branding alone will not be enough to sustain the viability of these trusted gateways. These gateways will only be successful if they provide content that is entertaining and engaging to the targeted audience.

VIDEO CONTENT CREATION

The advent of digital video has made the creation of digital content extremely easy and affordable. With the plummeting prices of powerful computer systems, barriers of access to the creative tools necessary to become a content producer have virtually disappeared. Almost anyone with the requisite hardware and talent can now produce quality digital video content. Even children are able to utilize these tools to create their own video expressions.

The widespread diffusion of digital video recording and editing equipment will allow for a vast amount of innovative digital video content to be made available to consumers. Anyone with a message or idea will be able to create some form of visual representation of this idea in the form of a digital video.

We are already witnessing this, as is evident from the increasing number of digital video clips and stories that are occasionally transmitted via the Internet. Some of these independently created videos are even catapulted to short-lived icons of popular culture. Word of these videos is quickly spread via e-mail messages, and these clips are viewed countless times before their novelty wears off. However, it is the unusual nature of the content that drives consumption of these clips. Once their popularity fades, the appeal, and thus any chances at sustainable marketability, vanishes.

The end result of this diffusion of digital media creation hardware and software is that many of the barriers that have heretofore limited entry into the business of video content creation have been removed. Even those with limited resources are able to utilize these available tools to create high-quality video content. Although producers of some of this content might be able to work out deals with larger distribution companies, the lure of the new digital environment, typified by Gilder (1990), promises to level the playing field and let anyone who can produce a digital video product become a distributor as well. However, the reality of distribution over current broadband networks might not quite fulfill Gilder's promise.

DISTRIBUTION NETWORKS

In this era of low-cost, high-quality production equipment, special interest groups such as educational institutions, parent groups, excetra, will easily be able to produce or pay for the production of high-quality video content for children. However, regardless of the ease and low costs associated with the creation of the video content, business models created to capitalize on this digital revolution can only be successful if they can generate income from the sale and distribution of this content to, at a minimum, remain sustainable. Although the high speed bidirectional models, (similar to today's Internet), discussed previously would appear to offer the perfect vehicle for distribution of all this content, significant economic barriers to entry remain.

At the surface, it would appear that by simply having a broadband Internet connection, anyone could distribute their video via the Internet. However, the upstream bandwidth requirements for quality digital content far exceed that allotted by today's broadband connections. These connections, typified by services such as DSL via copper phone lines and cable Internet delivered via existing coaxial networks, are typically asymmetrical in nature; allowing for much greater download speeds to the computer than they do for uploading content from the computer to the network.

The physical upload limits of these asymmetrical networks tend to favor the broadcast model of information distribution over Gilder's (1990) vision of a level playing field. These networks, in their very architecture, tend to favor consumption over production. Typical broadband connections offer up to 3-megabit-per-second download rates, but average 256 kilobytes-per-second upload speeds from the end-user's computer (Brown, 2004). The physical properties of these networks will not allow for upload speeds to increase much beyond this average. Although it might be possible for cable providers to provide upload speeds of up to 1.5 megabits-per-second, there would have to be some competitive reason for them to do so. Because the primary business of cable companies is the distribution of video content, it is unlikely they would willingly provide means for individuals to compete with them. However, the lure of voice-over-ip, allowing the cable companies to compete with telephone companies for local dial-tone, might be the impetus that drives the increase in bandwidth both to and from the home (Brown, 2004). By relying on these asymmetrical network models, individuals and smaller independent video production companies will not be truly able to compete with larger companies that have significant bandwidth available for distribution of video content. This could change in the future if complete end-to-end fiber networks are deployed, but given the costs and uncertainty of subscriber willingness to pay additional fees for such service, this conversion will take decades. Given the current environment, in order to reach more than a handful of viewers at a time, these independents will have to locate their content on computer servers with sufficient bandwidth connections to support the demand for their products.

The bandwidth costs to reach a significant market share are staggering for the independent video producer. One estimate (Sokol, 1993), suggests that even though the costs of bandwidth are shared by the video distributor and the consumer, the distributor is responsible for the share of the aggregate of users who choose to download the video content. For example, if the bandwidth cost for 1 minute of video at sufficient resolution was 20 cents, the consumer would pay 10 cents of this, usually as part of a flat, monthly subscription fee, whereas the producer would pay the remaining 10 cents. If the video distributor's content was viewed by just 5,000 viewers an hour, the bandwidth costs would be about $12,000 per day or $360,000 per month. When compared to current audience sizes for traditional broadcast content that typically run into millions of viewers, the costs associated with maintaining this level of audience would be enormous. Obviously, this type of distribution model would have to be supported through either subscriber subscriptions or advertisers. Either way, the reality of the costs of bandwidth would have a chilling effect on many considering entering into this business.

Saddled with these costs, many independent producers of video content, including videos targeted at children, seek different methods for the distribution of their products. One technique involves utilizing the Internet to market their product, but relying on more traditional ground-transport systems to actually distribute their video product. Because DVDs are inexpensive to produce, less than $1.00 per unit, and can be sent through the mail via regular postage rates, they are the favored distribution medium for many independent production companies (Wayner, 2004).

This distribution technique, although economically profitable, falls short of offering an on-demand experience for the end-user. In the on-demand environment, consumers should be able to choose what they want to watch when they want to see it. This can be accomplished through either subscriber pay-per-view or as part of a subscription offering or via some type of advertiser-supported system. The mass market appeal might be somewhat lessened if the consumer has to purchase a DVD of the program, usually at a higher cost than a pay-per-view, a few days in advance of when they actually receive the program. So, although this distribution model might work for some types of video programming, usually that aimed at niche markets, it may not be suited for wide-scale video distribution.

ALTERNATE DISTRIBUTION MODELS

What, then, are the chances for Gilder's (1990) vision of a truly open and competitive high-speed, bidirectional video network that could compete with traditional broadcasting oligopolies to become a reality? Actually, there is hope for the smaller video production company as well as the independent producer to find an economical way to offer on-demand video services over high-speed networks without incurring significant costs to do so. A relatively recent development in Internet technology called BitTorrent lies at the heart of this new technique. Developed by Brian Cohen, BitTorrent is able to speed up the down-loading of large files, including video, through the coordinated sharing of pieces of the file that exist on different "peer" computers (Vaughan-Nichols, 2005). Unlike traditional file downloading, in which a client computer is receiving a file from a single source, BitTorrent technology coordinates the sharing of a file between multiple users. The more users that are sharing the file, the faster the download completes. Since multiple users are both sending and receiving the file at the same time, the bandwidth is leveraged between all the "peers" so that individual bandwidth consumption is held to a minimum. The more "peers" involved in the transaction, the faster the download. This technique allows for very large transfers to occur, even when over limited band-width to the Internet. Because high-quality video files are typically very large, this technique is ideal for their distribution.

Although it is being cautiously monitored by media companies fear-ful that this technology be used to facilitate illegal sharing of copy-righted material, this technology holds great potential if it can be legitimatized for legal video distribution. Several fledgling initiatives are taking advantage of this peer-to-peer file-sharing technique to distribute video.

One such initiative that is just in its infancy is called the "Broadcast Machine" ("Internet TV is Open," n.d.). This project promises to make it affordable for anyone to share video via the Internet using BitTorrent technology. Additionally, the creators of the Broadcast Machine soft-ware claim that their software makes it possible to create a channel of content gathered from other sources, in essence allowing interested groups or individuals to create their own video portal. The Web site goes further to claim;

> Anyone can broadcast full-screen video to thousands of people at virtu-ally no cost, using BitTorrent technology. Viewers get intuitive, elegant software to subscribe to channels, watch video, and organize their video library. The project is non-profit, open source, and built on open stan-dards (Internet TV is open, n.d.).

If sufficient users adopt this technology and participate in sharing con-tent, inexpensive distribution of quality video might become a reality.

The "Broadcast Machine" is not the only developing initiative seeking to utilize BitTorrent technology to help distribute video content. The "Open Media Network" initially launched in April, 2005, was developed by Marc Andreessen and Mike Homer, formerly developers of the Netscape web browser (Konrad, 2005). This initiative also promises to help "broaden the audience for any amateur or professional producer of video or audio" (Konrad, 2005, p. 1). Google, Inc. has also announced that they are starting the "Google Video Upload" program that allows individuals and companies to upload video content of any length that will be available for purchase and playback from the Google site ("Google upload video F.A.Q," n.d.).

These initiatives and others that will surely follow, offer great promise in helping to make it affordable to distribute digital video content via broadband networks. These projects are especially attractive to agencies, individuals, and organizations that desire to increase the educational and prosocial values of children's videos but are not able to compete with mainstream media oligopolies.

If these initiatives take hold, Gilder's (1990) vision of a truly level playing field becomes one step closer to fulfillment. Over the near term, because of their ability to invest huge sums into marketing efforts, it appears that large media companies will most likely continue to be dominant providers of children's video. However, if local providers and trusted content gateways are allowed to develop by leveraging bandwidth via peer networking, they could slowly begin to erode the market share held by the traditional media giants. Only then will the true potential of the digital age be realized.

REFERENCES

Brown, E. S. (2004, July 8). Swimming upstream with uploads. *Technology Review*. Retrieved May 30, 2005, from http://www.technologyreview.com/articles/04/07/wo_brown070804.1.asp

Chan-Olmsted, S. & Louisa, Ha (2003). Internet business models for broadcasters: How television stations perceive and Integrate the Internet. *Journal of Broadcasting and Electronic Media, 47*(4), 597–617.

Chan-Olmstead, S. and Kang, Jae-Won (2003) Theorizing the strategic architecture of a broadband television industry. *The Journal of Media Economics, 16*(1), 3–21.

Gilder, G. (1990). *Life after television: The coming transformation of media and American life*. Knoxville, TN: Whittle.

Google upload video faq. (n.d.). from Google, Inc. website. Retrieved May 25, 2005 from https://upload.video.google.com/video_faq.html

Internet TV is open and independent. (n.d.). Retrieved June 01, 2005, from http://www.participatoryculture.org/

Kaiser Family Foundation (2005). *Generation M: Media in the Lives of 8–18 Year-olds.* Menlo Park, CA: Authors.

Konrad, R. (2005, April 28). Netscape veterans launch video startup. *Associated Press State & Local Wire.* Retrieved May 30, 2005, from Lexis-Nexis Academic database.

Sokol, John L. (1993, April 16). Economics of video and the Internet. Video Technology Magazine. Retrieved May 31, 2005, from http://www.videotech nology.com/econimics of video.htm.

Stipp, H. (1999): Convergence now?, *The International Journal on Media Management, 1* (1), 10–13.

van Dijk, Jan. (1999). *The network society, social aspects of the new media.* London, Thousand Oaks: Sage.

Vaughan-Nichols, Steven J. (2005, March 10). A More Business-Friendly BitTorrent. *eWeek.com.* Retrieved May 30, 2005, from/Lexis-Nexis Academic database.

Wayner, P. (2004, May 20). In the era of cheap DVD's, anyone can be a producer. *New York Times*, p. 1G. Retrieved March 24, 2005, from Lexis-Nexis Academic database.

IV

MONITORING CHILDREN'S TELEVISION

11

Kids' Media Policy Goes Digital: Current Developments in Children's Television Regulation

Dale Kunkel
University of Arizona

Television technology in the United States is on the verge of a fundamental shift from an analog to digital delivery system (Benton Foundation, 2005; New America Foundation, 2005). The new technology can deliver sharper pictures, more channels, and enhanced features such as viewer interactivity and video on demand. This changeover will occur in the latter part of this decade and holds far-reaching implications for all aspects of the television environment. New television receivers will be required for viewers to obtain programming delivered on digital channels because the frequencies broadcasters use to transmit their signal will change, as will the technical dimensions of the content they distribute. Broadcasting will become more diverse and dynamic as local stations will have the option to exploit the new technology using different configurations. For example, some are expected to transmit multiple channels simultaneously, whereas others are likely to concentrate more on enhanced features such as viewer interactivity.

What do these technological shifts mean for the child audience, and for the future of children's television programming and related public policy in the United States? Will broadcasters use them to benefit children by enhancing the educational elements of their children's programming efforts, or merely try to target children with potentially more powerful persuasive tactics incorporated in interactive advertising? Policymakers have already begun to lay the groundwork for adapting the "public interest" obligations of television broadcasters, first established in 1934, to this new futuristic environment. Just as television technology is on the cusp of dramatic change, so too are many aspects of children and television policy.

At the broadest level of analysis, there are three primary types of policy concerns in the realm of children and television: (1) policies designed to assure the adequacy of service to child audiences, (2) policies designed to protect children from adverse effects of exposure to potentially harmful program content, and (3) policies designed to protect children from advertising effects (Kunkel & Watkins, 1987; Kunkel & Wilcox, 2001). In the late 1990s, the V-chip was implemented as the key policy initiative to address the second of these three critical policy concerns (Kunkel, 2003). Although the overall efficacy of the V-chip remains unclear, the emergence of the V-chip ratings and electronic blocking technology have functionally diminished most policy debate in this realm while allowing adequate time to weigh the impact of this new initiative (Kaiser Family Foundation, 2004; Ventura, 2005). In contrast, both the first and third areas just noted, involving children's educational programming requirements as well as advertising protections, have been the focus of significant new policy activity related to the transition to digital television technology.

With little public attention or press coverage, the Federal Communications Commission (FCC) adopted an important new set of rules in late 2004 that will shape the future of children's television regulation for programming as well as advertising (FCC, 2004). The rules reflect an effort to adapt long-standing policies governing both children's programming and advertising to the new digital television environment. The agenda for this proceeding, however, is not yet fully complete. Moreover, the implications for much of the new ruling are uncertain because many aspects of digital broadcasting are not yet operational. Thus, the new policy framework warrants careful scrutiny to understand its long-term meaning and impact.

This chapter explores these recent developments in children and television policy and analyzes their implications for the future. In each topic area, some brief background is first provided to help the reader appreciate the history and context of existing regulation that precedes the latest policy developments.

EDUCATIONAL PROGRAMMING REQUIREMENTS IN THE DIGITAL ERA

Background

Age-related developmental differences in children's information processing capabilities affect how children learn in virtually all contexts.

For hundreds of years, educators have structured the school environment to group together in classrooms children of the same age and roughly the same level of cognitive capability. This separation of children by grade level is effective because it allows the use of developmentally appropriate pedagogical materials. No one would seek to use the same book to teach all children aged 2-to 12-years-old how to read. Similarly, no one should expect that television programming directed to all ages of children can hold optimal value for educating or informing such a diverse group of viewers.

Children benefit the most from programs that target narrow segments of the overall child population, such as when 2- to 5 to-year-olds watch *Sesame Street* or *Dora the Explorer*, two shows that are of great value to preschoolers but of little interest to youngsters beyond this age range. Yet the economics of the commercial broadcast industry historically have dictated that most television programs must be geared to attract the largest possible audience in order to maximize the advertising revenue obtained. That economic principle explains why most commercial broadcasters have aired only limited amounts of children's programming over the years, with most such efforts designed to attract the widest possible range of children (Palmer, 1987; Pecora, 1998).

Although the paucity of children's programming efforts on broadcast networks has persisted since the 1960s and 1970s (Turow, 1981), the shortage of educational programs for youth grew so acute in the 1980s that the Congress adopted the Children's Television Act (CTA) of 1990, which requires broadcast television stations to serve the educational and informational (E/I) needs of children as part of their public interest obligation (Kunkel, 1991). The statute makes no mention of any specific amounts for such service, leaving it up to the FCC to determine how much is expected from each station as well as what material qualifies as educational.

In the early years under the CTA, the commercial broadcast industry pursued only modest efforts to fulfill the law, both in terms of the quantity and quality of programming delivered (Center for Media Education, 1992; Kunkel & Canepa, 1994; Kunkel & Goette, 1997). This led the FCC to implement more stringent policies enforcing the Children's Television Act in 1996. Among the revisions was a more strict definition of what qualifies as educational programming, a 3-hour per week guideline for each station, and a requirement that educational/informational programming for children must be publicly identified with an E/I label or rating at the time it airs (FCC, 1996).

From 1996 to 2000, the Annenberg Public Policy Center of the University of Pennsylvania conducted an annual study assessing the quality of the educational programming efforts of the broadcast industry (Jordan, 1996, 1998, 2000; Jordan & Woodard, 1997; Schmitt, 1999). These evaluations provided a relatively mixed "report card" for the industry. Although a pattern of slightly improved performance was observed over time across these studies (Kunkel & Wilcox, 2001), the industry's overall evaluation still fared rather poorly. On a positive note, programs that the Annenberg Center rated as "minimally educational"—that is, they failed to meet basic educational benchmarks and "were unlikely to provide substantive lessons for the audience" (Jordan, 2000, p. 4)—decreased from 36% of all E/I claims in 1998 to 26% in 1999 to 23% in 2000. But despite the improvements, nearly one of every four programs claimed as E/I by broadcasters was judged to be of little if any value to children in the most recent Annenberg study. And that finding was obtained 4 years after the FCC strengthened its children's programming policies because of past shortcomings in industry performance, and 10 years after the law was first adopted by Congress.

Meanwhile, increased competition for child audiences from cable networks such as Nickelodeon, which enjoy dual revenue streams from both cable subscription fees as well as advertising revenue, makes it all the more difficult for broadcasters to air children's programming that is profitable for them. Children's programs on cable channels are often of high-quality, target narrow segments of the audience, and convey prosocial or educational messages that make them valuable contributors to the media environment for much of the nation's youth. However, 15% of U.S. households lack access to cable television and rely solely on over-the-air signals to watch television (FCC, 2005); thus, the children's educational programming on broadcast channels is likely to be the only such content available for viewing in many millions of homes. This concern, coupled with the principle that broadcasters must serve the public interest in return for the privilege of using the publicly owned airwaves, is the reason why each local television station is still required to air programs to serve the educational needs of children in their community.

Within this context, two important developments have occurred recently in the area of children's educational programming policy. The first involves formal action by the FCC to adapt the existing regulatory requirements for analog television established by the CTA in 1990 to the new digital technologies that are just now being implemented nationwide in the United States. The second relates to a new legal challenge filed by public interest advocacy groups questioning the adequacy of the children's programming efforts of some stations. Each of these two topics will be addressed in turn.

New Educational Programming Requirements for Digital Television

The new digital technology brings with it many new options for broadcasters (Advisory Committee on Public Interest Obligations of Digital

Television Broadcasters, 1998). One of the most important of these is the prospect of multicasting. With the shift to digital, each television station has been granted new spectrum space that will allow it to transmit a high-quality digital signal. The bandwidth required to accomplish that transmission is roughly six times greater than the bandwidth required for the old analog signals (Campaign Legal Center, 2005).

There are many controversies and uncertainties surrounding the question of how quickly the transition from analog to digital television service will be achieved in the United States. In a classic "chicken and egg" scenario, broadcasters are resisting the significant investments required to upgrade their technical capabilities when few viewers are capable of receiving their enhanced signal while viewers are hesitant to purchase expensive new receivers at a time when few broadcasters are offering the new, more sophisticated services. The Congress and FCC are anxious to see the transition to digital completed as expeditiously as possible. Once the changeover occurs, the government will receive back from the broadcasters their "old" analog frequencies, which can then be auctioned for other nonbroadcast uses, generating revenue expected to be in the billions of dollars (Clark, 2005; New America Foundation, 2005).

In the digital environment, broadcasters will have the freedom to air one high-definition (HDTV) signal, which would require their full digital bandwidth, or alternatively to carve that same spectrum space into smaller pieces by offering a number of standard definition television (SDTV) signals with different programming streams. This equation is complicated by the fact that the options may be varied by a station at different times of day. As the FCC explains:

'DTV broadcasters have the flexibility to vary the amount and quality of broadcast programming they offer throughout the day. For example, a broadcaster could air 4 SDTV channels from 8 a.m. to 3 p.m., switch to two higher definition channels from 3 p.m. to 8 p.m., and finish with one HDTV channel for prime-time and late-night programming.' (FCC, 2004, p. 7)

The key question the FCC faced in adapting the Children's Television Act to this new technological environment was whether to maintain the existing 3-hour rule for children's educational programming or to alter it in some way according to the programming options exercised by each station. In late 2004, the Commission adopted new rules that specify how the educational programming requirements from the Children's Television Act will be applied to the new digital broadcasting environment. The concept embodied in the ruling is best characterized as a "commensurate rule."

When stations choose to multicast (i.e., transmit multiple programming signals), they must count their total hours of programming on any stream and add them all up. Any increase in the overall programming time that results from multicasting incurs a proportional rise in the station's requirement for airing children's E/I programming, at a ratio consistent with the current expectation under the 3-hour rule. A week contains 168 hours, and FCC policy currently specifies that each station should provide a minimum of 3 hours per week of E/I children's shows. That requirement translates to one half-hour increment for every 28 hours of total time. Thus, under the new policy, for every 28 additional hours of programming a digital television station airs as a part of its multicasting efforts, it will now incur an additional half-hour obligation for children's educational programming. The rule is commensurate in the sense that if the station aired two full-time signals over an entire week (i.e., 168 hours of increased programming), it would be obligated to double its E/I efforts to 6 hours per week; triple it if it offered three full-time multicast channels; and so on.

All E/I programming in the digital environment must still meet the same standards established by the FCC in its previous rulings in this area, which include that it must:

1. have serving the educational and informational needs of children 16 and under as a significant purpose;
2. be aired between the hours of 7:00 a.m. and 10:00 p.m.;
3. be a regularly scheduled weekly program;
4. be at least 30 minutes in length;
5. have an age-specific target audience and learning objective; and
6. be identified at the time of broadcast with an E/I label or rating.

For stations that multicast, at least 3 hours of children's E/I programming must air on the primary channel. Rather than requiring that each additional programming stream or channel carry its "fair share" of E/I programming, the FCC has allowed that additional E/I content may be aired on any of the station's additional frequencies. This seems to make sense given that most industry analysts expect stations to specialize with their additional programming streams, such as offering an all-news service, an all-shopping channel, and so on. Indeed, observers have suggested that some broadcasters are likely to devote one of their multicast channels primarily to children's programming, and this new policy would seem to help facilitate that outcome.

Consistent with that prospect, several broadcast organizations that filed comments with the FCC on this issue requested that stations should be allowed to carry *all* of their E/I programming on a specialized children's channel. This request was opposed by child advocacy groups out of fear that such programming would either be less available to many families who may be slower to gain access to the digital television receivers required to watch such channels, or less visible in terms of a community's awareness of and access to the programming delivered on these part-time, secondary frequencies. The Commission sided with the advocacy groups on this point, and thus stations must still maintain the basic level of 3 hours per week of E/I programming on their primary channel regardless of their programming efforts on other digital multicast channels (FCC, 2004).

Along with the advent of digital broadcasting comes the prospect for viewer interactivity with the program content. For example, a child who is excited about dinosaurs in a television program he or she is watching could click on the screen and be connected to a Web site with more information the topic, such as the Web site of the Smithsonian Institute. In the children's digital ruling issued in 2004, the FCC declined to require that stations must offer interactive features to enhance children's educational programming, noting that it is too early in the evolution of this new technology to mandate such steps. The Commission observed that it may be necessary to offer incentives to promote such service in the future, such as the possibility of increasing the credit a station receives toward fulfilling its weekly quota of children's E/I material interactive programming efforts.

Finally, the FCC has adopted an important new initiative to improve parents' ability to locate educational and informational programming for their children to view. In 1996, the FCC first required that all programs aired to fulfill a station's CTA obligations should be identified at the time of broadcast, establishing the E/I designation used to indicate that a program holds educational and informational value for children. With no effort from either the FCC or the stations to explain this labeling approach to the public, it is not surprising that few parents understand it. One survey reported that only one in seven parents was able to correctly identify the meaning of the E/I symbol (Schmidt, 1999), whereas another pegged this level at just one in twenty (Kaiser Family Foundation, 2004).

As part of the new children's digital television policy, the Commission has now ordered that all programs designated by stations as educational shall display the E/I symbol on screen throughout the entire broadcast. In addition, the Commission has also ordered that public broadcast stations, which were previously exempted, must also display the E/I symbol during their children's educational programming. The

FCC believes that this shift should greatly improve parents ability to identify and locate children's educational programming, and that seeing the symbol displayed on public broadcast content that is clearly recognized as educational will help to reinforce viewer awareness of the meaning of the symbol. This new labeling policy took effect in September 2005, and the commensurate rule for multicasting is set to be implemented in January 2006.

The Issue of Quality: Holding Stations Accountable for Their E/I Claims

Ever since the Children's Television Act was first adopted by Congress in 1990, controversy has persisted in one form or another about the quality or legitimacy of some of the programs that stations have claimed as educational for children. In the early years, researchers identified clearly frivolous claims of educational value attached to programs like *The Flintstones, The Jetsons,* and *Yogi Bear* (Center for Media Education, 1992; Kunkel & Canepa, 1994). This situation led the FCC in 1996 to implement more stringent rules for enforcing the CTA, as just outlined. More recently, critics have questioned the extent to which certain sports programs (e.g., *NBA Inside Stuff, NFL Under the Helmet*) or comedy/dramas that claim to convey general prosocial lessons (e.g., *City Guys, Darcy's Wild Life*) properly qualify as E/I programming. Clearly, there are discordant perspectives between the industry and child advocates regarding what type of programming reasonably qualifies as educational for children.

The process by which stations are held legally accountable for their claims about the educational value of their children's programs is neither simple nor time-sensitive. Broadcast television licenses are currently granted by the FCC for a period of 8 years. It is only at the point when a station must apply for its license renewal with the FCC that the adequacy of its E/I programming is subject to review. And even then, the Commission will accept on its face a station's claims of educational value in the absence of any evidence to the contrary submitted to the agency by members of the public or interested parties in the community. In other words, unless someone steps forward and challenges a station's claims at the time of its license renewal proceeding at the FCC, then the Commission will accept by default that the CTA's educational programming obligation has been fulfilled, presuming that the requisite amount of such content is claimed by the station. The Commission never initiates on its own any independent evaluation of the quality or legitimacy of the program content claimed by a station to fulfill its E/I obligations.

In formal legal terms, if a party wishes to challenge a station's license renewal on the basis of poor performance in delivering children's educational programming, that individual or organization would file a document with the FCC known as a Petition to Deny. Historically, Petitions to Deny were filed extensively in the 1960s and 1970s by public interest groups pursuing efforts to improve broadcasters' service to a wide range of constituencies, including ethnic minority groups, women, the elderly, the disabled, and of course children (Cole & Oettinger, 1978). Stations that were targeted by such challenges would sometimes offer concessions to the aggrieved parties, but rarely if ever failed to successfully achieve their license renewal (Krasnow, Longley, & Terry, 1982). Perhaps due to their relative lack of success, the Petition to Deny a license renewal application has fallen out of favor as an advocacy group tactic. Since the Children's Television Act was first adopted in 1990, no serious challenge to a station's license renewal on the basis of E/I programming has yet come to public light.

That situation changed in 2004, when an elaborate Petition to Deny was filed in license renewal proceedings for two Washington, DC area stations. The challenges were lodged jointly on behalf of two public interest advocacy organizations: the Office of Communication of the United Church of Christ, a nonsectarian group with a long history of involvement in media issues, now headed by former FCC Commissioner Gloria Tristani; and the Center for Digital Democracy, a relatively new but highly active interest group that was centrally involved in successfully reversing the FCC's effort to deregulate national media ownership limits in recent years (Lee, 2003). Although technically the challenges apply solely to the two stations involved, the implications of the cases are potentially far-reaching, as the children's programming in question is distributed nationally and is aired on hundreds of local stations across the country.

WDCA, a UPN network affiliate owned and operated by Fox Television, relied heavily during the last 2 years of its license period on two programs, *Stargate Infinity* and *Ace Lightning*, to fulfill its Children's Television Act E/I obligations. Both of these syndicated programs were produced by DIC Entertainment, an independent children's programming firm that provided the network with assurances that the shows met all applicable FCC standards for E/I content.

The FCC defines qualifying E/I content as "any television programming that furthers the educational and informational needs of children 16 years of age and under in any respect, including children's intellectual/cognitive or social/emotional needs" (FCC, 1996, p. 10695). As just noted, to qualify as core programming required for the FCC's 3-hour guideline, a show must have serving the educational and informational needs of children as a "significant purpose" (FCC, 1996, p. 10699). The Commission has specifically stated that "entertainment programming with a minor or wrap around educational and informational message cannot correctly be said to have serving the educational and informational needs of children as a significant purpose" (FCC, 1996, p. 10701).

In the WDCA challenge, the petitioners assert that *Ace Lightning* fails to meet these basic standards. The program was originally produced in England by the BBC and based upon a videogame of the same name. The BBC's Web site provides the following overview of episodes 1 to 3 of the series:

> Mark Hollander is finding it hard enough to fit into his new American school. But when a burst of lightning transposes the characters from his computer game into the real world, life suddenly gets a lot more complicated. Lord Fear and his evil cronies, Staff Head, Lady Illusion, Anvil, Pigface, and Dirty Rat, are looking for the missing pieces of the Amulet, a magical artifact that will give them special powers. But the pieces are hidden around the Carnival of Doom and only Mark and the hero of the game, Ace Lightning, can stop them and save the world. A combination of real-life action and stunning computer graphics, this is an adventure that blurs the boundaries between games and reality and brings fantasy to life (BBC Shop, 2004).

In WDCA's license renewal application to the FCC, the station provided a mere two sentences to explain how this program qualifies as educational/ informational for children:

> *Ace Lightning* is a live action animated adventure series which follows 13-year-old Mark and his superhero friend Ace Lightning. The series promotes the idea that there is a little hero in each of us and examines the various qualities that 8–11-year-olds need to think about and develop in order to make such heroism emerge (WDCA, 2004).

The petitioners challenging the license renewal obtained an independent, *pro bono* evaluation of the educational value of *Ace Lightning* from the author of this chapter, and filed that report in support of their Petition to Deny. According to the report:

> The program holds no apparent value, either tangible or incidental, for serving children's cognitive/intellectual or social/emotional needs. ... More specifically, this series of programs has no palpable message, lessons, or curriculum at even the most modest level of depth that would contribute to a child's positive development in any sense. ... The clear emphasis of the content of the program is anti-social, including extensive scenes of violence, derisive and insulting comments among characters, callous treatment of the

ills and misfortunes commonly experienced by children such as fear and anxiety, and stereotypical portrayals of adult authority figures as being stupid and repugnant. (Kunkel, 2004, at para. 17–18)

A second program, *Stargate Infinity* was also challenged as failing to meet the standards required of E/I programming. The official Web site of this animated program set in outer space describes its premise:

> *Infinity* takes place 20 to 30 years [in the future], when the Stargate is tres- passed by a mysterious creature escaping a sinister alien race. Now Stargate Command must get the beguiling Draga back to her home planet while evading sinister alien soldiers and bounty hunters from Earth. (Gateworld, 2004)

In the station's license renewal application, the following explana- tion was provided to justify the show as educational/informational for children:

> In every episode, the Stargate Explorers enter another new world and encounter life forms and cultures very different from their own. The young explorers serve as models as they learn hard lessons about such things as trying to see the world from the perspective of other cultures, functioning as a team, the positive benefits of diversity or how to mesh their own strengths and abilities with those of others on the team. The series examines fundamental issues about how and why to get along with others and the kinds of abilities and strengths necessary to be a good Stargate explorer and a good person: (WDCA, 2003)

The independent evaluation of *Stargate Infinity* filed in support of the license challenge observes the following about the show:

> It includes extensive violence presented in a manner labeled "high-risk" by the National Television Violence Study (see National Television Violence Study, Vol. 2, 1998, pp. 121–154) for its propensity to increase aggressive- ness in child-viewers. Specifically, the violence involves attractive perpe- trators who offer role models for children; the violence is presented as justified; the violence occurs without punishment; the pain or harm to vic- tims of violence is not accurately portrayed; and the violence appears real- istic to audiences of young children, who do not discriminate effectively between fantasy and reality on television. ... In each episode, literally hun- dreds of acts of violence and aggression demonstrate a clear lesson that others are to be confronted and battled, directly contradicting the educa- tional message asserted by the licensee. (Kunkel, 2004, at para. 23, 29)

The license renewal of a second Washington-area station, WPXW, was also challenged by the same groups. This station, an affiliate of the Pax

Network, relied exclusively on multiple airings of a single program, *Miracle Pets*, to fulfill its children's educational programming obligations for a 3-year period from 2001 to 2004. At the time the license renewal was submitted to the FCC, the Pax Network Web site described *Miracle Pets* as a "family show" and "a winner for animal lovers of all ages" ("Petition to Deny, 2004, p. 10). In its license renewal application, WPXW offered the following statement as the entirety of its claims justifying *Miracle Pets* as an E/I program:

> *Miracle Pets* is a one-hour live-action program. This show is designed to meet the needs of children between the ages of 13 and 16. Each episode explores different short reenactments of pets/animals doing heroic, extraordinary acts. Children learn positive role models, prosocial values and the importance of taking care of the pets in their lives. (WPXW, 2002)

The independent evaluation of *Miracle Pets* filed in support of the license challenge asserted that the program "is obviously a general audience-oriented program that is designed to appeal to audiences of all ages, with a primary emphasis on adults" and thus fails to meet the criterion of being 'specifically designed' for children (Kunkel, 2004, at para. 11). This judgment was based on "the nature of the content itself, including the featured characters, vocabulary, approach to storytelling, music, and related production conventions, all of which are clearly oriented to the older adult population" (Kunkel, 2004, at para. 11). In addition, the report noted that the advertising inserted in the program includes only adult-oriented products, including Blue Cross Medi-Gap insurance to supplement Medicare coverage, law enforcement career training, mail-order moustache-trimming tools, mattresses, and automobile sales.

Both stations have contested the Petitions to Deny their license renewal and offered rebuttals in defense of the educational value of their programming. WDCA provided a statement from Dr. Donald Roberts of Stanford University, the principal children's programming consultant to DIC Entertainment, the producer of *Ace Lightning* and *Stargate Infinity*. Roberts described the process by which he devised the educational curriculum for these programs. For *Ace Lightning*, which was originally produced by the BBC and only later distributed in the United States by DIC, Roberts explained how he developed short inserts "to strengthen and highlight the educational and informational messages and themes" already found in the program when DIC purchased the rights to air it in the United States. (Roberts, 2004, at para. 14). These inserts were then added to episodes before they were broadcast in the U.S.

Roberts asserts that the two programs meet all FCC standards for E/I programming:

> It is flatly incorrect to suggest, as I understand that the Petitioners here do, that the pro-social educational elements are merely added on to or wrapped around entertainment content. The process is a great deal more comprehensive and complex, and the educational elements are both more pervasive and more subtly integrated into the stories than the Petitioners seem to understand. (Roberts, 2004, at para. 17)

In defense of the use of a violent theme for educational programming, Roberts observes that:

> Some age-groups are particularly attracted to programming that includes confrontation and conflict as part of the storyline. When handled carefully, action-adventure formats can be effectively used to attract young viewers who might not otherwise view pro-social programming. (Roberts, 2004, at para. 18)

In the case of the second license renewal challenge, WPXW's owner, the Paxson Corporation, hired an esteemed developmental psychologist, Dr. Steven Ceci of Cornell University, to evaluate the educational quality of *Miracle Pets* as part of its rebuttal to the Petition to Deny. In his report filed on behalf of the station, Ceci provided several claims of educational value associated with episodes of the program that he viewed. For example, he observed that the program may teach vocabulary, noting that in one episode the word "reverberate" is used in a manner that allows adolescents to learn its meaning; and that the program may also teach brief scientific concepts, such as a segment in which a police dog chases a criminal, allowing the viewer to learn that "adrenalized individuals emit more scent hormones that are detectable by tracking dogs than nonadrenalized persons" and that "concrete surfaces are the poorest medium for holding scents" (Ceci, 2004, at para. 6). Ceci concludes that "these two points, when coupled with the vocabulary decontextualization, provide educationally useful information, particularly given what we know about American adolescents' poor relative and absolute performance on science and literacy achievement tests" (Ceci, 2004, at para. 6).

In responding to Ceci's report, the petitioners noted that none of Dr. Ceci's observations supported the station's original claim that *Miracle Pets* offers children positive role models, teaches prosocial values, and emphasizes the importance of taking care of pets. They argue: "Instead, Dr. Ceci identifies two purportedly educational aspects of the program that were not even mentioned by Paxson" in their license renewal claims ("Reply to Opposition of Paxson Washington License, Inc.", p. 14).

Despite his judgment that *Miracle Pets* holds educational value, Ceci himself conveyed some consternation at the process of evaluating the fit of the program with the FCC's policy:

> As an expert and specialist in children's cognitive and intellectual development, I am struck by the absence of rigorous thinking in the crafting of the FCC guidelines. Based on this same expertise and specialization, however, I can identify from the episodes of *Miracle Pets* on the videotape numerous examples of information that I regard as educationally meaningful (e.g., the vocabulary and concepts described above). *Miracle Pets* satisfies the standards as articulated by the FCC. (Ceci, 2004, at para. 8)

Implications of the CTA License Renewal Challenges

From a broader perspective, the challenges filed in these two cases and the defenses provided by the stations raise some fundamental questions. Is it possible to argue that virtually any television program holds at least some educational value for children? And if so, is it possible to then hold television stations accountable for compliance with the educational programming requirements of the Children's Television Act in any meaningful sense? In the 1970s, when the FCC first considered the prospect of children's programming requirements, then-FCC Commissioner Nicholas Johnson (1971) observed with wry wit: "All television is educational; the only question is—what is it teaching?"

These two cases raise the question of whether the television industry has taken that adage too literally.

At this point, all submissions in the two license renewal proceedings are complete and it is up to the FCC to decide the cases. For each station, the Commission may choose to reject the Petition to Deny and to approve the license renewal, or to designate the license renewal proceeding for a hearing before an Administrative Law Judge (ALJ) employed by the agency, who would then weigh all evidence on both sides and render a tentative decision. That decision would then be subject to final confirmation by a vote of all FCC Commissioners. Should either case be designated for a comparative hearing before an ALJ, the FCC would then be able to consider intermediate options in addition to simple approval or rejection of the license renewal, such as a short-term renewal that is the functional equivalent of being placed "on probation." It is normative for the process of license renewal challenges to unfold over an extended period of years, with some cases requiring more than a decade to reach a final conclusion based upon appeals of FCC decisions in the courts.

From an overall media policy perspective, these two cases are noteworthy because they represent the first serious legal challenge to a station's license renewal based on questions about any programming performance issue since the 1980s, when the FCC deregulated most of its public interest requirements for broadcasters (Wiley & Sechrest, 2005). For those interested in children's television policy, the cases are highly significant as they hold the prospect of clarifying where and how to draw the line in terms of what programming may qualify as educational for children. No such precedent yet exists, and clearly there are major challenges in translating the conceptual to the operational in this domain, as evidenced by the diversity of opinion about the educational value of these children's programs. Depending on the outcome of these two license renewal challenges and the precedent they establish, these cases may well exert tremendous influence on the future of children's programming that is aired to fulfill the requirements of the Children's Television Act. However, it is likely to be several years before a final outcome is reached and the implications of these two cases become clear.

CHILDREN AND ADVERTISING POLICY IN THE DIGITAL ERA

Background

Television has long been the predominant medium that advertisers have chosen for marketing products to children. Expenditures have been estimated at $15 billion annually for television advertising targeted at children (Barboza, 2003; Healy, 2004), with the average child viewer expected to see as many as 40,000 television commercials a year (Kunkel, 2001). In addition to television, advertisers are forging new beachheads to reach child audiences in alternative environments. Marketing in the schools has become commonplace (Boyles, 2005; U.S. Government Accountability Office, 2004), and advertising to children on the Internet is starting to surge (Cai & Gantz, 2000; Pereira, 2004).

Because young children lack the cognitive skills and abilities of older children and adults, they do not comprehend commercial messages in the same way as do more mature audiences, and, hence, may be particularly susceptible to advertising influence (Gunter, Oates, & Blades, 2005). A substantial body of research evidence documents age-related differences in how children understand and are influenced by television advertising. For example, children do not develop a basic understanding of the inherent bias and persuasive intent that necessarily underlies all advertising messages until at least 7 to 8 years of age (John, 1999; Kunkel, 2001). Prior to developing such knowledge, children tend to interpret advertising claims and appeals as fair, balanced, and accurate information, which presumably leads to more favorable reactions to television commercials.

This body of research has formed the basis for a wide range of policies in the United States designed to protect children from advertising, including several FCC regulations that limit the amount of commercial time and restrict certain advertising tactics such as host selling and program-length commercials in children's programming (Kunkel & Roberts, 1991).

Interactive Advertising to Children: The New Policy Battleground

The transition to digital television brings with it the functional equivalent of a merging of previously separate media platforms such as television and computers. That is, with the advent of interactive television on the horizon, viewers will be able to control and manipulate content in a manner much more akin to the experience of networked computing, such as is currently accomplished via browsing the Internet. Once interactivity is functional, viewers who see something that interests them during television viewing are likely to be able to "learn more about it" by signaling their television set with a remote control command that will trigger access to some supplementary material. One such application might be to enhance the value of educational programs by allowing child viewers to obtain more information about an intriguing topic presented in the program. For example, a cartoon that involves time travel might provide information about important historical periods and events from the past. Another obvious application of this new technical capability is to facilitate interactive advertising, which might occur in many different forms (Mehta, 2005).

There are several reasons to be concerned about interactive advertising to children. First, marketers may use interactivity to target particular products or ad strategies to individual viewers in a manner that significantly increases their persuasive power. This tactic is already occurring on the Internet in marketing to children. For example, at one time the *Barbie.com* Web site asked visitors to indicate what color they like and what is their favorite sport. Later during the visit, the site would then suggest that the visitor should take a look at a particular doll that shares the user's interest in volleyball and love for the color green, mimicking the user's indicated preferences. Gathering such information from children does not violate the Children's Online Privacy Protection Act (COPPA) if it does not contain personal identification that allows tracking of users; so long as the child remains anonymous, gathering the preference information is permitted without parental consent. The tailoring of commercial "pitches" that becomes possible with interactivity significantly enhances the potential impact of such marketing on young children.

Another cause for concern involves impulse purchasing that will soon become possible with interactive advertising and marketing. Cutting-edge cable television systems with interactivity currently allow TV viewers to order pizza delivery with their remote control device, or to schedule a test drive of a new car, with the car salesperson meeting the potential customer at their home doorstep (Donahue, 2004). Such applications will expand dramatically in the near future. Although Internet commerce currently requires a credit card or similar form of payment (e.g., Paypal), interactive marketing via television is likely to be account-based, particularly on cable systems. This means that the bill for a pizza order could simply be added to the monthly cable fee. If that's a convenience for single adults, it's a worrisome prospect for parents whose children may now be able to order products without their knowledge or consent. Such a worry would be further enhanced for child-oriented marketing, whether for toys, foods, or any other products.

Although current FCC policy limits the amount of time that advertising is permitted during children's programs, interactivity would potentially allow children to spend unlimited time in highly commercialized environments with a quick click of the remote control. Companies such as Disney plan to create "walled gardens" as a first step in implementing interactivity linked to their television programming *(Petition for Reconsideration of the Walt Disney Company, 2005)*. A walled garden is the functional equivalent of a Web site, including "adver-games" and other interactive features that promote program-related products. The distinction between a walled garden and a typical Web site merely involves constraint on connectivity to other interactive environments. Whereas typical web browsers and Web sites allow users to move freely between any Internet-based locations at will, an interactive television link to a walled garden would mean, for example, that Disney programming could limit its interactive connections solely to Disney walled garden sites. This approach, which is widely anticipated, may ease parental concern and leave them more willing to allow their children to use interactive television technology as compared to "surfing" the Internet and worrying where they would end up.

In its 2004 Report and Order, the FCC noted that "With the benefits of interactivity, however, come potential risks that children will be exposed to additional commercial influences" (FCC, 2004, at para. 54).

Although the Commission declined to issue any final regulations in this area, it conveyed a clear signal that it believes some protections are needed: "We tentatively conclude that we should prohibit interactivity during children's programming that connects viewers to commercial matter unless parents 'opt in' to such services" (FCC, 2004, at para. 72). The FCC announced that a Further Notice of Proposed Rulemaking would be conducted to clarify the details of this policy. It is not clear how such an "opt-in" system might work, though the idea is close conceptually to the parental approval required before Web sites may solicit any personal information from children under COPPA.

This preliminary ruling by the FCC creates a unique situation. From a political perspective, marketers and the television industry must be wary of any interactive advertising to children even though technically it could still be allowed until the FCC's tentative ruling is made final. This situation should clearly chill the prospects for the development of interactive advertising to children, which is still in its fledgling stages, though such efforts will certainly proceed for advertising targeting adults. The outcome is a rare victory for child advocates who have succeeded in convincing the FCC that interactive advertising to children should not be permitted even before it has surfaced in the United States.

That achievement was accomplished through the efforts of an ad-hoc group known as the Children's Media Policy Coalition. The principal members of the group include the American Academy of Pediatrics, American Academy of Child and Adolescent Psychiatrists, American Psychological Association, Children Now, National Institute on Media and the Family, National Parent–Teacher Association, and Office of Communications of the United Church of Christ, among others. The coalition benefits from extensive *pro bono* legal support from the Institute for Public Representation at the Georgetown University Law Center, under the direction of Professor Angela Campbell. Children Now serves as the coordinating arm of the coalition and typically posts related documents and announcements on its Web site (www.children-now.org).

The implications of this recent development are hard to gauge until the FCC takes further action to specify the operational details of the conceptual foundation it has laid. Although the Commission says that it will "prohibit interactivity during children's programming that connects viewers to commercial matter" (FCC, 2004, at para. 72), it is not clear exactly how the term "commercial matter" will be defined in this context. If the program contained an interactive link to a Web site and that site was primarily a shopping mall for kids' toys, it seems obvious such a link would be prohibited. But what if the site that is linked interactively has only incidental commercial messages, such as billboards and pop-up ads that commonly populate children's Web sites? No doubt media industry officials would argue that such a link should be allowed, whereas child advocates would protest that the presence of commercial matter in any proportion would disqualify such an interactive link from being allowed during children's programming.

The answers to operational questions such as this, as well as the FCC's final position on restricting interactive advertising to children, should be forthcoming in the near future. The agency has already issued a Further Notice of Proposed Rulemaking on this topic, and the period for comments and reply comments closed in May, 2005. The FCC strives to issue rulings on cases such as this within a year or so following the conclusion of public comments, although it is not unusual for delays to occur and final decisions sometimes take several years to be achieved.

Promoting Web Site Addresses During Children's Television Programming

The growth of the Internet in recent years has included significant efforts to attract child audiences to this new electronic medium ("More preschoolers now going online," 2005). Consistent with this trend, many if not most television programs and networks that target children have developed ancillary Web sites that young viewers can visit after the program is over, or perhaps for sophisticated multitasking children even while the program is on! These Web sites serve several functions for the sponsor, including building "brand loyalty" with their audience while also generating revenue from both direct product sales of licensed merchandise as well as advertising presented by third-party sources.

This has led some networks, such as Nickelodeon, to display Internet Web site addresses in a text overlay that remains on screen during most of their television programming. Because most such Web sites include substantial amounts of commercial content, an issue is raised regarding the extent to which such Web site promotions are permitted given the time limits on advertising during children's programming established by the CTA.

In its 2004 Report and Order, the FCC took steps to insure that such Web site promotions are not primarily commercial in nature. Effective in 2006, extended on-screen Web site promotions during children's programming are permitted only if a four-part test is met. To be allowed, a Web site that is promoted on-screen must:

1. offer a substantial amount of bona fide program-related or other noncommercial material;
2. not be primarily intended for commercial purposes;
3. clearly label and distinguish the noncommercial from the commercial sections of the home page and other menu pages; and
4. have a "landing page" (i.e., the page to which viewers are directed) that is not used for e-commerce, advertising, or other commercial purposes.

Web sites that do not meet these tests may still be advertised on television, but any time devoted to their promotion would be counted toward the commercial limits established by the CTA of 10.5 minutes/hour on weekends, 12 minutes/hour on weekdays.

In a related move, the FCC has extended its host-selling policy, first established in 1974, to apply to the advertising of Web sites on television. Effective in 2006, the Commission will prohibit the display of Web site addresses during children's programming, as well as any commercial advertising for Web sites that appears during children's programming, if the site "uses characters from the program to sell products or services" (FCC, 2004, at para. 51). In other words, if the Nickelodeon Web site features *Spongebob Squarepants* in a product ad for Kraft Macaroni & Cheese, the Web site address could not be displayed during the *Spongebob Squarepants* television program nor could an ad for the Nickelodeon Web site appear during the same program. This policy should lead to significant changes in current Web site advertising practices targeting children if it is implemented as announced, although numerous industry organizations have petitioned the FCC to reconsider this decision (McConnell, 2004). Final resolution of this issue as well as all of the FCC's new policies on digital advertising to children is likely to take a period of several years to sort out, given the typically slow bureaucratic pace of the agency.

THE FUTURE OF CHILDREN'S MEDIA ADVOCACY

This chapter has chronicled two key developments in children's television policy that have remained quite transparent to date: the FCC's 2004 ruling in the "kids digital" proceeding, as it is often termed; and the license renewal challenge filed against two Washington, D.C. area stations for failing to adequately fulfill their children's programming obligations. Both of these recent developments demonstrate a strong, proactive, and relatively effective ongoing public interest advocacy effort prosecuted by an amalgamation of different parties. This situation stands in contrast to the past, when only a single organization held dominant voice in representing children and media concerns in the nation's capital (see Montgomery, chap. 12, this volume).

In the 1970s and 1980s, Peggy Charren led Action for Children's Television (ACT) as it lobbied the FCC and Congress to improve the children's media environment. Then throughout the 1990s, Kathryn Montgomery led the Center for Media Education (CME) as the designated heir to the mission pioneered by Charren once she ended her operation. Although both ACT and CME were extraordinarily visible and successful in advocating for children's media causes, each was driven primarily by their leader and neither of the two organizations survived once their principal departed. Thus, when CME ceased its ongoing efforts in 2003 when Montgomery returned to a full-time academic position, a leadership vacuum clearly existed in the area of children's media advocacy.

It now appears that void has been filled effectively by a number of different groups rather than a single dominant voice. Under the leadership of Children Now, an array of public health and child-oriented advocacy groups known as the Children's Media Policy Coalition has now established itself as a central participant in the Washington-based policy battles in this realm. Among the key participants in the coalition are the American Academy of Pediatrics, American Academy of Child and Adolescent Psychiatrists, American Psychological Association, National Institute on Media and the Family, National Parent-Teacher Association, and Office of Communications of the United Church of Christ. Efforts pursued both jointly and individually by these organizations have begun to bear fruit, as this chapter documents. And indeed, the FCC's ruling in the kids digital proceeding stands out as a rare instance in which child advocates succeeded in establishing a policy framework to protect children's interests even *before* the industry could seize the initiative with new technological innovations likely to prove detrimental, such as interactive advertising to children.

This unusual success by the child advocacy community has generated significant resistance and opposition from the broadcast and cable industries. Richard Wiley and Lawrence Sechrest (2004), senior legal advocates for the media industries, reflect this stance, calling the FCC's digital public interest rules for children "highly premature," leading to educational programming requirements that "far exceed any reasonable marketplace need" (p. 238). Meanwhile, numerous media corporations such as Nickelodeon, Disney, and Turner Broadcasting have filed formal requests with the FCC (known as Petitions for Reconsideration) asking the agency to reverse the new policies on advertising to children. These requests are still pending and it is possible that the Commission will yet cede ground to these remonstrations. It seems the policy battle is never-ending.

One final development worthy of note on the policy front is the emergence of a legislative proposal known as CAMRA, the Children and Media Research Advancement Act (S 579 in the 109th Congress). The bill would establish an ongoing federal program of research on children and media issues housed in the National Institute of Child Health and Human Development, funded at the level of $90 million over the first 5 years. By the time they graduate from high school, children spend more time with media than they do in the classroom. Yet despite this balance, the federal government currently invests hundreds of millions of dollars in educational research but has no programmatic effort to study the broad public health impacts of children's media use.

Scientific research is one of the best catalysts to both inform and influence public policy regarding children and media. The CAMRA proposal holds the prospect to dramatically enhance the academic community's efforts to study all facets of the relationship between children and media, including such new concerns as the role of food marketing as a contributor to childhood obesity (Institute of Medicine, 2005). Such an investment would provide a welcome counterweight to the extraordinary lobbying capabilities of the media industries that help to shape regulatory policy outcomes toward their interests (Glassman, 2004). At the same time, it holds the potential to yield significant benefits to the nation's youth, which is the ultimate goal of all children and media policy.

Were CAMRA to be approved by the Congress, the research activity it would stimulate almost certainly would exert a profound influence on the state of knowledge about children and media, as well as help to shape the subsequent debate about children and media issues. But with or without this proposal being adopted, there is little doubt the policy battles in this realm will continue actively into the future.

REFERENCES

Advisory Committee on Public Interest Obligations of Digital Television Broadcasters. (1998). *Charting the digital broadcasting future: Final report of the Advisory Committee on Public Interest Obligations of Digital Television Broadcasters.* Washington, DC: Office of the Vice-President of the United States. Retrieved from September 1, 2005, at http://www.ntia.doc.gov/pubintadvcom/ pubint.htm

Barboza, D, (2003, August 3). If you pitch it, they will eat. *New York Times*, Sec. 3, p. 1.

BBC Shop. (2005). *Ace Lightning: Episodes* 1–3. Retrieved from September 1, 2005, http://www.bbcshop.com/invt/ebbcv 7337&bklist=%3Cvenda_bklist 1%3E

Benton Foundation. (2005). *Citizen's guide to the public interest obligations of digital television broadcasters*. Washington, DC: author. Retrieved September 1, 2005, from http://www.benton.org/pioguide/index.html

Boyles, D. R. (2005). *Schools or markets? Commercialism, privatization, and school-business partnerships*. Mahwah, NJ: Laurence Erlbaum Associates.

Cai, X., & Gantz, W. (2000). Online privacy issues associated with web sites for children. *Journal of Broadcasting & Electronic Media, 44*, 197–214.

Campaign Legal Center. (2005). *Broken promises: How digital broadcasters are failing to serve the public interest*. Washington, DC: Author. Retrieved September 1, 2005, from http://www.campaignlegalcenter.org/FCC-112.html

Ceci, S. (2004). *Declaration of Professor Stephen J. Ceci*. Appendix to *Opposition to Petition to Deny*, submission of Paxson Washington License, Inc. Before the Federal Communications Commission, Washington, DC. FCC File No. BRCT-20040527AGS.

Center for Media Education. (1992). *A report on station compliance with the Children's Television Act*. Washington, DC: Author.

Clark, D. (2005, February 18). Spectrum wars. *National Journal Online*. Retrieved September 1, 2005, http://www.nationaljournal.com/pubs/techdaily/

Cole, B., & Oettinger, M. (1978). *Reluctant regulators: The FCC and the broadcast audience*. Reading, MA: Addison-Wesley.

Donahue, S. (2004, May 3). Quiet, nosy Navic may be watching. *Multichannel News*. Available at http://www.multichannel.com/article/CA414339.html

Federal Communications Commission. (1996). In the matter of policies and rules concerning children's television programming: Report and order. *Federal Communications Commission Record, 11*, 10660–10778.

Federal Communications Commission. (2004). In the matter of children's television obligations of digital television broadcasters: Report and order and further notice of proposed rulemaking. *Federal Communications Commission Record, 19*, 22943–22996.

Federal Communications Commission. (2005). *Annual assessment of the status of competition in the market for delivery of video programming: Eleventh annual report*. Washington, DC: Author. Retrieved September 1, 2005, from http://www.fcc.gov/mb/csrptpg.html

Gateworld. (2004). *Stargate infinity*. Retrieved September 1, 2005, from http://www.gateworld.net/infinity/index.shtml

Glassman, M. (2004, November 1). Broadcast industry increases lobbying budget, study says. *New York Times*, p. C7.

Gunter, B., Oates, C., & Blades, M. (2005). *Advertising to children on TV: Content, impact, and regulation*. Mahwah, NJ: Lawrence Erlbaum Associates.

Healy, M. (2004, January 24). Those sugary Saturday mornings. *Los Angeles Times*, p. D1.

Institute of Medicine of the National Academies of Science. (2005). *Preventing childhood obesity: Health in the balance*. Washington, DC: National Academies Press.

John, D. R. (1999). Consumer socialization of children: A retrospective look at twenty-five years of research. *Journal of Consumer Research, 26*, 183–213.

Johnson, N. (1971, September 10). Nicholas Johnson of the Federal Communications Commission. *Life Magazine.*

Jordan, A. (1996). *The state of children's television: An examination of quantity, quality, and industry beliefs.* Washington, DC: Annenberg Public Policy Center. Retrieved September 1, 2005, from http://www.annenbergpublicpolicycenter.org/05_media_developing_child/childrensprogramming/childrens programming.htm

Jordan, A. (1998). *The 1998 state of children's television report: Programming for children over broadcast and cable television.* Washington, DC: Annenberg Public Policy Center. Retrieved September 1, 2005, from http://www.annenbergpublicpolicycenter.org/05_media_developing_child/childrensprogramming/childrensprogramming.htm

Jordan, A. (2000). *Is the three-hour rule living up to its potential?* Washington, DC: Annenberg Public Policy Center. Retrieved September 1, 2005, from http://www.annenbergpublicpolicycenter.org/05_media_developing_child/childrensprogramming/childrensprogramming.htm

Jordan, A., & Woodard, E. (1997). *The 1997 state of children's television report: Programming for children over broadcast and cable television.* Washington, DC: Annenberg Public Policy Center. Retrieved September 1, 2005, from http://www.annenbergpublicpolicycenter.org/05_media_developing_child/childrensprogramming/childrensprogramming.htm

Kaiser Family Foundation. (2004). *Parents, media, and public policy: A Kaiser Family Foundation survey.* Menlo Park, CA: Author. Retrieved September 1, 2005, from http://www.kff.org/entmedia/entmedia092304pkg.cfm

Krasnow, E., Longley, L., & Terry, H. (1982). *The politics of broadcast regulation,* (3rd ed.). New York: St. Martin's Press.

Kunkel, D. (1991). Crafting media policy: The genesis and implications of the Children's Television Act of 1990. *American Behavioral Scientist, 35,* 181–202.

Kunkel, D. (2001). Children and television advertising. In D. Singer & J. Singer (Eds.), *Handbook of children and the media* (pp. 375–393). Thousand Oaks, CA: Sage.

Kunkel, D. (2003) The road to the V-chip: Media violence and public policy. In D. Walsh & D. Gentile (Eds.), *Media violence and children* (pp. 227–245). Westport, CT: Praeger.

Kunkel, D. (2004). *Declaration of Dale Kunkel, Ph.D.* Appendix to *Petition to Deny the License Renewal of WPXW and WDCA,* submission of Office of Communication of the United Church of Christ and Center for Digital Democracy. Before the Federal Communications Commission, Washington, DC. FCC File No. BRCT-20040527AGS.

Kunkel, D., & Canepa, J. (1994). Broadcasters' license renewal claims regarding children's educational programming. *Journal of Broadcasting and Electronic Media, 38,* 397–416.

Kunkel, D., & Goette, U. (1997). Broadcasters' response to the Children's Television Act. *Communication Law and Policy, 2,* 289–308.

Kunkel, D., & Roberts, D. (1991). Young minds and marketplace values: Research and policy issues in children's television advertising. *Journal of Social Issues, 47*(1), 57–72.

Kunkel, D., & Watkins, B. (1987). Evolution of children's television regulatory policy. *Journal of Broadcasting and Electronic Media, 31*, 367–389.

Kunkel, D., & Wilcox, B. (2001). Children and media policy. In D. Singer & J. Singer (Eds.), *Handbook of children and the media* (pp. 589–604). Thousand Oaks, CA: Sage.

Lee, J. (2003, June 3). Deregulating the media: Lobbyists' comments showed solid opposition. *New York Times,* p. C8.

McConnell, B. (2004, December 21). Nets fight kids' web-link ban. *Broadcasting & Cable Online.* Retrieved September 1, 2005.

Mehta, S.N. (2005, July 27). The future of advertising: How the web will save the commercial. *Fortune Magazine Online.* Retrieved September 1, 2005, from http://www.fortune.com/fortune/technology/articles/0,15114,1085996,00.html

More preschoolers now going online. (2005, July 1). *ESchool News Online.* Retrieved September 1, 2005, from http://www.eschoolnews.com/news/showStory.cfm?ArticleID=5750&CFID=1848388&CFTOKEN=66345713

National Television Violence Study, Volume 2. (1998). Thousand Oaks, CA: Sage.

New America Foundation. (2005). *Speeding the DTV transition: Facts and policy options.* Washington, DC: Author. Retrieved September 1, 2005, from http://www.newamerica.net/index.cfm?pg=docs&SecID=3&DocTypeID=5

Palmer, E. L. (1987). *Children in the cradle of television.* Lexington, MA: Lexington Books.

Pecora, N.O. (1998). *The business of children's entertainment.* New York: Guilford Press.

Pereira, J. (2004, May 3). Junk food games: Online arcades draw fire for immersing kids in ads. *Wall Street Journal,* pp. B1, B4.

Petition for Reconsideration of the Walt Disney Company. (2005). In the matter of children's television obligations of digital television broadcasters. Before the Federal Communications Commission, Washington, DC. MM Docket No. 00-167.

Petition to Deny the License Renewal of WPXW and WDCA on behalf of Office of Communication of the United Church of Christ and Center for Digital Democracy. Before the Federal Communications Commission, Washington, DC. FCC File No. BRCT-20040527AGS.

Roberts, D. (2004). *Declaration of Donald F. Roberts, Thomas More Storke Professor, Department of Communication, Stanford University.* Appendix to *Submission of DIC Entertainment Corp. in Support of Fox Television to United Church of Christ and Center for Digital Democracy Petition to Deny Application for Renewal of WDCA-TV, Washington, D.C.* Before the Federal Communications Commission, Washington, DC. FCC File No. BRCT-20040527AKL.

Schmitt, K. (1999). *The three-hour rule: Is it living up to expectations?* Washington, DC: Annenberg Public Policy Center. Retrieved September 1, 2005, from http://www.annenbergpublicpolicycenter.org/05_media_developing_child/childrensprogramming/childrensprogramming.htm

Turow, J. (1981). *Entertainment, education, and the hard sell: Three decades of network children's television.* New York: Praeger.

U.S. Government Accountability Office. (2004). *Commercial activities in schools.* Washington, DC: Author. Retrieved September 1, 2005, from http://www.searching.gao.gov/query.html?col=allsite&qt=advertising+in+the+

schools&charset=iso-8859-1&amo=9&ady=11&ayr=2004&bmo=9&bdy=12&
    byr= 2005
Ventura, E. (2005). Power chip: Why the right hates the V-chip. *The New Republic Online.* Retrieved September 1, 2005, from https://www.ssl.tnr.com/p/docsub.
    mhtml?i=w050509&s=ventura051205
WDCA. (2003). *FCC Form 398 Children's Television Programming Report for quarter ending December 31, 2003.* Washington, DC: Author.
WDCA. (2004). *FCC Form 398 Children's Television Programming Report for quarter ending June 30, 2004.* Washington, DC: Author.
Wiley, R. E., & Sechrest, L. W. (2005). Recent developments in program content regulation. *Federal Communications Law Journal, 57,* 235–242.
WPXW. (2002). *FCC Form 398 Children's Television Programming Report for quarter ending September 30, 2002.* Washington, DC: Author.

12

Advocating Children's Television

Kathryn C. Montgomery
American University

I had given this lecture on television violence many times in my more than 15 years of teaching communication. To illustrate my explanation of the theories and research on the subject, I had brought a videotape with clips of violent scenes from children's cartoon shows. But I wasn't in a university classroom. I was in a large, ornately decorated, ceremonial room in the Old Executive Office Building, directly adjacent to the White House. My "class" on this hot summer Washington afternoon—seated around a long, polished conference table—included the Vice President of the United States, several prominent Senators and Congressmen, and nine representatives from the leading national education, health and child advocacy organizations.

This impromptu lesson took place in June, 1997 during a month-long series of closed-door negotiations between television industry leaders and the children's television advocacy community. Our task was to hammer out some amendments to the new TV program rating system developed by the industry and announced a few months earlier. White House staff had hastily arranged this special private session with Vice President Al Gore, to which industry leaders had not been invited. Shortly after the meeting, the Vice President's office issued a press statement urging negotiators to "put the V back in the V-chip" ("Put V for Violence," 1997). The TV industry cried foul, charging the White House with inappropriate interference, and abruptly halted the negotiations. But the talks soon resumed and an agreement was finally reached a few weeks later. The resulting ratings system—a set of hybrid labels that combined age and content descriptors—was flawed at best. But the process that produced it was a quintessential case of Washington politics.

My involvement in the V-chip ratings negotiations was just one of many experiences as an advocate during 12 years at the helm of the Center for Media Education (CME), an organization I cofounded in 1991. Throughout the 1990s, CME worked with dozens of nonprofit groups, professional associations, academic institutions, and foundations to promote media policies on behalf of children and youth. During this turbulent decade, a series of technological, economic, and regulatory changes transformed the media system. The Internet and a host of accompanying digital technologies rapidly intruded into U.S. homes. An already fragmented electronic media culture exploded still further into hundreds of cable television channels and thousands of Web sites. The 1990s also witnessed the first major Congressional rewrite of the nation's telecommunications laws since the New Deal, sparking a flurry of intense political activity, as industry lobbyists, politicians, and interest groups competed to stake their respective claims in the new policy regime (Aufderheide, 1999). These simultaneous tectonic shifts—in both the media and the regulatory landscape—created particularly fertile ground for a renewal of long-standing debates over the role of media in the lives of children. At the same time, they presented fresh, new challenges to policymakers, parents, and advocates.

In the following pages, I discuss three major television and media policy issues with which the Center for Media Education was involved during this crucial decade, placing each case into historical and political context, explaining the strategy behind our advocacy efforts, and assessing their impact. I have also incorporated into my discussion some of the lessons that can be learned from these policy experiences, offering my analysis and insights from the perspective of both an advocate and a media scholar.

Throughout the 50-year history of television, many different organizations and individuals have engaged in communications policy advocacy on behalf of children. A number of these have been multiissue groups, for which improving children's television has been only one of a myriad of policy goals. They have included: media watchdog groups such as the National Association for Better Broadcasting and the National Citizens Committee for Broadcasting; professional associations such as the American Medical Association, the American Academy of Pediatrics, and the American Psychological Association; and parents groups such as the National PTA. Advocates have represented a broad spectrum of political perspectives, from the liberal National Education Association to the conservative Parents Television Council. From time to time, coalitions have formed to advocate for change in specific policy areas, such as television violence, advertising safeguards, or quality children's programming (Kunkel, 2001; Montgomery,

1989; Rowland, 1983; Suman & Rossman, 2000). Academic researchers have also played a significant role as advocates for children's media policy, contributing their scholarly work to the policy debate, and testifying before congressional committees, regulatory agencies, and other government bodies (Kunkel, 2001; Rowland, 1983).

The 1960s and 1970s witnessed a proliferation of "media reform groups," organized in the wake of the U.S. civil rights movement. Representing African Americans, Hispanics, women, homosexuals, and a host of other issues and constituencies, many of these organizations took their causes to the Federal Communications Commission (FCC), the agency charged with regulating broadcasting (Cole & Oettinger, 1978; Krasnow, Longley, & Terry, 1982; Montgomery, 1989). Action for Children's Television (ACT) was one of them. Launched in 1968, the small activist group of Boston mothers quickly rose to become the leading advocacy organization representing the interests of children in television policy.

For decades, ACT played a critical leadership role in defining and promoting a policy agenda for children—lobbying for advertising safeguards, improvement in the quantity and quality of children's programming, and support for public television. ACT's strategies and tactics were consistent with those of many other political organizations involved in social movements (Benford & Snow, 2000; Gamson, 1990; McAdam, McCarthy, & Zald, 1996; Ryan, 1991). The group worked collaboratively with the academic community, commissioning studies to document programming and advertising practices in children's television and using this research to spark press coverage, frame the public debate, and fortify its policy advocacy positions at regulatory agencies and in Congress. As a watchdog, ACT followed the television industry very closely, exposing egregious and questionable practices in the press, and chastising TV executives (both publicly and privately). The organization also gave awards and public kudos to networks and producers for their positive contributions to children. Though it often worked in coalitions with child advocacy, health, and education groups, ACT was a highly visible and outspoken advocate for free speech, refusing to join campaigns against television violence, and filing legal challenges against attempts to censor program content (Cole & Oettinger, 1978; Foote & Mrookin, 1980; Hendershot, 1998).

When Action for Children Television closed its doors in 1992, the Center for Media Education assumed the role of carrying on ACT's work. Our organization shared many of ACT's issues, strategies, and values, but there were also key differences. Whereas ACT had maintained its headquarters in Boston, CME was based in Washington, D.C. This enabled us to develop more routine ongoing relationships with a number of advocacy and nonprofit organizations. Our mission encompassed a broader set of media policy issues, with a particular emphasis on the technological changes that were ushering in a new digital media system. For example, we cofounded the Telecommunications Policy Roundtable, a coalition of civil liberty, education, and computer groups that advocated a set of "Public Interest Principles for the Information Superhighway." CME's children's television policy efforts were part of a constituency-building strategy to mobilize groups concerned about children in support of a policy agenda for the new technologies. As part of that effort, we encouraged education and library groups to become involved in the Congressional deliberations over the Telecommunications Act of 1996. Their participation in the proceedings ultimately led to passage of the so-called "e-rate" provisions, providing schools and libraries with affordable access to the Internet (Federal Communications Commission, [FCC], n.d.).

Policy advocacy is a challenging, messy, and far-from-perfect process. For public interest and consumer groups, engaging politically around media issues means taking on some of the largest corporations in the world, whose flowing campaign funds, enormous lobbying infrastructures, and access to the highest policymakers in the country pose daunting challenges to the tiny, underfunded nonprofit community. In a political world where media coverage is an essential tool for any campaign, advocates for media policies are presented with particularly formidable obstacles, struggling to gain the attention of news organizations whose corporate agendas may conflict with their journalistic responsibilities. Gaining media visibility requires careful strategy and relentless effort. Advocates must also remain flexible. No matter how much effort is put into planning strategies and tactics, plans will need to be adjusted or scrapped to take advantage of a new opportunity or respond to a sudden crisis. Often decisions must be made in haste, without time for reflection. When the public policies themselves are finally decided, they are frequently more a product of political expediency and compromise than thoughtful deliberation or research. In the final analysis, it may be a set of external circumstances entirely beyond the control of the advocates that proves to be the deciding factor in the resolution of a policy matter. And, in some cases, policies may work well as political solutions, but function poorly as remedies for the problems they were supposed to solve.

In my own experience as an advocate, I never found a one-size-fits-all policy framework to guide all of my decisions; in each case, I had to work out a position that fit my own values and those of my organization, choosing whether to take a lead on an issue, support the campaigns of others, take public positions in the media, or remain in the background.

The cases that follow revolve around three of the most visible and long-standing issues in the history of children's television advocacy. Each brief account illustrates some of the complexities and contradictions inherent in the policy advocacy process. In many ways, the campaigns with which the Center for Media Education was involved were influenced by political battles and policy decisions that preceded us. At the same time, the strategies, tactics, and ultimate outcomes of these later efforts were shaped by a unique set of technological, political, and economic developments that converged during the 1990s.

CHILDREN'S EDUCATIONAL PROGRAMMING

Quality children's programming has been a central issue in children's advocacy, public debate, and government policy for decades. As early as 1970, Action for Children's Television petitioned the Federal Communications Commission to require television broadcasters to air a minimum of 14 hours per week of programming designed for children, as part of each station's obligation to serve the public interest. Although the group's petition was never formally adopted as an FCC rule, ACT's advocacy efforts were successful on several fronts. The campaign generated extensive press coverage, fostering and framing a broad public debate about the quality of children's television that continues to this day. It also forced the issue of children's television programming onto the formal policy agenda at the FCC, where a special unit was established to conduct research and policy development on the issues. Although the resulting 1974 FCC policy statement was a vaguely worded document that lacked the force of law, it articulated the principle that addressing children's programming needs was part of a television station's responsibility to serve the public interest (Cole & Oettinger, 1978; Kunkel, 2001; Kunkel & Wilcox, 2001).

In the 1980s, under a new deregulatory FCC regime, many of the policies governing a broad range of public interest obligations for broadcasters, including children's television, were dismantled altogether. ACT responded by challenging the FCC rules in court, which, in turn, remanded some of the decisions back to the Commission for reconsideration. At the same time, the advocacy group took its cause to Congress, along with a coalition of children's educational and health groups. These efforts ultimately led to passage of the 1990 Children's Television Act, the first federal law to mandate that television stations address the programming needs of children. Under the CTA, all television stations are required to document to the FCC how they were serving the educational and informational needs of children through their overall programming when renewing their licenses. The law also stipulates that some of this programming must be "specifically designed" to educate. (Another provision of the Children's Television Act reinstated some of the earlier safeguards for children's advertising, including time limits '[Children's Television Act', 1990; Kunkel & Wilcox, 2001]).

Activists who lobbied for the CTA had hoped that the broadcast industry would take this obligation seriously, creating new educational programs for commercial television that would engage and enlighten children. Unfortunately, these hopes were not fully realized. In 1991, the television industry convinced the FCC to craft implementation rules for the CTA that significantly undermined the law's effectiveness (Kunkel, 2001).

My own involvement with this issue began the year before the Center for Media Education was established. As a consultant to a science education nonprofit organization, I conducted several interviews with producers and network programmers to assess their openness to the idea of creating children's programs about science. I was dismayed to learn that the networks had no intention of making any changes in their children's program schedules to comply with the Children's Television Act. I was instead advised to tell my client to develop "interstitials" about science—short 1 to 2-minute spots that could be inserted between programs without disrupting the existing schedule. "Children go to school all week," I was told repeatedly, "they don't want to have to go to school on Saturday morning."

In 1991, the Center for Media Education began laying the groundwork for what became a national campaign to strengthen the rules on the Children's Television Act. We approached ACT President, Peggy Charren, who encouraged our involvement in the issue. We also began developing allies with large membership organizations that could help us build a national and grassroots constituency. Although a broad coalition of health, education, and child advocacy groups had lobbied for passage of the Children's Television Act during the late 1980s, once it became law, these groups were directing their energies to other front-burner policy issues with which they were involved. Most had little time to pay attention to what was happening in children's television. CME began meeting with representatives of these organizations, explaining our concerns about the law's poor implementation and enlisting their support for our efforts to promote stronger enforcement.

In 1992, CME partnered with the Institute for Public Representation, a public-interest project at Georgetown University Law Center that trains attorneys in public interest law and provides pro-bono services to the advocacy community. Working with law students at IPR, we began examining the license renewal applications that had been submitted to the FCC by the first group of stations required to comply with the Children's Television Act. Our analysis revealed that most stations had done very little to fulfill their mandate to serve children's educational needs. Most of the programming that stations designated as educational contained only minimal content of a prosocial nature. In a number of cases, the stations had simply relabeled their standard fare of entertainment cartoons and reruns, writing up lofty-sounding descriptions of these shows for their license renewal forms. And although a handful of new educational programs had been created in response to the Children's Television Act, stations routinely scheduled these so-called "FCC-friendly" shows during predawn time slots between 5:00 and 7:00 a.m. (Center for Media Education [CME], 1992).

We wrote up our findings in a descriptive report designed to frame the problem in the press and publicly shame both the broadcasting industry and the FCC for their failure to carry out the mandate of the Children's Television Act. The 12-page document described the patterns we had found, providing illustrations and examples from the license renewal documents. We purposely identified the call letters, and quoted directly from the stations' applications to document the pattern of lackluster response, cynical reporting, and irresponsible scheduling. Emblematic of this pattern was one broadcaster's description of the 1960s cartoon series, *The Jetsons*, as a program "specifically designed" to educate children because it "teaches children what life will be like in the 21st century" (Center for Media Education, 1997, p. 3). CME's report ended with a call for specific policy actions at the FCC, including an investigation of license renewal applications, and a formal rule-making procedure to revise and strengthen the implementation rules (CME, 1992). (A subsequent content analysis of station license renewals, using social science methods, found similar programming and reporting patterns. [Kunkel & Capena, 1994]).

To ensure media coverage for the report, we assembled a group of representatives from well-known and respected organizations, including the National PTA, the National Education Association, and the American Academy of Pediatrics, along with Peggy Charren, for an event at the National Press Club. Working through existing relationships with reporters in both the trade and mainstream press, CME staff pitched the report for several weeks in advance of its formal release. The event was held in late September, 1992.

The report generated extensive media coverage, including a front-page story in *The New York Times* (Andrews, 1992). Within a few months, the FCC had conducted its own analysis, finding similar problems to those in CME's report, and launched a formal inquiry on the Children's Television Act (Federal Communications Commission, 1993).

There is little doubt that the election of Democrat Bill Clinton as President 1 month after the release of CME's 1992 report was a fortuitous event for children's television advocate. Under new leadership, the FCC was much more sympathetic to our cause than the previous administration had been. However, it wasn't quite that simple. Though the Clinton-appointed FCC Chair, Reed Hundt, did eventually take up the cause of improving children's television, his support was not immediate. In the early days of the campaign, the children's television coalition met repeatedly with Hundt and the other commissioners, supplying each of them with reams of academic studies on the benefits of prosocial and educational programming, in order to make the case for new rules. Congressional leaders such as Edward Markey (D-Mass), one of the sponsors of the children's television legislation, played a key role in encouraging FCC support, by conducting oversight hearings and jawboning the Commission. Nor is quality programming for children's television exclusively a partisan issue. Passage of the Children's Television Act required a buy-in from members on both sides of the aisle.

Over the next 4 years, the Center for Media Education, leading a coalition of more than 70 education, health, and child advocacy organizations, waged a campaign for stronger children's educational television requirements. Our efforts combined a full spectrum of political advocacy tactics, including: (1) continued monitoring of broadcast industry practices; (2) public education and outreach to the nonprofit community, educators, and parents; (3) grassroots efforts in several strategic broadcast markets; (4) an ongoing press and media campaign; (5) formal comments and testimony before the FCC and Congressional oversight committees; and (6) numerous meetings with staff and policymakers at the FCC, in Congress, and in the White House. We also took advantage of several opportunities that presented themselves during the time period when our campaign took place. For example, when Westinghouse announced a planned takeover of CBS, we filed a petition to deny the license transfer, extracting an agreement from the new company on children's programming that set a key precedent for a change in the rules (Andrews, 1995).

The broadcast industry, through its powerful lobbying organization, the National Association of Broadcasters, countered with its own press and political campaign. The industry also responded by adding new educational programs to head off stronger government regulations, hiring educational consultants to provide input and lend legitimacy to programming initiatives, and conducting its own studies of compliance (CME, 1997). In the final analysis, however, these efforts were unable to prevent regulatory action.

Ultimately, both the FCC and the White House realized that it was in the best political interests of the administration to take a leadership role in calling for quality children's media, particularly as the election year got closer, and internal political polls showed that these kinds of "family value" issues were appealing to both liberals and conservatives, and thus could be valuable to Clinton's reelection campaign.

The FCC reached its decision on the Children's Television Act rules in the summer of 1996, just a few months before President Clinton was reelected. The White House brokered a set of telephone negotiations with the National Association of Broadcasters, the FCC, and leaders of the advocacy community over a weekend. We were all urged to reach an agreement in time for a high-profile White House Summit on Children's Television scheduled for that Monday, which was designed to show that the Clinton Administration was doing something to help families. Passage of the Telecommunications Act of 1996 a few months earlier had also played a role in pressuring the broadcast industry—which had many issues on the table during the Congressional deliberations—to give in on the requirements for more educational programming (Levy, 1996).

The final FCC rule-making was issued a few months after the summer negotiations. The central provision was a new requirement that allowed television broadcasters who sought an automatic license renewal to certify they had provided at least 3 hours of children's educational programming per week (FCC, 1996; Kunkel, 2001). The advocates had originally called for 1 hour per day, speculating that we would be lucky to get half that amount. The "processing guideline" that we proposed and the FCC adopted was purposely designed to give broadcasters flexibility in responding to their obligations to serve children, preempting charges that the new rules were forcing stations to air a 'quota' of programming. The Commission also clarified its definition of what constituted an educational or informational program. The only programs that would count toward the 3-hour minimum were "core" programs, which were required to have: a "significant purpose" of educating children 16 and under; a clearly stated, written educational objective; and a target age group as the intended audience. Core programs also had to be at least 30 minutes in length, regularly scheduled, and broadcast between the hours of 7:00 a.m. and 10:00 p.m. (FCC, 1996).

For several years after the new rules took effect, the Annenberg Public Policy Center conducted follow-up studies to evaluate the effectiveness of the new policy, and held yearly conferences on the subject (Allen & Wolf, 2001; Davis, 1997; Schmitdt, 1999; Jordan, 2000). These efforts achieved a number of objectives: keeping the issue visible in the press, providing valuable research to the FCC the industry, and the public; and fostering more collaborative relationships among academic researchers and television industry professionals. Other nonprofits, such as L.A.-based Mediascope, worked cooperatively with the children's television production and programming community, supplying them with experts and research designed to facilitate and maximize industry compliance with the new programming requirements.

The combination of all these efforts appears to have had an effect on the quality and quantity of children's educational programming (Kunkel, 2001). Academic studies have shown that many of the new educational programs created after the stronger rules were implemented have had a beneficial impact on children's cognitive/intellectual and social/emotional learning (Calvert, 2003). A study in 2000 by the Annenberg Center found that a majority of television stations were providing at least 3 hours per week of core children's educational programming. However, nearly a quarter of these programs were only "minimally educational" (Jordan, 2000).

One of the linchpins of the law was the ability of community groups to challenge a station license where a broadcaster had not fulfilled its programming obligations to children. The new rules created several public accountability mechanisms designed to provide more information to parents about how they can get involved in making the law more effective (CME, 1997). However, although there have been numerous academic studies on the impact of the Children's Television Act, there has been very little grassroots political activism. Dependent on private foundations for support, the Center for Media Education was not able to acquire sufficient funds to coordinate such efforts at the local level, though we had done so as part of our campaign to strengthen the rules. Moreover, by 1996 we had already begun to focus our research and advocacy attention on the Internet and other new digital technologies. As a consequence, almost no oversight has been conducted, either by the public or the Commission. In 2004, the United Church of Christ's Office of Communication and the Center for Digital Democracy, working again with Georgetown University Law Center's Institute for Public Representation, challenged the licenses of several television stations in the Washington, D.C. area. Their petition was reminiscent of CME's study 12 years before, charging that shows such as *Miracle Pets* and *Ace Lightning* did not meet the FCC definition of children's educational programming ("Church Challenges," n.d.).

Recently, a coalition of advocacy groups led by Children Now was able to use the 3-hour CTA rule and other provisions of the programming guidelines as an important precedent for a campaign on public interest responsibilities for digital broadcast television. As a consequence, the 2004 rules on digital television included new mandates for additional children's educational programming, which could amount to 18 hours per week in some cases (Children Now, 2004). However, it remains to be seen whether the industry will invest the time and money to develop digital programming and services that truly serve children's educational needs.

TELEVISION VIOLENCE

Concerns about TV violence began as early as the 1950s, when Congress first took up the issue in hearings on juvenile delinquency. By the 1960s, social scientists in the growing field of mass communication had begun to accumulate studies documenting the nature and extent of the harms to children and youth posed by media violence. Over the years, several generations of academic experts testified before Congressional Committees. Dozens of bills were introduced aimed at reducing television violence, but none became law (Kunkel & Wilcox, 2001). In the private sector, boycott campaigns were waged against the TV industry from a wide spectrum of interest groups—from the National PTA to the American Medical Association to the National Federation for Decency. But although these efforts generated widespread press coverage, their impacts were transitory. Under heightened pressure, the TV industry would reduce violent content; but as soon as the pressure lifted, programming would return to business as usual and violence would rise to its previous levels (Montgomery, 1989). After decades of Congressional debate, millions of dollars in research, and repeated industry promises of self-regulation, no workable remedy had emerged for the longstanding problem of television violence.

Beginning in the1980s, a series of developments took place that laid the groundwork for a new regulatory regime to address the problem of television violence. As television fragmented through the growth of cable and satellites, more and more niche channels were created, bringing about a more competitive environment. With hundreds of channels competing feverishly for viewers' attention, television continued to push the envelope of acceptable content, triggering greater public concern. Industry mechanisms that had successfully deflected outside criticism—including the National Association of Broadcasters' "code of good practice"—were dismantled. Government deregulation of broadcasting, along with corporate takeovers and media mergers, had also resulted in cutbacks of the networks' standards and practices departments, whose job had been to maintain programming standards and deflect outside criticism. All of these changes prompted outcries from politicians, parents, and advocacy groups, who decried the deteriorating quality of the media culture (Montgomery, 1989).

In 1990, the same year that the Children's Television Act was enacted, Congress passed the first legislation aimed at addressing the TV violence problem. Introduced by Senator Paul Simon (D-Ill.), the law suspended the television industry antitrust provisions for 3 years to enable (and encourage) industry leaders to get together and work out a self-regulatory plan for curbing excessive violence in their programming (Kunkel, 2001). However, the TV industry did virtually nothing during the next few years. Only as the law was about to sunset in 1993, did the television networks respond to renewed pressures from Capitol Hill with a series of moves aimed at deflecting the rising tide of criticism. As Congressional leaders introduced numerous bills designed to reduce violence, industry executives responded by offering voluntary content guidelines, airing advisories, and funding academic research to assess the types and levels of violent program content (Eastin, 2001). In the meantime, several major child advocacy, health, and education groups had been meeting with lawmakers for years to push for some kind of government intervention on television violence. One of the proposals was to require that television sets be equipped with a chip that could block out violent programming. This "V-chip" had been developed in Canada and was becoming part of that country's policy for addressing the violence issue (Price, 1998).

In 1994, as Congress began deliberating a major overhaul of the U.S. telecommunications policy, legislators, working with public health and parents advocates, introduced legislative proposals for requiring a V-chip. When the Telecommunications Act of 1996 was finally signed into law, it contained a provision requiring, for the first time, that all new television sets be equipped with an electronic chip that would enable parents to block programs (Price, 1998). In the complex negotiations over the legislation, as various deals were struck between Republicans and Democrats, the "V-chip" had morphed into a device for blocking out not only violence, but also sex, and any other "indecent material" (Price, 1998).

The legislative language mandating the V-chip had been carefully crafted to walk a very thin First Amendment tightrope. In order for the chip to work, television programs would need to be rated. The law did not require the television industry to rate its programs, but if programmers chose to do so, then the ratings signal would have to be transmitted. Any guidelines developed by industry would be submitted to the FCC, which was required to consult with "public interest groups and individuals in the private sector" in order to determine whether the guidelines were "acceptable" (FCC, 1997). If the proposed system was judged by the FCC to be unacceptable, or if the industry did not come up with a ratings system within 1 year, then the Commission was required to step in and convene an advisory group to develop a ratings system (Price, 1998).

Congress and the White House found ways to encourage cooperation from the TV industry, which had much to gain from the deregulatory provisions of the Telecommunications Act. Immediately after the law's passage in February 1996, TV industry leaders announced at a White House summit that they would develop a set of voluntary parental guidelines to work with the V-chip (Price, 1998).

Although the Center for Media Education had participated in some of the meetings with Congressional leaders and other advocates prior to passage of the legislation, for the most part, we had remained on the side-lines during the early stages of this debate. Like Action for Children's Television, we were reluctant to endorse any policy proposals that might restrict speech. At the same time, however, we shared the concerns of advocacy colleagues who were alarmed by the rise in popular children's programs such as *The Mighty Morphin Power Rangers,* in which violence had become a dominant theme (Levin & Carlsson- Paige, 1995). It was not until a number of months after the industry had announced its ratings system that we became directly involved in the V-chip issue.

The Motion Picture Association of America, (MPAA) under the leadership of its President, Jack Valenti, had assumed the role of developing the new television ratings system, to be modeled on the MPAA's movie ratings (G, PG–13, etc.). The groups that had been working on the television violence issue for many years, on the other hand, wanted a system that would enable parents to identify which programs contained violence, as well as the nature or level of violence. This type of labeling system was already in use on pay-cable television networks such as Home Box Office (HBO). The content-based approach had also been supported by several academic studies, as well as public opinion polls (Cantor, 1998; Kaiser Family Foundation, 1998). The MPAA agreed to conduct a series of consultations with public health experts, educators, children's advocates, and academic experts, in order to seek input on the design of the new system. Within a few months, however, it was clear to many people involved in the process that the industry had no intention of making any substantial changes in its plans, and was moving forward with its age-based system. Sometime during this process, an FCC attorney approached the Center for Media Education and urged us to organize a political intervention before the whole matter ended up in the hands of the FCC. The Commission clearly wanted to avoid having to develop a TV ratings system, he explained. This was uncharted constitutional territory into which the government agency did not want to venture.

In early December, 1996, Valenti conducted one of his last consultative meetings, this one at the Washington, D.C. headquarters of the National Association of Broadcasters, where representatives from a variety of educational institutions and nonprofit advocacy groups had been invited, including the Center for Media Education. That same morning, however, *The Washington Post* had already published the industry's plan for the new age-based system, which had been leaked to one of its reporters (Farhi, 1996). When confronted with the article, Valenti vehemently denied that the system had been decided on, insisting that he was there to listen to ideas from the participants. But from his remarks during the remainder of the meeting, it was obvious that the industry had no intention of changing its plans. The new guidelines were scheduled to be released in the next few weeks, and Valenti was asking the groups that had been included in the consultations to endorse the plan, suggesting it would be a good form of publicity for them.

Although there was widespread dissatisfaction among the participants at this meeting, up to this point, there had been no organized political opposition to the industry's plans. Working with the National PTA, the Center for Media Education decided to take action. Though we knew it was probably too late to get the industry to make any changes, we believed it was important to make a public stand. We contacted all of the groups on the MPAA's list and urged them not only to refuse to endorse the industry proposal, but also to sign an open letter to Jack Valenti, opposing the age-based system and calling for a rating system that would label the content in the individual programs.

In the meantime, the White House was planning a large, high-profile "photo-op" celebration to announce the new V-chip ratings, inviting several families to participate, along with representatives from various public interest groups. The Clinton administration had already made a major political investment in the V-chip during Bill Clinton's successful bid for reelection earlier that year. The President had made a special reference to the V-chip in his January State of the Union address, and had highlighted the new provision in the Telecommunications Act the following month, when he signed it into law. To drive a wedge between the White House and the television industry, we organized a small delegation of representatives from several national education and public health organizations to meet with the Vice President, expressing our unhappiness and warning him that we were planning a major campaign against the industry plans. After our visit, the White House downsized the planned event and the Vice President's subsequent remarks to the press were less enthusiastic than they had been before.

When the new ratings system was unveiled at the National Press Club later in December, we organized a "counterpress conference" immediately following the event, inviting not only our advocacy group allies, but also Congressman Markey and other influential lawmakers who had been pushing for the ratings system. When the television industry released its public opinion poll that day, showing that parents supported the age-based system, we countered with our own "rapid response" strategy, working with academic experts to critique the methodology, and publicizing results of other polls documenting parental preference for content labels ("Markey Vows," 1996).

Our press campaign continued well into the following year, generating a great deal of media coverage, as well as overwhelming editorial support in major newspapers around the country. Amid this controversy, the FCC moved forward with its process of seeking formal comment on the proposed ratings (FCC, 1997). On April 9, our coalition submitted a letter to the FCC, urging the Commission to reject the ratings. In addition, Congressman Edward Markey (D-Mass), along with 15 other representatives and 7 senators, sent a letter to the FCC arguing that the system was unacceptable.

By early summer, the FCC had not yet acted on the industry proposal and several prominent lawmakers—including Senators John McCain, Joseph Leiberman, and Samuel Brownback, as well as Congressman Markey—were again rattling their legislative sabers, threatening to introduce new legislation to regulate television violence. Industry leaders had begun to soften their positions somewhat, and were making public comments indicating a willingness to discuss some adjustments in their system, which Valenti was now calling a "work in progress" (Bolliek, 1997). Sometime in June, Congressman Markey called representatives from some of the key groups together in his office on Capitol Hill to inform them that industry representatives were willing to begin meetings to discuss possible changes in the system. However, it was also made clear that it would not be possible to get the industry to scrap the system altogether; rather, some modifications could be made in the form of additional "content descriptors." Although the advocates who were invited to participate in these discussions were not terribly enthusiastic about the prospects of modifying the age-based system, we knew that just getting the industry to sit down and talk with us was a victory in itself. For CME's part, negotiating for alterations in a flawed proposal would be far better than getting the federal government involved in rating the content of television programs.

Within a few weeks, representatives of 10 advocacy groups had begun meeting with the top executives of the three trade associations representing key components of the television industry.[1] From the beginning of the negotiations, it was clear that the process and its outcome would be complex. It was one thing to work out a new plan for labeling television violence, for which there was considerable research to guide our deliberations. But the expanded mandate to include descriptors for sexual behavior, language, and other kinds of questionable content was far more challenging, forcing us into the realm of values and ideology rather than science.

The television industry was particularly reluctant to put content descriptors on children's programs. It had created a special label, TV-Y7, for programs aimed at children 7-years-old and older, hoping that move would preempt any further criticism. From the outset of our deliberations, the industry tried to keep the matter off the table altogether. But the advocates were adamant about making sure violent children's programs were rated. It was not until the industry leaders were shown clips from shows such as *The Mighty Morphin Power Rangers*, along with research on why this particular kind of violence was of concern to parents, that they realized they might have a public relations problem if they refused to label these "sinister combat violence shows," as a broadcast industry-sponsored UCLA study had called them (Television Violence Monitoring Reports, 1995). But the decision about *how* to rate the violence in children's programming became very contentious. Negotiators finally agreed to add a violent content descriptor only to the combat genre of children's programs. The advocates wanted a simple "V" but the industry insisted there be a "modifier" to distinguish the violence in children's programs from that in adult shows. Various proposals were placed on the table, and more arguments ensued. Finally, Valenti suggested that the term '*fantasy*' be added to the "V" in children's programming to indicate that this was a special category of children's programs. The proposal caused a serious rift among the advocacy representatives; nine of the representatives thought it a bad idea while one of them sided with the industry. At this point, the entire process nearly fell apart. Finally, the advocates, who had already put in weeks of effort into the negotiations, decided reluctantly to accept the confusing "fantasy violence" label. Our fears were

[1]The industry was represented by: the Motion Picture Association of America, National Association of Broadcasting, and the National Cable Television Association. The advocacy group coalition was comprised of: the American Academy of Pediatrics, the American Medical Association, the American Psychiatric Association, the American Psychological Association. Center for Media Education, Children Now, the Children's Defense Fund, the National Association of Elemantary School Principals, the National Education Association, and the National PTA.

later confirmed when we heard that some families participating in studies about the V-chip, as well as some of the reporters covering the issue, thought the letters stood for "family values."

What emerged from this highly politicized process was a confusing set of labels, probably only fully understood by the 14 participants in the negotiations. The written text of the agreement described each of the categories, but there were unwritten agreements embedded in the system that was finally adopted. Some of the highly technical issues had been argued over for weeks. In the middle of the process, another letter was tossed into the already-confusing alphabet soup. In addition to the "S", "L", and "V", industry negotiators insisted on adding a "D" for sexual innuendo. It was implied that adding this rating might give NBC, which had refused to participate in the process, some incentive to join the pack and agree to run the content descriptors. But the network never did, though it did use the age-based ratings. (The cable network, Black Entertainment Television, refused to participate in the ratings system altogether.)

Throughout the negotiations, the advocacy groups found themselves in the middle of a highly intense political tug of war, as Democratic lawmakers lined up against their Republican counterparts, and the White House competed with members of Congress over who would take public credit for the final resolution. At one point during the last few weeks of the process, before the negotiators had come to an agreement, several Senators called a press conference on Capitol Hill to announce that the process was finally over. It did not end, however, for at least another week. The amended "TV Parental Guidelines" were unveiled at a White House event on July 10, 1997, and the new content labels began appearing on television programs in the fall of that year.

It came as no surprise to the participants who had been involved in the V-chip negotiations when later studies documented major problems with the system. A 1998 report released by the Henry J. Kaiser Family Foundation found widespread failure on the part of the television industry to apply the content descriptors accurately. More than three out of four shows with violence (79 %) and nine out of ten shows with sex (92%) did not receive the "V" or "S" content descriptors (Chetwynd, 1999; Jensen, 1999; KFF, 1998). Another Kaiser study 3 years later revealed that although parents had begun to rely on the complicated icons that appear during the first 15 seconds of every program, many remained confused about the meaning of the symbols and expressed a desire for a uniform system for all media (KFF, 2001). Research on V-chip usage found that parents were often frustrated with the complexities of the process, and many families with V-chip equipped televisions did not even know they had the devices (Rutenberg, 2001).

During the first few years after the V-chip mandate took effect, neither the television industry nor the manufacturers did very much to educate the public about it. Under pressure from the FCC and advocacy groups, the television industry produced a handful of public service announcements to explain the ratings to parents. Though these spots appeared from time to time—often in the middle of the night—they were probably seen more often in Congressional and FCC hearings than they were on television. Several TV industry insiders told me that although labeling the programs had not caused much disruption or concern, no one in the business really wanted to encourage parents to *use* the V-chip itself to actually block the programming.

In 2004, when the CBS Network found itself in trouble over a "wardrobe malfunction" during the Super Bowl half-time show, and broadcasters were once again under siege by the FCC and the public over indecent content, the V-chip and the TV ratings suddenly rose to prominence again. The industry created a new print ad and PSA campaign to promote the V-chip; television representatives proudly invoked it in their Congressional testimony; and industry lawyers referenced it in their formal comments at the Federal Communications Commission (Hernandez & Elliott, 2004).

CHILDREN'S ADVERTISING

The policy debate over children's advertising, like that over television violence, has been a long, polarized struggle. Despite intense advocacy efforts and substantial research, public policy safeguards have been minimal. Action for Children's Television's 1970 petition to the Federal Communications Commission had called for the elimination of advertising in children's programs, arguing that the practice was inherently unfair. But the broadcasting and advertising industries fought successfully against the proposal, and the 1974 Children's Policy Statement contained only time-limit provisions and guidelines on a handful of particularly egregious practices, such as host-selling (Kunkel, 1988). The Children's Television Act, for the first time, legislated time limits on children's TV advertising for both broadcast and cable television, but neither Congress nor the FCC adequately addressed the more troubling trends of overcommercialization in children's programming (Kunkel, 2001).

When advocates took their cause to the Federal Trade Commission during the 1970s, they were met with sympathetic regulators. But the ultimate outcome was disastrous. In response to a petition filed by Action for Children's Television and the Center for Science in the Public

Interest, the agency issued a proposed rule-making offering several possible policy options, including a ban on television advertising directed at children. These regulatory moves aroused the ire of the powerful, well-funded lobbyists representing a wide range of industries—television, advertising, and major companies that produced and sold products to children. The lobbyists went directly to Congress to thwart the FTC's efforts, pushing through legislation that not only forced the Commission to terminate the rule-making procedure on children's television advertising, but also stripped the Commission of its powers to develop broad-based rule-making procedures on any issue. The press played a pivotal role in the controversy. One of the final straws that helped to crush the FTC's rule-making proceeding was a now-famous *Washington Post* editorial, accusing the Commission of trying to be the "national nanny" ("FTC as National Nanny," 1978).

By the time the Center for Media Education began its work in Washington, the "KidVid" advertising wars had become part of the folklore of the advocacy community, a cautionary tale with very important lessons for anyone trying to take up the cause in the 1990s. Even though there had been widespread concern among parents and educators, as well as mounting research documenting the special vulnerabilities of children to advertising, earlier activists had launched their regulatory campaigns when children's advertising had already grown into a thriving and profitable business. Both the broadcasting and the advertising industries had weathered numerous attacks from public interest and consumer groups for decades, and had built up large, professional lobbying organizations armed with a full arsenal of counter strategies designed to deflect, disarm, and undermine outside criticism (Stole, 2000).

Rather than open up old battles over television advertising—where a powerful army of D.C. industry operatives lay in waiting—the Center for Media Education made a decision to fight for advertising safeguards on the frontiers of the new digital media landscape. In the mid-1990s, as the Internet rapidly made its way into American homes, television itself was about to undergo a major transformation. With spending among children and teens—the "early adopters" of new technologies—at a peak level, marketers and television networks were establishing Web sites designed for this lucrative demographic group. The Internet was becoming a test bed for an array of new interactive services, all of which would become part of the new "converged" digital television of the 21st century (Montgomery, 2001).

In 1994, CME began researching the emerging new marketing practices on the Internet. Our investigation revealed a number of disturbing practices that were already becoming established in the Web sites for children. Some of the largest children's television advertisers of food, toys and candy had created online playgrounds—"branded environments" in the lingo of the industry—where children were invited to frolic with products and icons, and develop "personalized relationships" with "spokescharacters."

One of the most alarming trends was the widespread collection of personal data from children. Interactive advertising in the new media is rooted in the concept of "one-to-one marketing." The strategy is based on the principle of developing unique, long-term relationships with individual customers in order to create personalized marketing and sales appeals based on their individual preferences and behaviors. At the heart of this system is the ongoing collection of personal information and tracking of online behavior, in order to "microtarget" the individual customer (Montgomery, 2001). This new digital marketing paradigm was very much in evidence in the emerging online landscape of the mid-1990s. Many commercial children's Web sites in CME's study engaged in a variety of ways to elicit personal information from children. Some used incentives, promising free gifts such as T-shirts, mousepads, and screensavers, in exchange for children's e-mail addresses, street addresses, purchasing behavior and preferences, and information about other family members. Other Web sites required children to complete registration forms and questionnaires in order to enter the site (Montgomery & Pasnik, 1996).

Because this new digital media culture was still in its early fluid stages, we saw both opportunities and challenges. If actions were taken quickly, we might be able to establish some policies that could help influence how marketing and advertising to children developed in the new digital media. Waiting too long posed risks. Once marketing practices were in place, they would become fixed into the economic and business plans and processes of the industry and would be staunchly defended against any threats to regulate them. At the same time, the very newness of the Internet meant that the children's online marketplace was a well-kept secret for much of the public. While TV commercials had become an all-too-familiar part of the contemporary media environment, many parents and policymakers were not even aware that there *was* advertising targeted at children online. Policymakers and industry alike were promoting the so-called "Information Superhighway" as a noncommercial, educational alternative to television (Information Infrastructure Task Force, 1993).

Drawing from CME's analysis of children's Web sites, as well as our investigation of trends in the online marketing industry, we wrote a report, describing in vivid terms the new digital marketing paradigm for the future. As we had done with our first report on the Children's

Television Act, we incorporated into our analysis numerous specific examples of advertising and data collection practices that revealed both the strategies and the tactics of online marketers, identifying individual companies and Web sites. The report purposely did not call for a ban on all advertising to children in cyberspace; rather, we laid out a set of principles to guide the development of regulations for online advertising and marketing to children. Among them were: prohibitions against personalized data collection from children; clear mechanisms to distinguish advertising from content; and measures to prevent interactions between children and product spokescharacters (Montgomery & Pasnik, 1996).

Released to the press in March of 1996, *Web of Deception* generated extensive media exposure, including stories in the major newspapers and TV news, as well as online publications. The report caught the new online industry off-guard. We were told that one food company with a long-established presence in children's television was about to launch its new Web site for kids on the very day that the report hit the press. The launch was immediately called off when the company realized the new site would "violate all of CME's principles."

Though the Federal Trade Commission was limited in its authority to develop industry-wide rules, it could act on individual complaints against "bad actors." CME partnered with the Institute for Public Representation to prepare a case. Based on legal research, we determined that the FTC's jurisdiction over "deceptive" advertising was the strongest tool available. In May, 1996 we filed a formal complaint against a children's Web site called KidsCom, charging that the company had engaged in deceptive advertising by billing itself as "a communications playground for kids age 4 to 15," when the site's primary purpose was data collection for market research (FTC, 1996). A year later, after investigating the case, the FTC issued a ruling in our favor, and ordered the company to cease its deceptive practices (FTC, 1997). This decision laid the groundwork for a more comprehensive government policy.

CME also formed an alliance with Consumer Federation of America, one of the most prominent consumer organizations in the United States. Early on in the campaign, CME and CFA drafted a joint set of rules on children's online privacy, which we submitted to the Federal Trade Commission. This document was designed to preempt industry self-regulatory proposals and to set a high bar for establishing government rules. Among other things, our guidelines called for full disclosure of data collection practices on all children's Web sites and for advance parental permission before Web sites could collect personal information from children (Center for Media Education and Consumer Federation of America, 1996).

Over the next 3 years, CME participated in numerous hearings and public events at the FTC, the Department of Commerce, and the White House. We worked proactively with the press and continued to monitor practices in the online industry, releasing periodic updates, which generated further exposure for the issue. We sought out other consumer and child advocacy groups to join our cause, and enlisted the support of health professionals and academic experts to testify in public forums and serve as press spokespersons. When the White House drafted its policy statement on e-commerce—which was a treatise on self-regulation—we lobbied successfully to insert special language into the document that would leave open the possibility of government action to protect children (*Framework for Global Electronic Commerce,* 1997).

By June of 1998, the Federal Trade Commission asked Congress to pass a new law granting the agency authority to develop rules to protect children's privacy on the Internet. The Children's Online Privacy Protection Act was signed into law 3 months later and took effect the following year. COPPA limits the amount of information that can be collected on commercial children's Web sites; requires these sites to post prominent privacy policies; and forbids them from collecting personally identifiable information from children under the age of 13 without prior parental approval (Children's Online Privacy Protection Act, 1998).

As in the other two cases discussed in this chapter, external developments played an important role in the ultimate outcome of our campaign. In the case of COPPA, two broader policy debates were particularly significant. One was triggered by the European Union passage of a data directive in 1995. That directive laid out a strong set of policies to govern privacy protection in the EU member states and forbade EU member states from engaging in "data transfer" with other countries if those countries were not providing an adequate level of protection (Bennett, 1997). Pressure on the U.S. government to bring its privacy safeguards into "harmony" with those of EU countries created a political opening for privacy advocacy on behalf of children. Accordingly, we decided that focusing on the privacy aspects of these new interactive marketing practices would be the most effective way to organize. In addition to working closely with Consumer Federation of America, the National PTA, and several other groups that had been part of our children's television advocacy efforts, we joined forces with a coalition of privacy groups, the most prominent of which was the Electronic Privacy Information Center. Ultimately, the United States was able to work out an agreement with the EU to allow for self-regulatory mechanisms to take the place of new laws. However, in the case of children's privacy, avoiding government policy became untenable.

Passage of COPPA coincided almost to the day with the deadline for compliance with the EU data directive.

Our campaign was also influenced by the intense public obsession over "cyberporn" and online safety that began during Congressional deliberations over the controversial 1996 Communications Decency Act. Though the CDA was successfully challenged by civil liberty groups and subsequently struck down by the courts, concerns over child safety on the Internet dominated the public debate throughout the 1990s. The White House held several summits on the issue. Online companies launched numerous public education initiatives, and a new cottage industry of filtering software companies sprang up. Congress made several further attempts to regulate pornography and indecency on the Internet (Heins, 2001). CME was opposed to the CDA and other similar pieces of legislation, though we kept a low profile on that issue during the debates. However, the concerns we raised about online privacy were repeatedly conflated with concerns over online safety. The press and policymakers frequently invoked the frightening prospects of children's personal information falling into the hands of online predators.

When the Children's Online Privacy Protection Act was passed, it became part of a larger legislative vehicle that included a similar sounding law aimed at online indecency, called the Child Online Protection Act. For years afterward, the public would confuse COPPA with COPA. But the two laws had almost nothing in common. Civil liberty groups immediately attacked COPA, successfully challenging it in the courts on First Amendment grounds (Savage, 2004). Passage of COPPA, on the other hand, had required a series of public and private negotiations among a wide range of stakeholders—including privacy and consumer advocates, online companies, Web site creators, direct marketers, and civil liberty groups. When it took effect the following year, there was some brief grumbling from a handful of children's Web site companies that were forced to alter their data collection practices, but it was not subjected to court challenges or large-scale protests.

Though the final outcome of the campaign to regulate children's marketing on the Internet was a narrower policy than what we had originally wanted, COPPA has had a significant impact on the emerging practices targeted at children in the digital media. CME conducted an analysis of industry practices one year after the law took effect and found that, although there was still considerable room for improvement, a significant number of industry practices had been changed or curtailed as a result of the law (Center for Media Education, 2001).

In the years immediately following the COPPA's passage, the Federal Trade Commission investigated several children's Web sites and issued fines for failure to comply with the law (FTC, 2001a; FTC, 2001b; FTC,

2002). The legislation contained a "safe harbor" mechanism designed to shift much of the responsibility for enforcement to the industry itself. Before formally approving any self-regulatory guidelines, the FTC called for public comment from the consumer and public interest community. The Center for Media Education and Consumer Federation of America carefully scrutinized each of the proposals and called for changes in some of them before offering our endorsement to the Commission. As a result, industry groups such as the Children's Advertising Review Unit (=CARU=), the Entertainment Software Ratings Board (=ESRB=), and TrustE are involved in ongoing public education and monitoring of children's marketing and data collection practices on the Internet. These efforts have helped encourage widespread adoption of the safeguards, which have been integrated into the institutionalized practices for marketing to children in the digital media (CARU, n.d.; ESRB, n.d.; TRUSTe, n.d.).

Neither self-regulation nor government regulation, however, will remain effective in the long run, without the active involvement of the advocacy community. After the Center for Media Education closed, other consumer and public interest groups have carried on some of the important watchdog work on children's privacy. For example, in April of 2003, the Electronic Privacy Information Center, and a coalition of 11 other groups filed a complaint against Amazon.com, charging the company with violation of COPPA (Electronic Privacy Information Center, 2003). But the Federal Trade Commission denied the complaint ("FTC Fails to Enforce Children's Privacy Law," 2004). EPIC has also had to devote considerable attention to a host of other critical policy issues, particularly as threats of government invasion of privacy have become greater in the post-9/11 era (EPIC, n.d.).

One of CME's original goals in releasing our 1996 report was to create a framework of safeguards for children's marketing in all digital media, including television. In our formal comments at the Federal Communication Commission's rulemaking proceeding on "Children's Television Obligations of Digital Television Broadcasters," CME and other groups called for a set of new rules to govern digital TV marketing practices targeted at children (CME, 2000). But, while acknowledging the concerns raised by children's advocacy groups, the FCC chose not to issue rules on interactive TV advertising practices in its 2004 Report and Order. Rather, the agency postponed any regulatory action, issuing another rulemaking procedure on the matter to be decided upon sometime in the future (FCC, 2004). A new Children's Media Policy Coalition, led by Children Now, has vowed to continue the campaign for children's marketing safeguards in digital television (Children Now, 2004).

THE FUTURE OF ADVOCACY

As the electronic media penetrate further into children's lives, long-standing policy battles over issues such as violent content, indecency, and advertising are likely to continue. But the rapid explosion of digital technologies calls for a fresh approach to children's media advocacy. Because so much of the policy debate has been fashioned to protect the vulnerabilities of children (with a focus on young children), we have not paid enough attention to fostering their positive development, nurturing the attributes that children need to grow through adolescence and into adulthood. In a media culture dominated by consumer values, we have also tended to conceptualize children only as *consumers* of media products and content. Though these concerns remain important, it is time to expand our thinking to include a view of children as producers and contributors to the media culture and, in turn, to the society at large (Montgomery, Gottlieb-Robles & Larson, 2004).

As we consider the policy issues for the Digital Age, the goal of fostering a healthy, democratic media culture for young people must be a top priority. To ensure their well being, children must be understood as key stakeholders in the future of the digital media. This requires engaging in a variety of policy issues that have not traditionally been part of the children's media policy agenda. Though some of these issues—such as open architecture, digital rights management, and spectrum allocation—may seem too technical and complex, they are nonetheless fundamental to the preservation and growth of an open and participatory digital media system for the 21st century.

REFERENCES

Allen, C., & Woolf, K. D. (2001). *The 5th Annual APPC Conference On Children and Media: A Summary.* Philadelphia, PA: The Annenberg Public Policy Center of the University of Pennsylvania.

Andrews, E. (1992, September 30). Broadcasters to satisfy law, define cartoons as education. *The New York Times,* p. A1.

Andrews, E. (1995, November 22). FCC approval seen today for Westinghouse-CBS Deal. *The New York Times,* P. D2

Aufderheide, P. (1999). *Communications policy and the public interest.* New York: Guilford Press.

Benford, R., & Snow, D. (2000). Framing processes and social movements: An overview and assessment. *Annual Review Of Sociology 26,* 611–639.

Bennet, C. (1997). Convergence revisited: Toward a global policy for the protection of personal data. In P. Agre & M. Rotenberg M. (Eds.), *Technology and privacy: The new landscape.* Cambridge (pp. 99–123). Cambridge, MA: MIT Press.

Bolliek, B. ((1997, April 7). Senators: U.S. should demand content ratings. *The Hollywood Reporter.*

Calvert, S. (2003). Lessons from children television: The impact of the Children's Television Act on children's learning. *Journal of Applied Development* 24, 275–335.

Cantor, J. (1998). *Mommy, I'm scared!* San Diego, CA: Harcourt Brace.

CARU Privacy Program. (n.d.). *Children's Advertising Review Unit, Better Business Bureau.* Retrieved November 15, 2004, from http://www.technology.gov/digeconomy/framework.htm.

Center for Media Education. (1992). *A report on station compliance with the Children's Television Act.* Washington, DC: Center for Media Education.

Center for Media Education. (1997). *A field guide to the Children's Television Act.* Washington, DC: Center for Media Education.

Center for Media Education. (2000). *CME calls on FCC to ensure DTV rules on children are meaningful.* Washington, DC: Center for Media Education.

Center for Media Education. (2001, April). *COPPA: The first year. A Survey of Sites.* Washington, DC: Center for Media Education.

Center for Media Education and Consumer Federation of America (1996, June 5). *Guidelines for the collection and tracking of information from children on the global information infrastructure and in interactive media.* Washington, D.C: Center for Media Education/Consumer Federation of America.

Chetwynd, J. (1999, May 11). Parents not equipped with ratings savvy. *USA Today*, p. 1D.

Children Now. (2004). *Digital television: Sharpening the focus on children.* Retrieved November 14, 2004, from http://www.childrennow.org/media/dtv-convening/dtv-convening-report-2004-highlights.cfm.

Children's Online Privacy Protection Act, (1997) S.2326, 105th Cong., 2d Sess.

Children's Television Act H.R. 1677, 101st Cong., 2d Sess., Cong. Rec. H8535.

Cole, B., & Oettinger, M. (1978). *Reluctant regulators.* Reading, MA: Addison Wesley.

Church challenges license renewals on children's programming issue. (n.d.). Retrieved October 29, 2004, from http://www.ucc.org/news/u090104.htm.

Davis, D. (1997). *The second annual Annenberg Public Policy Center's conference on children and television: a summary.* Philadelphia, PA: The Annenberg Public Policy Center of the University of Pennsylvania.

Eastin, M. (2001). The onset of the age-based and content-based ratings systems: History, pressure groups, Congress and the FCC. In B. Greenberg (Ed.), *The alphabet soup of television program ratings.* (pp. 1–18). Cresskill, NJ: Hampton Press.

Electronic Privacy Information Center. (2003, April 22). *Before the federal trade commission Washington, DC. In the matter of Amazon.com, Inc. epic complaint and request for injunction, investigation, and for other relief.* Retrieved November 15, 2004, from http://epic.org/privacy/amazon/coppacomplaint.html

Electronic Privacy Information Center. (n.d.). *Privacy by topic: the A to Z's of privacy.* Retrieved November 13, 2004, from http://www.epic.org/privacy/#topics.

ESRB Privacy Online. (n.d.). *Entertainment Software Review Board.* Retrieved November 15, 2004, from http://www.ersb.org/privacy.asp

Farhi, P. (1996, December 3). TV industry agrees on rating system; age-based system is similar to that used for movies. *The Washington Post,* p. A1.

Federal Communications Commission. (n.d.). *E-rate.* Retrieved November 15, 2004, from http://www.fcc.gov/learnnet/welcome.html

Federal Communications Commission. (1993). *Notice of inquiry: Policies and rules concerning children's television programming. Federal Communications Commission Record, 8,* 1841–1843.

Federal Communications Commission. (1996). *In the matter of policies and rules concerning children's television programming: report and order. Federal Communications Commission Record, 11,* 10660–10778.

Federal Communications Commission. (1997). *Public Notice 97–34: Commission seeks comment on industry proposal for rating video programming.* Retrieved November 15, 2004, from http://www.fcc.gov/Bureaus/Cable/ Public_Notices/ 1997/fcc97034.pdf

Federal Communications Commission. (2004). *FCC adopts children's programming obligations for digital television broadcasters.* Retrieved November 13, 2004, from http://hraunfoss.fcc.gov/edocs_public/attachmatch/DOC-251972A1. pdf

Federal Trade Commission. (1996). *Complaint and request for investigation, in the matter of deceptive Internet sites directed toward the young child audience, before the Federal Trade Commission.* Washington, DC: Author.

Federal Trade Commission. (1997). *FTC staff sets forth principles for online information collection from children.* Retrieved November 13, 2003, from http://www.ftc.gov/opa/1997/07/kidscom.htm

Federal Trade Commission. (2001a). *FTC announces settlements with web sites that collected children's personal data without parental permission.* Retrieved November 13, 2004, from http//:www.ftc.gov/opa/2001/04/girlslife. htm

Federal Trade Commission. (2001b). *Web site targeting girls settles FTC privacy violation charges.* Retrieved November 13, 2004, from http://www. ftc.gov/ opa/2001/10/lisafrank.htm

Federal Trade Commission. (2002). *Popcorn company settles FTC Privacy violation charges.* Retrieved November 13, 2004, from http://www.ftc.gov/2002/ 02/popcorn.htm.

Foote, S., & Mrookin, R. (1980). The "Kid Vid" crusade. *Public Interest 61,* 90.

Framework for global electronic commerce. (1997, July 1). Retrieved November 15, 2004, from http://www.technology.gov/digeconomy/framewrk. htm

FTC as National Nanny. (1978, March 1). *The Washington Post,* A22.

FTC fails to enforce children's privacy law against Amazon. (2004). *Electronic Privacy Information Center, Latest news.* Retrieved November 29, 2004, from http://www.epic.org

Gamson, W. (1990). *The strategy of social protest.* Belmont, CA: Wadsworth.

Heins, M. (2001). *Not in front of the children: "Indecency," censorship and the innocence of youth.* New York: Hill & Wang.

Hendershot, H. (1998). *Saturday morning censors: Television regulation before the V-chip*. Durham, NC: Duke University Press.

Hernandez, R., & Elliott, S. (2004, March 31). An effort to promote V-Chip for television. *The New York Times*, C4.

Information Infrastructure Task Force. (1993, September 15). *The national information infrastructure: Agenda for action*. Retrieved November 15, 2004, from http://www.ibiblio.org/nii/goremarks.html

Jensen, E. (1999, November 9). What are kids doing 38 hours a week? TV still wins most of their time, despite the net. *Chicago Sun Times*.

Jordan, A. (2000). *Is the three-hour rule living up to its potential?*. Retrieved from the Annenberg Public Policy Center of the University of Pennsylvania Web site: http://annenbergpublicpolicycenter.org/05_media_developing_child/childrensprogramming/3hour-rule.pdf

Kaiser Family Foundation. (1998). *Major new study of the V-chip TV rating system*. Retrieved February 9, 2003, from http://www.kff.org/content/archive/1434/ratings.html

Kaiser Family Foundation. (2001). *Few parents use V-Chip to block TV sex and violence, but more use TV ratings to pick what kids can watch*. Retrieved July 24, 2001 from http://kff.org/content/2001/3158/V-Chip%20release.htm

Krasnow, E., Longley, L. D., & Terry, H. A. (1982). *The politics of broadcast regulation*. (3rd Ed.) New York: St. Martin's Press.

Kunkel, D. (1988). Children and host-selling television commercials. *Communication Research 15*, 71–92.

Kunkel, D. (2001) Children and television advertising. In Singer, D., & Singer, J. (Eds.), *Handbook of children and the media*. (pp. 375–394). Thousand Oaks, CA: Sage.

Kunkel, D., & Capena, J. (1994). Broadcaster's license renewal claims regarding children's educational programs. *Journal of Broadcasting and Electronic Media 38*, 397–416.

Kunkel, D., & Wilcox, B. (2001) Children and media policy. In Singer, D., & Singer, J. (Eds.), *Handbook of children and the media*. (pp. 589–604). Thousand Oaks, California: Sage.

Levin, D., & Carlsson-Paige, N. (1995). The Mighty Morphin Power Rangers: Teachers voice concern. *Young Children 50* (6), 67–72.

Levy, S. (1996, February 12). Now for the free-for-all. *Newsweek, p. 42.*

Markey vows that fight over age-based TV ratings has just begun. (1996, December 20). *Communications Daily*, p. 1.

McAdam, D., McCarthy, J., & Zald, M. (Eds.). (1996). *Comparative perspectives on social movements: political opportunities, mobilizing structures, and cultural framing*. Cambridge, UK: Cambridge University Press.

Montgomery, K. (1989). *Target: prime time. advocacy groups and the struggle over entertainment television*. New York: Oxford University Press.

Montgomery, K. (2001). Digital kids: the new on-line children's consumer culture. In Singer, D., & Singer, J. (Eds.), *Handbook of children and the media* (pp. 635–650). Thousand Oaks, CA: Sage.

Montgomery, K., Gottlieb-Robles, B., & Larson, G. (2004) *Youth as e-citizens.* Center for Social Media. Retrieved November 20, 2004, from http://www.centerforsocialmedia.org/ecitizens/index2.htm

Montgomery, K., & Pasnik, S. (1996). *Web of deception.* Washington, DC: Center for Media Education.

Price, M. (1998). *The V-Chip debate: Content filtering from television to the Internet.* Mahwah, NJ: Lawrence Erlbaum Associates.

Put V for violence back in V-chip, Gore urges as ratings talks continue. (1997, June 20). *Communications Daily.*

Rowland, W. (1983). *The politics of TV violence.* Beverly Hills, CA: Sage.

Rutenberg, J. (2001, July 25). Survey shows few parents use V-Chip to limit children's viewing. *The New York Times, p. E1.*

Ryan, C. (1991). *Prime time activism: Media strategies for grassroots organizing.* Boston: South End Press.

Savage, C. (2004, June 30). Justices bar curbs on explicit websites. *Boston Globe,* p. A1.

Schmitt, K. (1999). *The three-hour rule: Is it living up to expectations?* The Annenberg Public Policy Center of the University of Pennsylvania.

Stole, I. (2000). Consumer protection in historical perspective: The five-year battle over federal regulations of advertising 1933–1938. *Mass Communication & Society 3,* 351–372.

Suman, M., & Rossman, G. (Eds.). (2000). *Advocacy groups and the entertainment industry.* Westport, CT: Praeger.

Television Violence Monitoring Reports. (1995). Retrieved November 14, 2004, from Digital Media web site: http://www.digitalcenter.org/webreport94/iiie2.htm

TRUSTe: Make Privacy Your Choice. (n.d.). *TRUSTe: Consumer and business privacy advocacy.* Retrieved November 15, 2004, from http://truste.org

13

Advocates for Excellence: Engaging the Industry

David W. Kleeman
American Center for Children and Media

In the United States, the presence of strong policy advocacy organizations in children's television was instrumental to the current state of the medium in many respects. From the early and relentless spotlight shone by Action for Children's Television, to the regulatory savvy of the Center for Media Education, to the ongoing digital media work of a coalition led by Children Now, public interest groups captured, and then channeled into action, the attention of parents, press, legislators and regulators. Beyond their concrete achievements—the Children's Television Act of 1990 and its 2004 update that embraced the technological potential of digital television—the regulatory advocates made it impossible for broadcasters to escape scrutiny of their service to young people. (See Montgomery, chap. 12, this volume, for more about policy advocacy organizations).

The laws they instigated made concrete the quantity of educational programming demanded from every broadcaster. At the time of this writing, however, as the first broadcasters face scrutiny of their efforts for children as part of license renewal, arguments over the quality of that programming has revealed the limits of regulatory solutions. Lawmakers can create an environment in which excellence can flourish, but they cannot directly improve quality.

In other words, the government can—and did—demand more children's programming and educational substance; it cannot mandate or enforce that the resulting shows be "good." Quality depends on those who create the content, having internalized motivation to produce beneficial works, supported by the skills, resources, knowledge, connections, and leadership needed to fulfill that desire.

Therefore, one might argue that policy-based advocacy is necessary but not sufficient. The industry needs balancing forces, operating independently but collaboratively, that define excellence and foster best practices by studying, dissecting, promoting and honoring good works. Without pressure groups, however, there would be little impetus for the industry to be receptive to such resources.

Parallel in time to the advocacy groups' efforts, a number of U.S. organizations established positive, practical methods for engaging the industry's executives and creators. These groups sought to advance understanding of high-quality children's programming, to characterize best practices, and to encourage production in keeping with these standards. This chapter will profile four of those organizations, that represent the range of unique tools and strategies various entities brought to bear in the service of similar goals.

- *The American Center for Children and Media* (ACCM), founded in 1985 as a biennial competition to choose the country's best children's programs, evolved into a broad-based professional development and resource center encompassing TV and digital media. Established by public broadcasting executives, the ACCM fosters creative "best practices" in production and programming among media, education and child development experts.
- *Mediascope,* founded in 1992 as a research and policy organization promoting issues of social relevance within the entertainment industry, working more broadly than just with children's content. Mediascope was established by a social sciences communication specialist to promote thoughtful integration of research-based knowledge into entertainment media properties. Mediascope closed in 2004, taking time to reevaluate its service model in the face of industry and societal change.
- *Children Now,* founded in 1988 as an advocate for the overall well-being of children, working in areas such as health care, education, and economic policy. One facet of its work is a broad-based "Children and the Media" program devoted to improving the quality of news and entertainment media, both for children and about children's issues with particular attention to images of race, class and gender. Children Now also leads a coalition of health and welfare groups advocating for regulatory media reforms. The "Children and the Media" program of Children Now, launched within a lobbying organization, often works at the intersection of public policy and content.

- *The Kaiser Family Foundation's* "Program for the Study of Entertainment Media and Health," which conducts research, evaluations, and analysis on the impact of media on the public's health. Of particular interest for this chapter is the program's massive anti-AIDS campaign in cooperation with Viacom and its many TV networks. The founding director of Children Now's media program created Kaiser's entertainment media division; and the Ad Council was also a major influence.

Examination of these organizations reveals that each was constructed in a unique image—often influenced by a founder or antecedent organizations—that guides its choices of strategy, audience, and objectives.

This chapter examines the origins, missions and evolution of these four organizations, each in its own way engaging, prodding and inspiring the children's media industries. To add international perspective, it will touch as well on recent global network building by the world's longest-standing industry-engaging group—the worldwide children's television festival, PRIX JEUNESSE.

THE AMERICAN CENTER FOR CHILDREN AND MEDIA

The American Children's Television Festival—the Ollie Awards—laid the foundation for the professional development and resource center that later emerged. James Fellows—a longtime public broadcasting executive and communication professor—founded the ACTF in 1984. As International Advisory Board Chair for the worldwide PRIX JEUNESSE festival, he had long wondered why America's extensive children's TV industry had no national analogue to the global contest, where hundreds of producers and executives gathered to screen, discuss, and vote for the prize winners. Fellows established the U.S. festival within the Central Educational Network (CEN), a public television programming and resource center for which he was President.

These influences—the highly democratic world festival and public service media development—shaped an organization that engaged industry leaders and workers, educators, and researchers, in rigorous processes to evolve measures of excellence and reward work that exemplified those standards.

The festival concept fit the mid-1980s, as well: Cable was emerging, and system operators believed that children's programming could convince parents to adopt their services. With channels like Nickelodeon and Disney launching, public television expanding its children's services, the networks still producing Saturday morning fare, and still-healthy local programming, the sheer volume of children's TV was sufficient to support a diverse and competitive festival. Moreover, the trend toward media deregulation under President Reagan's Federal Communications Commission Chair, Mark Fowler, made it necessary to find and engage people who were internally motivated to do good work.

In 1988, the author of this chapter became Festival Director, after spending 5 years in program development, operations, and scheduling at the Public Broadcasting Service. His expertise and interest, like Fellows', was in building professionals' skills, motivation, and resources.

Ollie Awards competitions took place in 1985, 1987, 1989, and 1993 before being suspended for lack of funding. To sustain the Ollies' "workshop" atmosphere between competitions, the Festival organized its first seminars in 1989: *Teenagers and Television: New Alliances* with the Carnegie Council on Adolescent Development, and *Public Policy to Improve Children's Television: What Other Countries are Doing*, with the Annenberg Washington Program.

These early convenings established organizing principles on which the Center still relies, ensuring that its services and activities respect its constituents' professional stature, creative vision, and busy schedules. The guidelines include:

1. Provide clear information, supported with practical advice for applying it in a creative setting.
2. Supply timely information: Quality can't be added at the end of a production.
3. Build from strengths rather than lecturing about weaknesses.
4. Use visual examples to teach visual creators.
5. Respect the financial pressures under which children's media professionals work.
6. A spark can't exist in a vacuum: Connecting people with shared interests and vision yields dynamic exchange and inspires new approaches.
7. Support producers' creative visions: Don't usurp people's ideas, but endow them with the best available knowledge.
8. Keep children first: It doesn't matter if a work satisfies educators, researchers, or politicians if children don't enjoy, engage with, and benefit from it.

In 1991, the Festival separated from its founding organization, CEN, established a new Board made up of entertainment industry senior executives, and became the American Center for Children's Television. Because the Center was industry-guided and supported, it carried on the Festival's tradition of avoiding issue advocacy. The rare occasions when it did touch on regulatory issues offered alternative, creative insights. For example, even before Congress mandated V-chips in new televisions, the ACCM hosted a panel on constructing rating systems that would help parents find the right programs for their children, rather than simply blocking what they didn't want. When the Children's Television Act established a National Endowment for Children's Educational Television, the Center convened a panel on "Endowing Excellence," with industry and academic experts suggesting how to spend the funds most effectively.

With its roots in PRIX JEUNESSE and ties to the World Summits on Media for Children, looking worldwide for best practices is a Center hallmark. In an increasingly global media environment, it's only practical to focus on the relationship between media and culture. International perspective also supports children's ability to navigate in a culturally diverse world, a core 21st century literacy skill, for media producers as well as children.

Consistently, the organization's most popular events have been its screenings featuring children's programs from around the world. These "mini-festivals" are infinitely adaptable. Some last 2 hours, and others several days; some have a topical, genre, or regional focus whereas others provide a "tasting menu"; the Center has produced screenings for media professionals, academics, students, and families. For a U.S. industry that often chases trends until its audience becomes oversated, the screenings are meant to reveal techniques or content unlike American programming, particularly risk-taking efforts that presume an active and engaged audience.

Festival entries generally don't reflect children's daily viewing, however; most companies submit special productions. The bulk of broadcasters' budgets (and children's viewing time) is devoted to daily and weekly series—"bread and butter" television. In an effort to enhance the quality of these programs, the ACCM invented "A Toast to Bread & Butter." Held in 1999, 2001, and 2003, these noncompetitive international screening conferences established a practical venue for producers from around the world to exchange insights about the creative and financial realities of making everyday TV.

The Center's mission goes beyond strengthening today's children's media; it seeks to endow a strong next generation of creators, too. With New York's Center for Communication, the ACCM produces "Careers in

Children's Media" panels on topics ranging from young-adult fiction (in print and electronic media) to screenwriting, to the range of skills that must come together to create a TV series.

Change may be ahead for the American Center. In early 2005, its Board recommended strategic planning toward a new direction, as more of an "executive roundtable" of children's media executives—a gathering place for the top minds of the industry to look at how to act responsibly as an industry.

MEDIASCOPE

For founder Marcy Kelly, establishing Mediascope in 1992 represented the integration of several previous positions. As a press and communications officer for the U.S. Department of Health and Human Services, Kelly fielded inquiries from television writers and producers on a variety of topics. Seeing dialogue she had suggested turn up in an episode of "All in the Family" made her aware of the power of incorporating accurate and beneficial health messages into entertainment programming. Kelly continued that work as Executive Director of the Scott Newman Foundation, counseling the industry on unintentional glamorization of drug and alcohol use, then concentrated on teen pregnancy prevention for the Center for Population Options (CPO).

"I learned that the key was to approach the industry in an objective manner. It is more effective to present controversial topics as public health issues and provide supportive data than to criticize" (M. Kelly, personal communication, January 6, 2005). Initially, Kelly worked with network Standards and Practices executives, and, over time began to connect directly with writers and producers, eventually expanding her reach to include music and film.

After CPO, Kelly opened her own firm, and Mediascope evolved from its consulting contract with the Carnegie Corporation of New York, part of a multifaceted effort to counter adolescent violence. At first, she was concerned about discussing media violence with the industry, because it was such a sensitive subject often associated with the fervor of the religious right. Testing the waters with small roundtables, Kelly was pleased to find writers and producers receptive.

"No one was deliberately trying to be irresponsible; they just didn't comprehend how young people interpreted the violent behavior they saw on the screen. We presented violence as a public health issue, as objectively as we could, and focused on its consequences, which was absent from a lot of television and film" (M. Kelly, personal communication, January 6, 2005). In fact, the creative experts were often shocked by what they learned from the researchers and violence prevention teachers Mediascope brought to Hollywood. Over time, many began incorporating more responsible story lines. "Conflict is the essence of story telling and sometimes showing it is necessary. Mediascope's priorities included not using violence as the first response to a conflict, and letting the audience see that a violent act has consequences, like pain and loss" (M. Kelly, personal communication, January 6, 2005).

As Mediascope dug deeper into the subject, it found gaps in the research data. "Statistics on teen pregnancy and data on its effects were easier to translate for the entertainment community. We could overwhelm people with information and show how media role models affected young girls' lives and decision making," said Kelly (M. Kelly, personal communication, January 6, 2005). "The information on violence did not always make a compelling argument. For one thing, the industry felt many studies were too old and not relevant to current programming … I always saw myself as an information broker, making social science and public health findings available to those who could incorporate it into entertainment and—through them—to the public" (M. Kelly, personal communication, January 6, 2005). Mediascope's most recent President, Donna Mitroff, described this function as facilitating a "knowledge transfer equation" (D. Mitroff, personal communication, January 28, 2005), in which Mediascope connected knowledge creators and knowledge users.

There was a translation factor, as well—taking complex and lengthy information and synthesizing it down to a useful form for busy people. Kelly recalled "we sought experts and speakers who would not start talking to an audience of writers by saying, 'I don't watch television' or 'I never let my children watch.' This was not as uncommon as you might think and it was insulting to the audience we were tying to reach" (M. Kelly, personal communication, January 6, 2005).

Under pressure from Congress, the National Cable Television Association commissioned Mediascope to conduct a 3-year investigation of media violence in quantity and context, "The National Television Violence Study." This was the only time Mediascope accepted industry funding, and only with extensive protections against any perception of outside influence.

"We never allowed the industry to participate in our studies although we did seek their advice in the development phase," Kelly clarified. "We had to get it right. I didn't want the work to be rejected because of technical flaws relating to programming. We even listened to strong critics of our work, because we had to understand their point of view and create the information so they would accept it" (M. Kelly, personal communication, January 6, 2005).

Over time, Mediascope conducted a range of other studies: on media rating systems; substance abuse in popular media; weapons in movie advertisements; and primetime television popular with adolescents. It also convened industry roundtables from which came two sets of children's programming guidelines: "Building Blocks: A Guide for Creating Children's Educational Television" and "Special Considerations for Creators of Children's Media."

These latter works, and Mitroff—a Fox Family and Disney veteran—becoming Mediascope's President, led it into more work with children's and teen media. Mitroff remembered that "our work with the UCLA School of Public Health on modeling of health behaviors influenced Disney's Standards and Practices department to revise its guidelines and alerts to inappropriate health behaviors" (D. Mitroff, personal communication, January 6, 2005).

Mediascope developed strategic guidelines for its industry interactions, many similar to those used by the American Center for Children and Media. They included:

- Establishing itself as an independent organization with an objective voice;
- Presenting issues as concerns of public health, never of taste, morality or personal opinion;
- Seeking new and more effective ways to present research findings;
- Exploring the common perception that violence equals financial profit;
- Acknowledging conflict as essential to storytelling and focusing only on irresponsible and gratuitous depictions;
- Making every effort to find material to praise; never singling out individuals or titles to criticize;
- Taking no public advocacy positions;
- Identifying uncharted areas to explore, rather than competing with other nonprofit organizations, and always being open to working with others.

The organization always kept a low profile. "If people wanted to give us credit, that was fine," Kelly explained, "but we never pursued press. There was always the possibility that it might backfire. Reporters wanted us to name names, identify the bad boys or a specific show that was irresponsible. It was important to us that writers, producers, and studio executives knew we didn't operate that way. If they took our advice that was wonderful, if not, we were still happy to work with them" (M. Kelly, personal communication, January 6, 2005).

In August 2004, Mediascope closed its doors. "It was a confluence of things," explained Kelly, "political change in Washington, redirection of priorities at funding sources, deregulation, the erosion of the independent television producer and consolidation of the entertainment industry" (M. Kelly, personal communication, January 6, 2005). Asked if Mediascope might reemerge, Kelly said, "It's possible. An organization like Mediascope will always be needed. One of the things we did best was to forge understanding and relationships between disparate worlds. Face to face. The technologies so common today didn't exist when we started. The Internet provides instant access to information, and is a great resource. But ultimately the media is about communicating stories that resonate with an audience. I think the result of Mediascope's work was that some of those stories were more thoughtful, accurate, and responsible" (M. Kelly, personal communication, January 6, 2005).

CHILDREN NOW

Creating a Children & the Media Program actually followed Children Now's first efforts to engage the industry. In 1994, the organization planned a one-time conference on news coverage of children's issues and children's opinions about news. A memo detailing the Children & the Media Program's history recalls the realization that "the three relevant players—advocates for children, academics who study the media, and national media executives—met amongst themselves to discuss issues concerning the impact of media on children but had never been brought together in a collaborative environment to exchange views" (Prunty, 1998, p. 1).

Having been founded in 1988 as a policy and advocacy center, Children Now was already distinguished by its strong communication focus. Its efforts to bring children's issues—particularly those disproportionately affecting low-income families and people of color—to the forefront of news coverage had resulted in strong relationships with media organizations. Convening the people responsible for producing and presenting the news was therefore "a common sense approach," according to Victoria Rideout, the consultant hired to organize the conference. "Producers and editors were immediately receptive. As with Hollywood, there's a group of people who care, and if you can reach them you're ahead of the game" (V. Rideout, personal communication, December 21, 2004).

The interest in that initial conference, and the attention to the research conducted to support it, convinced Rideout that more was possible and needed. For the next 2 years, the Children & the Media Program extended its successful conference model to new corners of the media. In 1995, it looked at the values conveyed to young people by entertainment television—both children's programs and prime time series—and built around a poll on what values children said they received from TV and a content analysis of children's portrayals. In 1996, the topic was advertisers' role in promoting quality children's programming.

The department developed slowly around the projects. "Our initial entrepreneurial way evolved to more focused, ongoing program commitments," recalled Lois Salisbury, then-President of Children Now (L. Salisbury, personal communication, December 21, 2004). For example, based on recommendations from the conferences, Children Now began organizing briefings on children's media themes for reporters, writers, and producers.

Simultaneous with its engagement activities, the Children & the Media Program was working with the coalition of advocacy groups urging the Federal Communications Commission to codify the mandates of the Children's Television Act. "We tried to be critical in the regulatory arena while being constructive and thoughtfully provocative in our relationship development," Salisbury detailed. "We were providing data they weren't aware of and perspectives they needed to hear, that hopefully would result in a win-win" (L. Salisbury, personal communication, December 21, 2004).

In spring of 1996, integrating its advocacy and engagement roles, the Children & the Media Program conducted a survey of leading experts from industry, advocacy, and research, on designing television rating systems, while Congress was debating the legislation that mandated the V-Chip. It was the V-Chip debate, however, that brought about the greatest tension between Children Now's dual functions of engaging and challenging the industry.

According to Salisbury, because of the perception that the blocking device was a first step toward government content censorship, "the creative types in Hollywood really bristled around the V-Chip, more than the top management people" (L. Salisbury, personal communication, December 21, 2004). At the same time, Salisbury added, "the V-Chip ratings battle was a perfect example of how hard it is for legislation to deal with quality. Regulatory incentives to produce quality are nil; the marketplace incentives are the only power" (L. Salisbury, personal communication, December 21, 2004).

In 1997, Children Now launched the MediaNow newsletter, intended—similarly to Mediascope's publications—to translate academic findings into practical terms for media professionals. The newsletter usually featured an industry perspective on the topic at hand. For example, "ER" Executive Producer Neal Baer, MD, wrote about children's health and advertising; then Nickelodeon President Herb Scannell authored a commentary on diversity on television.

Strategic change to the Children Now conferences came about. Instead of focusing on a single genre, the topic was media messages to girls across the full range of technologies and content. According to the memo detailing the Program's history, this change had two effects: it suggested to the industry the cumulative mass of formative messages girls encountered in a typical day, and it fostered a less defensive atmosphere as "no one industry felt targeted ... and all of the media leaders could see how their product became part of a much larger picture in girls' lives" (Prunty, 1998, p. 5). The cross-platform approach continued for 2 more years, with conferences on portrayals of race and class in 1998, and images of masculinity in 1999.

In 1999, the Children & the Media Program refined its mission. To its original statement that the program "works to improve media for children and about children's issues," Children Now added "paying particular attention to media messages about race, class and gender" (P. Miller, personal communication, January 2, 2005). For Salisbury, this specific focus was crucial. "The ethnic and race issues were the best example of how our work was unique; it's work I'm very proud of. The industry hadn't thought about how the absence of diversity affected all kids. Even White kids saw the world differently; when primetime TV looked all White, it was like regression for them" (L. Salisbury, personal communication, December 21, 2004).

To bring this perspective to producers, in 1999, Children Now began releasing an annual research study of primetime TV diversity, known as *Fall Colors*. Current Children & the Media Program Director Patti Miller explained that "the study served as a benchmark of primetime television's progress, or lack thereof, over time. It was a natural extension of our race and class work, especially because children watch television during primetime more than any other time of day" (P. Miller, personal communication, January 24, 2005).

After 1999, Children Now stopped holding annual conferences. An independent evaluation determined that the meetings demanded most of the program staff's time to reach relatively small audiences, and that fundraising and organizational time would be better spent on more frequent, wider reaching efforts like roundtables and research projects. "Supporting Children in the Digital Village," at Stanford University in 2000—a smaller, more-focused convening model aimed at developing specific action plans for increasing quality content—was their first such effort.

In recent years, the Children & the Media Program's advocacy work has taken the forefront, with Children Now leading a coalition lobbying for children's programming requirements in the digital television environment. In seeking to increase both the quantity and the quality of children's media, the organization found that it was easier to gain quantity through the regulatory arena, but quality from working with the industry.

KAISER FAMILY FOUNDATION

In January 1997, Victoria Rideout left Children Now to establish an Entertainment Media and Public Health Program at the Kaiser Family Foundation. The Foundation is an independent philanthropy that analyzes and disseminates information on health issues. Rideout's program conducts research into how young people use entertainment media of all types, and the health-related messages they're getting from its content. Knowing those patterns, it seeks opportunities within media properties to convey research-based messages about healthy behaviors.

Because sexual health is a key part of Kaiser's agenda, the Entertainment Media program is targeted more often at teens and young adults than children. The program's research often deals with younger audiences, however; its surveys of what media technologies are present in homes, and how they are used, are fundamental and often cited in industry, advocacy, policy, and journalism. Initially, the Kaiser Family Foundation program used familiar strategies, such as briefings and roundtables to present and discuss research findings, and providing Public Service Announcements (PSAs) to telecasters. "Our model evolved more from the Ad Council than from Children Now," Rideout noted (V. Rideout, personal communication, December 21, 2004).

Kaiser quickly learned the benefits and the limitations of PSAs. "Broadcasters have to serve the public interest. In doing so, they can distribute PSAs, but they don't have to. So, if that's your strategy, you really have to engage the industry. With some campaigns, we found we just weren't getting airtime, or we were getting it in the middle of the night" (A 2002 Kaiser Family Foundation survey found that broadcast and cable networks devote only one half of one percent of all airtime—15 seconds per hour—to public service announcements (Berger, 2002, p. 1).

From this lesson emerged the Entertainment Media and Public Health Program's seminal project—its partnership with MTV Networks. Much as advertisers are finding enhanced efficacy through product placement in programming, the Kaiser Family Foundation found it achieved greater reach and recognition by incorporating heath information naturally into existing programming, and partnering in development of unique program and outreach efforts. "They have the creative expertise and we provide the facts, figures and collateral materials," Rideout described. "The project includes PSAs as well as full-length shows; one-off shows as well as episodes of series they're doing anyways" (V. Rideout, personal communication, December 21, 2004).

The partnership began only with MTV, and then was adopted by Viacom's Black Entertainment Television (BET) network. Under the guidance of Foundation vice president Tina Hoff, the Viacom partnership expanded dramatically in 2002, with the launch of the KNOW HIV/AIDS campaign. This campaign involved the full range of the company's channels—MTV, BET, CBS, UPN, Showtime, VH1, and even Nickelodeon and its tween-audience offshoot, The N, at age-appropriate levels.

The effect was remarkable. By the end of campaign's first year, 44% of U.S. adults over 18-years-old recognized the KNOW HIV/AIDS brand, or had seen a PSA. Moreover, 135,000 information booklets had been mailed or downloaded, and more than 7 million unique visitors had come to the campaign Web site. "The idea snowballed within Viacom," Rideout explained. "Our ability to pitch ideas to a sequence of channels came about because of our success with the first channels" (V. Rideout, personal communication, December 2, 2004).

Organizations that collaborate with the entertainment industry often find themselves questioned about companies' influence on their objectivity. Rideout says:

> we've walked that line often at the Foundation. There's a tacit understanding that we'll do the research we do and we'll state it plainly. ... We are thoughtful to our partners—we give them a heads-up that the results are to be released—but we let the chips fall where they may. We said they weren't giving enough time to PSAs, even while we were working with them on PSA campaigns. Our obesity research affected their bottom line. But, it's useful to be an honest broker of information—we hold their feet to the fire, but we give them a path to do better" (V. Rideout, personal communication, December 1, 2004).

Kaiser's work with MTV raised different questions. "There's no question that there are music videos on MTV and BET sending messages about women and sexual relationships that aren't the same as what we're sending," Rideout admitted. "But we'd rather have balance than have those messages going out by themselves. We've to go where the eyeballs are; kids live in a sexualized environment and having content that is real to them is crucial" (V. Rideout, personal communication, December, 2004).

The Kaiser Family Foundation campaigns now reach worldwide. "All the content we produce is available rights-free, globally," according to the campaign's director, Tina Hoff (cited by V. Rideout, personal communication 12/21/04. In 2004, United National Secretary General Kofi Annan and Viacom Chairman Sumner Redstone convened the first-ever "Creative Summit," drawing executives from the world's major media companies. The Kaiser-MTV model was central to this gathering on exploiting media in the fight against HIV and AIDS, and the conference resulted in new Foundation partnerships in India, China and Russia.

PRIX JEUNESSE

The concept of engaging the industry works on an international level, as well. For more than 40 years, the international children's television festival—PRIX JEUNESSE—has used the competition programs as a launch pad for extensive creative seminars and workshops, often focusing on affordable and sustainable production models.

A coalition of broadcasters and German governments established the PRIX JEUNESSE Foundation in 1964, because even in television's early years, children's and educational programming received "short transmission periods, small staffs and modest budgets" (PRIX JEUNESSE, 1989, p. 6). A festival, the coalition believed, could "assess the achievements of TV in the area of education and at the same time provide incentive for further efforts" (p. 20).

For 30 years, the Foundation's principal focus was the biannual festival, with occasional academic seminars and research publications. From the beginning, the festival was conceived as the premier gathering point for the world's channel commissioning executives and producers, using the entries as fodder for reviewing and assessing the current state of children's TV. The winners were important, but the heart of the gathering has always been its welcome to media professionals from all regions and cultures, and its "market of good ideas," emphasizing cost-effective and sustainable models.

Even as the industry has become fiercely and globally competitive, PRIX JEUNESSE has sustained its atmosphere of a safe oasis for frank, open exchange. In a letter written for the festival's 40th anniversary, James Fellows, President of the American Center for Children and Media and then-chair of the PRIX JEUNESSE International Advisory Board, put that spirit into words: "Children's TV is not a calling for those who wish to become rich or famous. Rather, it is for those who both like and respect children, and want to harness the power of the media to engage, entertain, and inspire them. Even in a highly-competitive industry, most children's TV professionals love sharing experiences and insights about their work" (Watchwords online, vol. 8), Spring 2003, retrieved from www.prixjeunesse.de/watchwords/index.html).

After Ursula von Zallinger's appointment as Secretary General in the early 1990s, PRIX JEUNESSE industry development work expanded greatly. Having organized the festival since its inception, Von Zallinger had unparalleled perspective on the cultural, professional, political and technological foundations of children's TV in different world regions. She also knew myriad writers, producers, directors, animators, and development executives, particularly which could teach their craft to others. A decade later, the result is an expanding network of PRIX

JEUNESSE-supported coalitions, resource centers, and coproductions on every continent, custom built to each area's unique needs and resources.

The largest PRIX JEUNESSE-supported initiative is the continent-by-continent expansion of children's program "item exchanges." For more than 25 years, European Broadcasting Union member broadcasters have exchanged short films for use in magazines. Each broadcaster produces a small number, conforming to simple rules, and gives broadcast rights to the other members in return for their works.

Because Asian broadcasters need to fill a lot of airtime with little budget or facilities, PRIX JEUNESSE helped introduce the item exchange to the Asia-Pacific Broadcasting Union. The festival sponsored workshops in Asia taught by Europeans, and the two regions began sharing items.

With help from PRIX JEUNESSE and the EBU, URTNA (the pan-African Broadcasting Union) established an item exchange in 2002, and an informal Latin American exchange emerged in 2004. The ultimate goal is a "World Bank" of items that any member could draw from—a cost-effective and self-sustaining production model with the added benefit of introducing children to other cultures.

Post-war Balkan television is composed of multiple channels serving Kosovo, Serbia, Montenegro, Albania, and Macedonia. None offered programming encouraging children to break down language, culture, and religious barriers that have plagued previous generations. In 2002, PRIX JEUNESSE supported workshops to develop a Balkan children's TV magazine coproduction, knowing it would take years of meetings simply to build the necessary trust across cultures. The program premiered in October 2004 in all the regions just mentioned, available to millions of Balkan children.

In Latin America, with no broadcasters' or producers' umbrella organization, PRIX JEUNESSE identified and connected the region's dedicated children's program makers, both independent and within broadcasters. From this network emerged MIDIATIVA—the Brazilian Center on Media for Children, launched at the Fourth World Summit on Media for Children, in Rio in May 2004. Mediativa serves all Latin American producers, broadcasters, educators, researchers, and families, using an extensive library of books, publications and exemplary programs from around the world. In 2003, Chile hosted PRIX JEUNESSE IberoAmericano, the first regional children's TV competition and workshop with entries and participants from well over a dozen countries. A second festival is scheduled for 2005.

Children's TV in Africa is hindered by severe lack of funds and facilities for making indigenous programming, opening the door to imported shows that fail to accurately represent African children or cultures. The

PRIX JEUNESSE Foundation helped locate funding for a multicountry coproduction, "BMW African Pen Pals." The series built African producers' skills, made effective use of scarce resources, and created positive and diverse images of African children and childhood by and for African children. A similar co-production—"Trip to My City"—is currently in development among Arab countries.

Space limitations prohibit giving each PRIX JEUNESSE adjunct described here the unique section it deserves. Each, however exemplifies the core idea that only producers and programmers truly can improve the quality of children's media, and only when they receive ongoing training and learning to build their abilities and motivation.

CONCLUSION

The children's media industries are going through revolutionary times. The advent of digital TV is expanding channels, but those options are owned by a shrinking number of companies. At the same time, the explosive rise of console and computer gaming is shifting power from traditional producers and distributors to newer interactive companies. Personal, portable, and programmable devices give young people considerable control over their media options. Simultaneously, childrens' worlds are becoming more complex. The core elements and stages of their development may maintain a consistent arc over time, but the environment in which young people grow and learn changes radically. Under these conditions, there has never been a more important time for organizations like those just profiled. Each in its own way offers a retreat where people in an intensely competitive field can step back from daily pressures and ensure that children's needs, interests, and abilities are put first.

For years, the American Center has talked about "5 C's" that are necessary conditions for sustaining excellence in children's media. Three of the five must emanate from within the industry—Cash (adequate support for varied and well-made programs), Clout (people in positions of power who care about doing the right thing for kids) and Continuity (staying with a program, project, or person until it has a fair chance to prove itself). The final two conditions, however, invite the efforts of supportive organizations like the American Center, Children Now, the Kaiser Family Foundation, Mediascope, and PRIX JEUNESSE. Competence—lifelong learning—and Connections—feeling oneself as part of a professional community—are vital to success in what is by nature a collaborative profession, one that demands an alchemy of expertise in creative arts, child development, education, sociology, and business.

REFERENCES

Berger, W. (2002, February). "Public Service Advertising in America: An Overview." *In Shouting to be heard: Public service advertising in a new media age: Background papers.* Kaiser Family foundation.

Fellows, J. A. "Parting Thoughts From the Chair." Watch Words Online, Volume 8, Spring 2003. Retrieved from www.prixjueunesse.de/watchwords/index.html.

MediaScope. (2004). *Who we are.* Retrieved December 13, 2004, from: http://www.mediascope.org/whoweare/index.htm.

PRIX JEUNESSE. (1989). *PRIX JEUNESSE 1964–1989.* Munich, Germany: PRIX JEUNESSE.

Prunty, M. (1998). *Transition memo.* (Unpublished) (Provided by *Children Now*). San Francisco, CA: Children Now.

14

Super-Sized Kids: Obesity, Children, Moral Panic, and the Media

Rebecca Herr Stephenson
Sarah Banet-Weiser
University of Southern California

In the last few years, there has been an increasingly sensationalized public discourse about the "epidemic" of childhood obesity in the United States,. Recent headlines point to the seriousness of the problem ranging from "Parents Might Outlive Obese Children" (Gillis, 2005) to "Fat Kids 'May Be Eating Away to Early Death'" (Sommerfeld, 2005). Reports about the future ill health of obese kids has led to a general hysteria over what the future will bring and the threat of high-profile obesity lawsuits has caused food companies to think hard about liability and public scrutiny. Together, these concerns have fueled the emergence of a moral panic about childhood obesity and have pointed to the media (television in particular) as the primary culprits corrupting children's bodies.

This latest moral panic draws upon a dichotomous understanding of children as *either* innocent victims of media influence *or* savvy media users. Those who blame television for the childhood obesity epidemic clearly adhere to the idea of children as innocent victims, and have proposed increased regulation of content and advertising as the solution to the problem. Simultaneously, under pressure to do something to address this moral panic, children's media companies have undertaken several initial efforts to combat childhood obesity and mold their young viewers into morally and physically virtuous citizens, indicating their embrace of the idea of children as savvy media users.

To better understand the dichotomy of children as innocent victims versus children as savvy media users, it is helpful to track advertising and programming trends as well as some of the FCC's policy decisions, all of which have a role in creating and sustaining a broader cultural view of the child audience. Since the 1950s, broadcast networks have aired children's programming in the early morning and late afternoon (afterschool) hours, providing child viewers with content tailored to their needs and interests while, at the same time, allowing advertisers to focus marketing efforts on timeslots during which a child audience is guaranteed. As Mittel (2003) argues, the "exile" of children's cartoons to Saturday morning established a viewing programming context not only for who would be watching television at this time, but also what kind of television would be available. Because the Saturday morning audience was defined as children, and the reigning assumption at the time was that children were both an uncritical audience and enjoyed watching repeats, this timeslot became a financially lucrative one for broadcasters. Advertisers were just beginning to understand the economic value of reaching the child audience in the late 1950s, and the Saturday morning timeslot allowed networks to incur fairly negligible production costs— reruns were common and popular, and programs involved very few financial risks. The move to Saturday morning, then, effectively designated cartoons as primarily kid fare, thus simultaneously creating and supporting the child audience as uncritical and in need of protection from adult material. Cartoons were regarded as "harmless entertainment" and the narratives and creative style of cartoons were shaped to fit the (perceived) unsophisticated child audience (Mittell, 2003, p. 50).

More and more advertisers began to tap into the market potential of the child audience between the 1960s and the 1980s, increasing the merchandise tie-ins with children's television programs (see Tashjian & Naidoo, chap. 9, this volume, for more on licensing and merchandising in children's television). The environment of media activism in the 1960s and 1970s (led primarily by Peggy Charren and Action for Children's Television [ACT]) challenged the presence of advertising in children's television programs, voicing criticism of the content and style of the ads as well as the practice of promoting merchandise featuring the characters of the program. Due in part to these protests, the FCC prohibited the airing of television programs based on licensed characters in 1969, declaring them "program-length commercials" (Englehardt, 1986, p. 74). Nonetheless, with the widespread deregulation of the communications industries in the 1980s under the Reagan administration, this FCC restriction was lifted to allow for a different kind of "public interest" broadcasting, where every member of the audience, including both young children and advertisers, was considered "equal" in the free market of the media.[1] This led to a boom in the merchandising tie-in business, prompting yet another FCC intervention several years later with the 1990 Children's Television Act (CTA). One of the major goals of the CTA was to increase the quantity of educational and informational broadcast television programming for children, and to force broadcasters to serve the child audience as part of the obligation to the public interest.[2] The CTA eventually produced the 3-Hour Rule, mandating that commercial broadcast stations air a minimum of 3 hours per week of programming that fulfills the educational and informational needs of the child audience. Commercial broadcasters are required to comply with the 3-Hour Rule in order to qualify for expedited license renewal (Jordan, 1996, 2000).

The federal enforcement of "educational" television is clearly connected to a more general understanding of the symbolic power of the medium. Because children are culturally and politically understood as future citizens as well as both innocent and impressionable, television programming has, through ideology, narrative, and aesthetic style, encouraged this kind of subjectivity. In the 1960s, public broadcasting in the United States sought to redress some of the problems of broadcast television in terms of its dependence on advertising, the increasing ties with toy companies, and the general low quality of children's programming. The famous "vast wasteland" speech on May 9, 1961,[3] by then-FCC president Newton Minow was inspired by a concern for children and the ways television was failing them in providing a model for informed citizenry.

In the contemporary media environment, despite Minow's lament about the future of television, the children's media market is even more impressive, generating billions of dollars in revenue each year in the United States. In this environment, children are recognized—at least by advertisers—as an "empowered" group, one capable of making important purchasing decisions for themselves as well as their families.

---

[1]For more on this shift in public interest broadcasting, see Robert Horwitz, *The Irony of Regulatory Reform: The Deregulation of American Telecommunications* (1991) and Robert McChesney, *The problem of the Media: U.S. Communication Politics in the 21st Century* (2004.)

[2]See http://www.fcc.gov/cgb/consumerfacts/childtv.html

[3]See http://www.americanrhetoric.com/speeches/newtonminow.htm

However, what it means, exactly, to empower children within the context of a liberal capitalist media-driven culture is ideologically complex. One of the most powerful symbols of the current media age has been the use of children as both metaphorical and literal figures to signify a variety of moral agendas involving the future, the past, hopes, fears, anxieties, and national identity. Within this ideological framework, children are often situated as innocents in need of protection—often (indeed, especially) from the media.

At the same time as the use of children in the media has functioned powerfully to shore up dominant ideologies, children in the contemporary era have also *used* the media more than ever before. Clearly, one of the factors that characterizes the current generation of children is their acuity with multimedia. Technological skills are encouraged at a very young age; Internet use is common in elementary schools; there are now videos and software packages designed for infants as young as 6 months, and there is a whole new genre of digital technologies ranging from cell phones to portable DVD players to PDAs designed specifically for kids. As new media use becomes normalized within youth culture, children as new "experts" of the media occupy a position of agency that challenges the historical (and federally legislated) stance of protecting children from the media. Children increasingly use the media as producers themselves, in a culture where DIY (Do-It-Yourself) cultural production (such as blogs and 'zines) is more accessible and common (Ito, forthcoming). This is not to suggest that children have historically only had access to a passive relationship with the media, but it does indicate that the early 21st century offers a different kind of moment to theorize the dynamic between children and the media.

We witness yet again in the early 21st century the recognition of children as an important consumer group. Children have their own purchasing power as well as an important influence over parents' purchasing. Within this cultural economy, where an increasingly sophisticated advertising climate taps into significant (and not always traditionally mainstream) elements of youth identity in order to sell products, the economic power of the child audience is shaped within a different environment than was relevant earlier in the political history of the United States.

The various ways in which children are constructed in relation to the media in the United States—the child in need of protection from the media, the child as future citizen, the child as savvy media user, and the child as consumer—have come to define the American experience of childhood itself. Because children have been recognized as one of the most lucrative commercial markets, it makes sense to analyze the ways that children are targeted as particular kinds of consumer citizens in the current media environment.[4] This youth community, coined *'tweens'* in marketing parlance, are particularly engaged in brand culture, where multinational corporations (such as Viacom or Disney) appeal to them on terms that invoke lifestyle, experience, and identity more powerfully than the characteristics of actual products and material goods. Moreover, in a generation that has been widely characterized (by popular media, politicians, and educators, among others) as politically apathetic or, less generously, as "slackers," marketers have been remarkably efficient in using tropes of youthful rebellion, irony, and "cool" to appeal to contemporary youth identities. Within these complex interconnections between youth identity, political subjectivity, and commercial culture, it is simply does not make sense to make precise distinctions between the commercial and the political, and to then locate youth identities as either commercially mainstream and superficial *or* politically alternative and meaningful. Simply put, commercial brand culture has become expert in incorporating the politically alternative as appealing to the commercial mainstream.

In the last two decades, branding has taken on increased importance in advertising due to the saturation of products on the market. Branding has been especially important for media companies, as expansion beyond existing media runs the risk of losing viewers. The effectiveness of branding in influencing children's consumption habits has been documented in various contexts, and brand awareness has been demonstrated in children as young as 3 years of age (Gunter, Oates, & Blades, 2005).

For companies producing media products for children, the extension of the network brand to the supermarket is an important form of promotion for shows and movies. Many child-oriented foods use licensed characters from children's television shows or movies to simultaneously draw attention to the products and advertise the program. For example, one can purchase Betty Crocker fruit snacks featuring Disney's Buzz Lightyear, Shrek, or Winnie the Pooh. Similarly, sugared cereals have a long-standing history of using licensed characters for advertising purposes. The vast majority of kid-friendly products, from juice and cereal to candy and fast-food kids' meals, feature characters from media properties (Brownell, 2004).

THE WAR ON FAT

Childhood obesity is the most recent in a long history of moral panics in the United States about the role of media use in the health and

---

[4]For more on marketing to children, see James McNeal (1992), *Kids As Customers: A Handbook of Marketing to Children,* Norma Pecora (1998), *The Business of Children's Entertainment,* and Ellen Seiter (1995), *Sold Separately,* and Tashjian and Naidoo (chap. 9, this volume).

well-being of children. Reports from the Centers for Disease Control, the Kaiser Family Foundation, the American Academy of Pediatrics, and others, have argued that this latest "epidemic" to hit the United States is connected to both the amount of time that children sit in front of television sets and to the content of television advertisements geared toward children. Such studies have prompted parents, educators, and media advocates to demand the FCC's attention to the issue.

Although the FCC has not yet imposed new regulations, cable and broadcast networks have moved quickly to quell this recent panic in ways that prove to be profitable. Using a kind of "social marketing" strategy similar to the antismoking campaigns developed by Phillip Morris, Inc., some television networks have created not only new programming and public service announcements, but also have joined in "strategic alliances" with food corporations such as Kraft and McDonald's. Such strategic alliances allow corporations to diffuse public panic about the nation's unhealthy children while simultaneously keeping those same children in front of the television and eating fast food. McDonald's and Burger King are now offering fruit and milk alongside of soda and fries, and children's television programmers such as Sesame Workshop, the Disney Channel, and Nickelodeon are leveraging the strength of their brands to address the issue through new programming, products, and licensing agreements to encourage activity and good nutrition without discouraging television viewing.

In order to make this strategy seem logical, television programmers tap into dominant ideologies about childhood itself. Specifically, these media strategies rely on the construction of children as either victims or savvy media users two cultural discourses simultaneously: the idea that children are innocent and in need of protection from the media, and the contradictory idea that children are savvy media users. Within the moral panic surrounding childhood obesity, these discourses are used to frame conflict over the control of children's bodies, a conflict that becomes especially important in terms of cultivating physically, socially, and morally healthy future citizens.

Public discussion of childhood obesity frequently employs the trope of the innocent, naïve child—the child who knows nothing about nutrition or exercise and who, if left to his or her own devices, would play video games all day and eat junk food for every meal. Children's naivety necessitates guidance and protection from parents and trusted media sources. In this way, discourse surrounding childhood obesity is not so different from discourse about other adult fears such as technology or violent and sexual media (Banet-Weiser, 2004). Like the protective technologies available to parents to control children's access to potentially corrupting content (i.e., net filtering software or ratings systems), a variety of programs and products designed to help parents control their child's food intake, decrease sedentary activities, and increase time spent exercising have been developed.[5]

In addition to recognizing the potential market of concerned parents, media companies and marketing firms readily recognize the purchasing power of children, a characteristic of the child audience that has been valued since the early days of television (Pecora, 1998). Campaigns that emphasize kids' roles in improving their fitness and nutrition through the purchase and use of products within a network brand or from allied partners, therefore, tap into the power children have in personal and family purchases. It is through this process that television networks capitalize on the youth television audience and commodify the moral panic concerning childhood obesity, so that this panic discourse is transformed from a critical movement in opposition to goals of the network to being an important part of children's television brand identities.

Identifying childhood obesity as a kind of moral panic that is supported by the media does not indicate our refusal to recognize a concern about unhealthy foods and lack of physical activity among U.S. children. Neither does it indicate our complete dismissal of the value of media responses thus far. However, we are interested in the *kind* of response that this "epidemic" has generated within children's media, in particular, we are interested in the ways in which the responses of media corporations have become elements in specific network brand identities. How is this most recent moral panic perceived—through what set of assumptions and histories? Or according to whose standards or values? What does the public attention to this "epidemic" have to do with current cultural definitions of childhood?

Rather than arguing with the logic of bringing public attention to the issue of obesity, it makes more sense to query *why* it is that this particular anxiety—one that revolves around children as future citizens and as a potentially corrupt social body—has taken hold with such force in American culture. One important reason is, of course, economic: Television programmers certainly found a market in the culture of fear and anxiety that surrounds media coverage of childhood obesity. In fact, Barry Glassner (2000) argues that a "culture of fear" in contemporary American culture has been legitimated because of the immense profit to be made off of adult insecurities.

---

[5]For example, Weight Watchers published *Weight Watchers Family Power: 5 Tips for a Healthy-Weight Home* in late 2005, a book that encourages parents to adapt some of the principles of the Weight Watchers program to the family diet. Products such as the Cateye game bike (see http://www.videogamebikes.com) combine game play with exercise, while products such as the Eyetimer (see http://www.eyetimer.com) allow parents to control the amount of time children are allowed to watch television, play video games, or use the computer.

Those who are economically savvy enough to capitalize on the "culture of fear" are skilled in tapping "into our moral insecurities and [supplying] us with symbolic substitutes" (p. xxviii).

We begin our investigation of the assumptions shaping public discourse regarding the childhood obesity epidemic by examining ongoing concerns about children's bodies as signifiers of adult society. We then investigate the processes by which children simultaneously have been constructed as innocent victims and savvy media users throughout the history of children's media. The final section of this chapter highlights several of the initiatives undertaken by various television networks in response to childhood obesity. The examples given are just a few of the initial attempts to address the issue, but nonetheless provide useful evidence of the complex construction of the responses to this issue.

CHILDREN AND THE BODY

Some concern about childhood obesity is, of course, rightfully rooted in medical evidence. Research has indicated that overweight and obese children are at greater risk for a variety of health problems, including Type 2 diabetes, high blood pressure, heart disease, orthopedic problems, and depression (Kaiser Family Foundation, 2004; Kirk, Scott, & Daniels, 2005). The vast majority of these studies advocate the same intervention to treat obese children: diet and exercise. However, these medical interventions, although effectively prescribing treatment for the physiological problem, largely ignore the psychological and social aspects of obesity. It is these aspects that fuel the moral panic about childhood obesity. Abby Ellin writes in *Teenage Waistland* (2005):

> Fat hysteria has swept the nation. ... You can't go anywhere without hearing that childhood obesity is near epic proportions, an epidemic (as if fat could be transmitted from one person to the other through the sheer force of our cultural anxiety), a national health risk, a code orange of young people. ... The mission of the new millennium seems clear: *Help the fat kids, help the fat kids!* (p. xxxi)

When we consider the psychological and social aspects of childhood obesity, especially, the way in which the issue is framed in public discourse, it becomes clear that the crisis of childhood obesity involves children's bodies in much more than a physiological sense. The moral panic around childhood obesity relies on the use of children's bodies as signifiers of control (or loss of control) and morality.

As scholars such as Kathryn Rowe Karlyn (1995) and Susan Bordo (1995) have pointed out, society sees the overweight body as something that is morally corrupt, and the obese person is someone who has lost control of his or her body and thus his or her life. Indeed, recent obsessions that many men and women (and boys and girls) have with fat and flab can be argued to be a metaphor for something else; we interpret the presence of fat on our bodies to be a metaphor for anxiety about internal processes out of control. As Bordo describes, fat stands for "uncontained desire, unrestrained huger, uncontrolled impulse" (p. 189). In contrast, the physically fit person represents a tight and contained moral subjectivity—a person in control of his or her body and his or her life. The body, in short, is read as a transparent statement of the interior moral qualities of individuals.

When the obese body is that of a child, anxiety about his or her moral subjectivity is heightened. Healthy, thin, athletic, disciplined children's bodies are especially important because they act as "the dominant signifier and a locus of control for adult society" (Aitken, 2001, pp. 74–75). Adults rely on outward appearances to judge a child's development, an assessment that has become very important due to the codification of benchmarks for physical, cognitive, social, and moral development assumed to be universal within "normally" developing children. Children's bodies that do not match the expectations for universal development are not only viewed as abnormal, but often also as a result of substandard care from parents or caregivers. The increase in popularity of parenting manuals and the perceived authority of parenting experts in the early 20th century contributed significantly to a change in cultural expectations for competent childrearing (Hulbert, 2003). New standards expected parents to intervene in developmental processes more frequently and in very specific ways, thus allowing the emergence of a cultural climate in which a child's parents are assumed to be, in part, liable for any deviation from normal development, thereby emphasizing adult stewardship of future citizens.

The links between the role of the child body as signifier of adult competence and adult society and the construction of the child as innocent victim and future citizen help explain some of the adult anxiety about childhood obesity. Some of the anxiety is out of genuine concern for obese children, but an equal (or greater) part of the anxiety—and the part responsible for fueling the moral panic—is that adults ultimately have more to lose if the "crisis" is not resolved.

Childhood obesity is not the first issue to call attention to a loss of control over children's bodies. Concerns regarding the bodies of specific young people—called juvenile delinquents at the time—were investigated in a series of Congressional hearings in the 1950s (Hoerrner, 1999). By the 1990s, the line between delinquent bodies and mentally ill bodies was blurred, and moral panic around an epidemic of Attention Deficit

Hyperactivity Disorder (ADHD) dominated discussion of problematic child bodies (Miller & Leger, 2003). Childhood obesity is also not the first issue to link this loss of control to media and technology. The media are often implicated in situations in which young bodies become out of control. In addition to anxiety about children's exposure to sexual and violent content, and the activities it might encourage in impressionable young people, the advertising of alcohol, tobacco, and non-nutritious foods to children and teens has been of perennial concern to adults. Control of children's bodies and cultivation of healthy future citizens obviously holds great importance to adults. It is because of this cultural significance that childhood obesity has been elevated to the stage of moral panic.

CHILDHOOD OBESITY: WHOSE FAULT?

The response of the children's media industry to the childhood obesity "crisis" thus far has comprised an interesting conflation of the commercial marketing practice of branding and social marketing. For the children's television industry, adding concern for fitness and nutrition to the network brand is both an effective way to connect with viewers (and their panicked parents) and an essential weapon in deflecting the blame placed on television for the increase in childhood obesity. However, because the industry's profits are, in part, based on viewers eating branded snacks while viewing, promoting activity and healthy food can be a dangerous undertaking. For now, the benefits of including healthy habits in network brands seem to outweigh the drawbacks, as the new focus has helped to encourage further brand loyalty in both viewing and purchasing habits. In addition, it has opened up opportunities to expand product lines with healthy snacks and branded equipment for kids' new, active lives.

Examples of social marketing (or entertainment education, as it is sometimes called) can be seen in the increase of programs and PSAs encouraging healthy eating and activity habits. Through social marketing, topical information is woven into the story of a program, modeling behaviors and providing factual information about the desired behavior. For example, a recent episode of Disney's pre-teen comedy *That's So Raven* titled "Food for Thought" addressed concerns about the presence of fast-food outlets in school cafeterias, a prevalent practice in schools across the country. In this episode, a student organizes her peers to protest the renovation of the school cafeteria into a fast food court.[6] Similarly, a recent

---

[6]See http://www.tvtome.com/ThatsSoRaven/Season3.html

episode of *The Simpsons,* titled "The Heartbroke Kid," (Maxtone-Graham & Moore, 2005) questioned the practice of vending machine contracts in schools. The potential for weight gain and resultant health problems is (in typical *Simpson's* style) exaggerated and satirized through Bart's experience consuming a diet of vending machine treats.[7] Although the positive effects of social marketing have been noted for a variety of social and health related topics, the technique provides limited long-term attention to the issue. In order to have real "sticking power" in the minds of young viewers and consumers, the message must become an integral part of the network brand.

The VERB campaign created and executed by the Centers for Disease Control and Prevention (CDC) is an example of the merging of social marketing and branding. According to the program's Web site, VERB's objective is to "encourage[s] young people ages 9–13 (tweens) years to be physically active every day".[8] The campaign is entering its second phase and expanding its reach through additional advertising and marketing in the form of PSAs, printed ads, and regularly scheduled events in conjunction with community organizations such as the National Recreation and Park Association. The campaign has been deliberately constructed in a way that utilizes corporate branding strategies. Careful design of the messages, media products, and events have led to the establishment of VERB as "multicultural, inspirational, motivational and a source of great ideas for activities that get tweens' bodies moving."[9] The use of humor and sarcasm, appealing visuals, popular music, and celebrity involvement have contributed to the "cool factor" of the campaign.

In addition to its own branding, VERB has established strong relationships with several children's media companies including Disney, Kids' WB, and Nickelodeon. Each of these networks air customized PSAs featuring the network's characters. In addition, VERB sponsors events in conjunction with these networks such as Nickelodeon's *Worldwide Day of Play.* There is a synergistic relationship between the VERB brand and the network brands, which provides the opportunity for both parties to extend and shape their brands in a positive way. Through the mutual constitution of the brands, VERB increases its reputation as cool, hip, and part of the 'tween culture while the network brands incorporate activity and efforts to reduce childhood obesity.

Nickelodeon has made several additional efforts to incorporate healthy habits into the network brand. For example, the network has

[7]See http://www.tvtome.com/Simpsons/season16.html

[8]See http://www.cdc.gov/youthcampaign

[9]See http://www.cdc.gov/youthcampaign/advertising/index.htm

created "Nicktrition," a series of health and wellness suggestions for children and parents, to assist in rebranding existing food products to be consistent with its new dedication to health and fitness.[10] Nicktrition tips, which range from control of portion sizes to encouraging family activity, appear on the packaging of many Nickelodeon-branded products, from *Dora the Explorer* fruit snacks to *SpongeBob Square Pants* Pop Tarts. Although the intentions behind "Nicktrition" are good, the campaign has been criticized for presenting young consumers with conflicting messages—as labels advising kids to drink water and eat vegetables on the back of boxes of Macaroni and Cheese are bound to do (Kiley, 2005). Recent licensing agreements with Boskovitch Farms, Grimmway Enterprises, and LGS Specialty Sales will allow Dora, SpongeBob, and characters from Nick's new program *Lazytown* to appear on bags of spinach, carrots, and fruit (Hill, 2005). These agreements are also well-intentioned steps in the right direction, but open the network up to criticism for using the same characters to advertise processed junk food and produce at the same time (Kiley, 2005).

Nickelodeon has also emphasized support for physical activity in its brand. The network's *Worldwide Day of Play* and *Let's Just Play* initiative encourage viewers to turn off the television in favor of active play. *Let's Just Play* is a long-term effort that was begun in 2003 to encourage and "celebrate active, physical play" for the fun and health of it. The initiative includes PSAs, grants for schools and community organizations to implement activity programs, and events sponsored by the network with its partners, the Boys and Girls Clubs of America and the National PTA. *The Worldwide Day of Play* is one such event. In October 2004, Nickelodeon went off the air for the first time in its 25-year history, showing instead 3 hours of graphics encouraging families to go outside and play. This programming decision, like the decision to encourage healthy eating and exercise, is antagonistic to the network's larger mission. However, the *World Wide Day of Play*, now a national event, has become a key part of Nickelodeon's identity as a network concerned with child health. Although Nickelodeon and other networks are encouraging their viewers to turn off the television, the concern with viewer well being ensures that when viewers return to the couch, they will resume watching that network's offerings (Lemonick, 2004).

This new brand identity extends to program offerings. Nickelodeon's show *LazyTown*, an import from Iceland "designed to give kids the power to go play, move, dance, sing, make new choices and feel really good about it.'[11] The show's archetypical characters such as the hero

---

[10]See http://www.nickjr.com/home/nicktrition/nicktrition_tips.jhtml
[11]See http://www.nickjr.com/home/shows/lazytown/lt_about_lazytown.jhtml?minibar=true

"Sportacus," a super-fit super-hero, and Robbie Rotten, described as "the world's laziest super-villian" enact a 21st Century morality play for viewers. Disney's preschool program *JoJo's Circus* also has as its mission encouraging activity in its young viewers. *JoJo's Circus* is described as "TV's first movement-focused series ... designed to engage young children in activities that develop posture, balance, coordination, movement and spatial orientation, and build familiarity with exercise"(US Newswire, 2005, p. 1). In addition, Disney's preschool program, *Breakfast with Bear*, focuses on healthy habits including nutrition, hygiene, and activity. In this program, the character Bear (from *Bear in the Big Blue House*) will visit children's homes throughout the country to observe and participate in their daily morning routines (Romano & Becker, 2005).[12]

Despite its history as a noncommercial network, PBS is also using commercial branding techniques to incorporate activity and nutrition into its preschool lineup. For example, in the summer of 2005, PBS premiered *Happy Healthy Summer*, a programming block highlighting PBS Kids programs that address healthy habits, including nutrition, exercise, rest, and hygiene. At the center of this effort is Sesame Workshop's *Healthy Habits for Life* initiative, which shapes content for *Sesame Street*'s curriculum as well as online resources at the Workshop's Web page and a growing group of related DVDs and other products. Segments focusing on healthy habits such as exercise, healthy eating, and the importance of a good night's rest are included in each episode. In addition, new characters related to healthy habits are slated for appearances in upcoming episodes. These long-term changes to the curriculum of the show reflect the incorporation of health consciousness into the Sesame Workshop brand. Perhaps the most poignant signifier of this change in the brand is Cookie Monster's new policy on cookie consumption—moderation (Weinberg, 2005).

The examples just noted are just a handful of the industry responses to the moral panic over childhood obesity. In addition to the networks mentioned, many independent production companies have produced videos, Web sites, and other interactive media that utilize social marketing to deliver messages about childhood obesity. Undoubtedly, such products will continue to appear in the marketplace until the panic is declared "solved." Until that time, the conflation of social marketing and commercial marketing/branding will continue to merge at the junction of the network brand. Nickelodeon will continue advertising its *SpongeBob Squarepants* spinach alongside *SpongeBob Squarepants*

---

[12]See also http://www.muppetcentral.com/news/2005/030105.shtml

macaroni and cheese. Television advertisements and programs will continue to be used to discourage television viewing. Children raised with media brands will learn to associate healthy habits with their favorite networks and programs, and the actions of parents and networks will be reinforced by cultural understandings of children as innocent (yet media savvy) future citizens.

REFERENCES

Aitken, S. C. (2001). *Geographies of young people: The morally contested spaces of identity.* New York: Routledge.

Banet-Weiser, S. (2004). Surfin' the net: Children, parental obsolescence, and citizenship. In M. Sturken, D. Thomas, & S. Ball-Rokeach (Eds.), *Technological Visions* (pp. 270–292). Philadelphia: Temple University Press.

Bordo, S. (1995). *Unbearable weight: Feminism, Western culture, and the body.* Los Angeles: University of California Press.

Brownell, K. D. (2004). *Food fight.* New York: Contemporary Books.

Ellin, A. (2005). *Teenage waistland.* New York: Perseus.

Engelhardt, T. (1986). The Shortcake strategy. In T. Gitlin (Ed.), *Watching television* (pp. 68–110). New York: Pantheon.

Food for thought. (2005). [Television series episode]. In S. McNamara & D. Brookwell (Executive Producers), *That's so Raven.* Burbank, CA: Disney Channel.

Gillis, M. (2005, May 6). Parents might outlive obese children [Electronic Version]. *Ottawa Sun* (Final Edition), p. 28. Retrieved July 14, 2005, from Lexis Nexus Academic Universe.

Glassner, B. (2000). *The culture of fear: Why Americans are afraid of the wrong things.* New York: Basic Books.

Gunter, B., Oates, C., & Blades, M. (2005). *Advertising to children on TV: Content, impact, and regulation.* Mahwah, NJ: Lawrence Erlbaum Associates.

Hill, M. (2005, July 14). SpongeBob Squarepants, other cartoons to be used to market vegetables to children. *Associated Press Worldstream.* Retrieved July 14, 2005, from Lexis Nexis Academic Universe.

Hoerrner, K. L. (1999). The forgotten battles: Congressional hearings on television violence in the 1950s. *Web Journal of Mass Communication Research, 2:3.* Retrieved February 12, 2005, from http://www.scripps.ohiou.edu/wjmer/vol102/2-3a-B.htm

Horwitz, R. B. (1991). *The irony of regulatory reform: The deregulation of American telecommunications.* New York: Oxford University Press.

Hulbert, A. (2003). *Raising America: Experts, parents, and a century of advice about children.* New York: Vintage Books.

Ito, M. (forthcoming). Mobilizing the imagination in everyday play: The ease of Japanese media mixes. In S. Livingstone & K. Drotner (Eds.), *International handbook of children, media, and culture.* Thousand Oaks, CA: Sage.

Jordan, A. B. (1996). *The state of children's television: An examination of quantity, quality, and industry beliefs* (Annenberg Public Policy Center Report Series, No. 2). Philadelphia: University of Pennsylvania, Annenberg Public Policy Center.

Jordan, A. B. (2000). *Is the three hour rule living up to its potential?* Philadelphia: University of Pennsylvania, Annenberg Public Policy Center.

Kaiser Family Foundation. (2004). *The role of media in childhood obesity.* Washington, DC: Author.

Karlyn, K. R. (1995). *The unruly woman: Gender and the genres of laughter.* Austin: University of Texas Press.

Kiley, D. (2005, Feb. 17). SpongeBob: For obesity or health? *Business Week Online.* Retrieved July 14, 2005 from Lexis Nexis Academic Universe.

Kirk, S., Scott, B. J., & Daniels, S. R. (May, 2005). Pediatric obesity epidemic: Treatment options. *Supplement to the Journal of the American Dietetic Association, 105* (5), S44–S51.

Lemonick, M. D. (2004, June 7). Nickelodeon turn-off time [Electronic Version]. *Time, 163*(23), 104. Retrieved July 14, 2005, from Lexis Nexis Academic Universe.

Maxtone-Graham, I. (Writer), & Moore, S. D. (Director). (2005). The heartbroke kid [Television series episode]. In A. Jean (Producer), *The Simpsons.* Los Angeles: Fox Broadcasting Company.

Mc Chesney, R. (2004). *The problem of the media: U.S. Communication politics in the 21st century.* New York: Monthly Review press.

Mc Neal, J. (1992) *Kids as customers: A handbook of marketing to children.* Lanham, MD: Lexington Books.

Miller, T. and Leger, M. C. (2003). A very childish moral panic: Ritalin. *Journal of Medical Humanities, 24*(1/2), 9–33.

Mittel, J. (2003). The great Saturday morning exile: Scheduling cartoons on television's periphery in the 1960s. In C. A. Stabile & M. Harrison (Eds.), *Prime time animation: Television animation and American culture* (pp. 33–54). New York: Routledge.

Pecora, N. (1998). *The business of children's entertainment.* New York: Guilford Press.

Romano, A., & Becker, A. (2005, March 14). Kids TV's health kick [Electronic Version]. *Broadcasting & Cable, 135* (11), 16.

Seifer, E. (1995). *Sold separately: Parents and children in consumer culture.* New Brunswick, NJ: Rutgers University Press.

Sommerfeld, J. (2005, March 27). Fat kids 'may be eating away to early death' [Electronic Version] *Courier Mail (Queensland, Australia),* p. 1. Retrieved July 14, 2005, from Lexis Nexis Academic Universe.

Weinberg, H. (2005, April 19). Cookie Monster eating fewer cookies to combat child obesity epidemic. *University Wire,* DC Bureau. Retrived June 5, 2005, from Lexis Nexis Academic Universe.

US Newswire (2005, March 28). *YMCA Healthy Kids Day calls kids, families to 'put play in your day'.* Retrieved June 5, 2005, from Lexis Nexis Academic Universe.

Author Index

Subject Index